About the Authors

Charles Austin Stone, PhD, and **Anne Zissu, PhD,** are the founding editors of *The Financier* (www.the-financier.com), *The Securitization Conduit* (www.asset-backed.com), and *The Arbitrageur,* publications providing commentary on corporate finance, risk management, securitization, and related topics. Stone is a visiting professor at Université Paris Dauphine, where he teaches a course on securitization. Zissu is a professor of finance at Temple University in Philadelphia. They have edited several books on finance, and their research has appeared in leading academic journals including the *Journal of Derivatives,* the *Journal of Applied Corporate Finance,* and *Financial Markets, Institutions and Instruments.* They share their time between residences in Philadelphia and Paris.

THE
Securitization Markets
Handbook

Also available from
BLOOMBERG PRESS

Fixed-Income Securities and Derivatives Handbook:
Analysis and Valuation
by Moorad Choudhry

PIPES: A Guide to Private Investments in Public Equity
edited by Steven Dresner with E. Kurt Kim

Inside the Yield Book:
The Classic That Created the Science of Bond Analysis
by Sidney Homer and Martin L. Leibowitz, PhD

Due Diligence for Global Deal Making:
The Definitive Guide to Cross-Border Mergers and Acquisitions,
Joint Ventures, Financings, and Strategic Alliances
edited by Arthur H. Rosenbloom

Dealing with Financial Risk
by David Shirreff

A complete list of our titles is available at
www.bloomberg.com/books

ATTENTION CORPORATIONS

THIS BOOK IS AVAILABLE for bulk purchase at special discount. Special editions or chapter reprints can also be customized to specifications. For information, please e-mail Bloomberg Press, **press@bloomberg.com**, Attention: Director of Special Sales, or phone 212-617-7966.

THE
Securitization Markets Handbook

Structures and Dynamics of
Mortgage- and Asset-Backed Securities

Charles Austin Stone
AND
Anne Zissu

BLOOMBERG PRESS

NEW YORK

First edition published 2005
3 5 7 9 10 8 6 4 2

Library of Congress Cataloging-in-Publication Data

Stone, Charles A. (Charles Austin)
    The securitization markets handbook : structures and dynamics of mortgage- and asset-backed securities / by Charles Austin Stone and Anne Zissu. -- 1st ed.
        p. cm.
    Includes index.
    ISBN 1-57660-138-2 (alk. paper)
    1. Mortgage-backed securities. 2. Asset-backed financing. I. Zissu, Anne. II. Title.

HG4655. S76 2005
332.63'23--dc22   2004020399

To our children, Ben and Hava Stone—
we hope that books will always be
as large a part of their life as this one has

And in memory of Ben Zissu and Allan Stone,
the grandfathers of Ben and Hava

Contents

P a r t   O n e

Key Structures and Cash Flow Dynamics

Part Two

Corporate Debt and the Securitization Markets

Part Three

Securitization of Revolving Credit

Part Four

Searching for Value in the Mortgage- and Asset-Backed Markets

List of Exhibits

Acknowledgments

WE WOULD LIKE TO THANK Kathleen Peterson and Tracy Tait at Bloomberg Press. Kathleen had the confidence in our idea and the patience to work with us on the manuscript. Tracy was dedicated and hard-working in bringing the project to successful completion; she has been the closer on this book. We also thank all those at Bloomberg Press—especially Barbara Diez Goldenberg, JoAnne Kanaval, and Mary Macher—who have worked so diligently to make this book more valuable.

Introduction

SINCE 1991 we have lectured on the market for mortgage- and asset-backed securities, to students and faculty at universities in Europe and the United States and to practitioners at banks, and we have, lecture by lecture, come to understand which questions are foremost in our audience's mind when they begin to study this subject. This book addresses those questions. Our students have included bankers, accountants, and financial engineers as well as those who have yet to enter the job market but are well versed in various finance case studies, empirical finance literature, and the modern theory of finance.

Although securitization is a specialized field of banking and finance, teaching students in first- and second-level banking courses about the mechanics of securitization can be a very good pedagogical tool. Securitization of financial assets requires that lawyers, accountants, bankers, and financial engineers come together to build a funding structure from the ground up, designing an efficient capital structure that can be raised in the capital and money markets. Contrasting a bank's balance sheet and all the attendant risks with the risk of a securitization vehicle's capital structure reveals many important distinctions between general funding and securitization. The balance sheet of a bank is not constrained the same way a securitization vehicle is. A manager of a general-purpose balance sheet can allocate funds across a broad range of assets in a dynamic fashion, whereas a special-purpose vehicle used in a securitization transaction is only equipped to fund a quantitatively and qualitatively predefined pool of assets or flow of assets. As to risk, a bank may be managed conservatively, investing predominantly in fixed-rate mortgages that it sells forward to the Federal National Mortgage Association (FNMA). However, with a change in management or in management's preferences, the assets of the bank may be reallocated from warehousing fixed-rate mortgages to investing in high-yield tranches of commercial mortgage-backed securities (MBSs) or, for that matter, to forming the majority interest in a movie studio. Equity owners and creditors of the bank are exposed to this risk shift.

Our choice of subject matter and the style of its presentation are intended to offer valuable guidance to the first-time student of securitization as well as to the experienced financier, legal expert, corporate treasurer, accountant, or money manager who is constructing a securitization/asset-backed strategy. This strategy may simply involve allocating funds to the market for mortgage- and asset-backed securities. Or it may aim more broadly at developing a financial institution's ability to liquidate certain dimensions of its balance sheet or to hedge interest-rate and prepayment risk, or at expanding an industrial company's source of capital by tapping into the asset-backed commercial paper (ABCP) market. In addition, professionals trying to garner new legal, accounting, or financial consulting business involving securitization will want to read this reference.

For the securitization expert who is busy analyzing, constructing, marketing, or trading securitization transactions, this book is something that, we hope, will reduce some of the expenses associated with training a person to join a securitization team. The largest share of this saved expense will be the expert's time.

THE DEMAND TO UNDERSTAND the intricate and valuable segment of the capital and money markets that this book covers is driven by the phenomenal growth in the market for mortgage-backed securities (MBSs) and asset-backed securities (ABSs). No longer is asset securitization a marginal source of funds; it is a fundamental source of short- and long-term funding and liquidity for a broad range of firms all over the world. No longer are ABSs and MBSs an esoteric, illiquid investment; they are, or should be, basic components of all fixed-income portfolios and serve as benchmark securities for other segments of the fixed-income market. It would be difficult to find a money market fund that does not invest in ABCP, or a bank that has not securitized assets or sold assets to an institution that securitizes them. Finance companies use securitization as one component of a diversified capital structure.

The need for *The Securitization Markets Handbook: Structures and Dynamics of Mortgage- and Asset-Backed Securities* is thus a reflection of the size and continued growth of these markets. Other books exist on the topic, but this book's approach is unique, offering in-depth analysis of both the supply and demand sides of U.S. markets for ABSs and MBSs. We use market data, case studies, and original detailed exhibits to teach the reader how and why specific companies have securitized their assets, the factors that affect the values of the resulting MBSs and ABSs, and the securitization structures that were employed.

Good supplements to this book are the general corporate Securities and Exchange Commission (SEC) filings of Ford Motor Credit Corporation or any other significant securitizers of assets, such as GM, GE, Wells Fargo, and Citicorp, among others, as well as issue-specific filings, such as monthly servicer reports for a series; prospectuses; and prospectus supplements. These documents can be found in the SEC's EDGAR data base. FNMA and the Federal Home Loan Mortgage Corporation (Freddie Mac) put the offering circulars and prospectuses for their MBS and collateralized mortgage obligation (CMO) securities at their respective websites. Once readers have taken the time to review an offering circular or prospectus, they will likely have many questions regarding the structure and mechanics of the transaction and the dynamics of the offered securities. As was noted at the outset, this book is an attempt to anticipate and answer such questions as well as to explain the information that is published in SEC filings.

Documents filed by companies that use securitization but have less diverse capital structures than large banking organizations and finance companies also make for informative reading; securitization in fact is often the lifeblood of these smaller financial institutions. Specifics of the securities and quantitative elements of the securitization transactions sponsored by such companies, including the size and type of credit enhancement and the cost of warehouse facilities, differ significantly from those issued by special-purpose securitization vehicles sponsored by larger financial institutions with a more diversified funding base and more constant flow of receivables. Likewise, the N-30D annual and semiannual shareholder reports of mutual funds filed by the management companies are yet another good source of information on securitization, concerning, in this case, how money managers allocate funds to the MBS and ABS segments of the fixed-income markets.

Investors, fund managers, corporate treasurers, and asset/liability managers must be educated about the value securitization offers and the ways of tapping this value. They must understand general market constraints and asset-specific and issuer-specific constraints. Unfortunately, these constraints are not static; on the contrary, they are constantly being revised and reinterpreted by regulators, rating agencies, accounting standards boards, and often courts. We touch on the primary constraints—for example, the Employment Retirement Income Security Act (ERISA), Financial Accounting Standards Board (FASB) 140, Fin 46, risk-based capital regulations, and rating agency qualifications; however, investors and issuers must engage professional legal and accounting advisers before allocating funds into the ABS and MBS market and before calculating the relative cost of raising funds by means of securitization.

Fund managers must be able to value an MBS or ABS relative to a Treasury bill, note, or bond. Corporate treasurers must be able to calculate the cost of raising funds via securitization relative to on-balance-sheet forms of fixed-income funds, such as commercial paper and medium-term notes. Asset/liability managers should consider using the MBS and ABS market for constructing certain interest-rate and prepayment hedges. Retail investors, too, need to understand how MBSs and ABSs may enhance returns, but they, like all market participants, must also understand the risks particular to these securities.

The Securitization Markets Handbook is designed to be a valuable resource within the finance section of libraries of prospective, as well as active, issuers and investors. Practitioners of finance, law, and accounting also will find the book of value as they allocate their scarce education budgets. We have attempted to offer a practical and detailed picture of a select number of asset classes, securitization structures, and pricing techniques. The assets presented represent the largest and most liquid segments of the market, and the structures we review comprise the most general financial architecture for securitization transactions. These same schemes also apply to asset securitizations not specifically covered here, such as commercial mortgages, home equity loans, corporate loans, and corporate debt. We have written this book so that it will serve as a reference and a stepping-off point to more specialized texts on the subject of asset securitization.

AS HAS BEEN NOTED, this book approaches the topic of securitization from dual sides of the market: the supply side, or the side where assets are securitized and MBSs and ABSs are issued, and the demand side, or the side where investors decide which classes of MBSs and ABSs will enhance their portfolios or serve as efficient hedges.

In Part One, Key Structures and Cash Flow Dynamics, we present the tools and examples that will teach the reader how to value mortgage- and asset-backed securities across various payment and interest-rate scenarios. The first four chapters are targeted more to the demand side of the market, to prospective investors, who must have a general understanding of the source of the securities, the securitization structure, and the motivation of the issuer to correctly assess an investment strategy involving the securities. Of course, the entity that is pooling assets for securitization is also quite concerned with the value the assets can be sold for when they are packaged and placed as MBSs or ABSs. Issuers must be able to value future MBS and ABS issues correctly in order to plan a meaningful funding program.

In Chapter 1 we introduce the scheme that links the primary and secondary mortgage markets. With this information the reader can see how the integration of the capital and money markets with the retail market for mortgages has opened up new and deeper sources of capital for mortgage originators. We explain how the pricing of mortgages in the primary market translates into the pricing of securities backed by these mortgages that are offered on the secondary market. After discussing the cash-flow mechanics of a mortgage and a corporate bond, we present the tools necessary to calculate measures of duration and convexity for a pool of mortgages. Convexity and duration are used to evaluate the risk profile of fixed-income securities with respect to changes in interest rates.

Also covered are the ways in which fixed-rate mortgages differ from fixed-rate corporate bonds and how these differences translate into different values and risk profiles for each. Before modeling the cash flows and valuing the mortgage contract and the corporate bond, the chapter reviews the agency and nonagency segments of the secondary mortgage market. The secondary mortgage market is dominated by FNMA and Freddie Mac. Their pricing of mortgages in the primary market determines the terms that MBSs will be offered at in the secondary market. The yield that investors receive will be a function of not only the pool of mortgages securitized but also the interest rates and risk spreads that exist at the time the securities are placed. Risks include interest-rate and prepayment risk. As is discussed, the source of prepayment risk is the embedded call option in the mortgage contract.

Chapters 3 and 4 build on the earlier analysis and extend it to the valuation of mortgage pass-through securities, interest-only (IO) strips, principal-only (PO) strips, and various classes of CMOs. Chapter 3 presents the fundamental material necessary to understand how cash flows from mortgage pools are directed to finance MBSs and those securities derived from MBSs. Once the reader understands how cash flows from mortgage pools are passed through to investors net of servicing and credit-enhancement fees, our book then models the cash flows for various securities issued to fund similar pools of mortgages. We examine a pass-through MBS issued by Freddie Mac, as well as an IO strip and PO strip created from this same pass-through security. With real-time and historical data from Bloomberg, we illustrate how the pass-through security, the IO, and the PO behave across various prepayment and interest-rate scenarios. We measure the convexity and duration of each security and examine the meanings and value of each measure.

Chapter 4 uses a hypothetical pool of mortgages to create a four-class CMO. This simple example serves to introduce the basics of evaluating different classes of CMOs. Once we model the cash flows for each of the four classes of the hypothetical CMO, we present Bloomberg analytics to examine the cash flows of various classes of actual CMOs, including how cash flows and the weighted average life of CMO classes are affected by changes in the rate at which the underlying mortgage collateral prepays. Comparing IOs and POs is illuminating, offering insight into how the risk profiles of MBSs are fundamentally different from those of corporate and government bonds. We decompose the cash flows generated by a mortgage pool into its interest component, principal component, fees for mortgage servicing, and credit enhancement to study how each component is affected by the change in the term structure of interest rates and by the rate at which the mortgages are refinanced.

In Part Two, Corporate Debt and the Securitization Market, Chapter 5 examines how and why Ford Motor Company uses securitization. We look at the financial structure of Ford Motor Credit (FMC) and discuss how securitization fits into the company's overall capital structure. The chapter moves from a general discussion of Ford's use of asset securitization to coverage of a specific securitization transaction of retail automobile loans. This review introduces fundamental issues and elements that underlie all securitization structures, such as achieving a true sale of assets, bankruptcy, remoteness of the securitization vehicle, and reallocation of risk across multiple classes of securities. Also covered are the financial architecture of the securitization transaction and the financial engineering of the ABSs that are issued by the special-purpose vehicle to finance the purchase of assets from FMC.

The purpose of Chapter 5 is to show how one of the most active issuers of ABSs structures its securitization transactions and how the securities issued to efficiently finance pools of finance receivables are designed to appeal to investors. While the focus is Ford Motor Credit, the analysis can easily be applied to other large captive finance companies, general finance companies, and banking institutions.

Also in the corporate debt context, Chapter 6 discusses the supply and demand of asset-backed commercial paper (ABCP). This important segment of the money market provides financial, industrial, and service firms with a vital source of liquidity. Firms use the ABCP market when they are priced out of the conventional CP market due to their low credit rating, and also to diversify and increase their sources of working capital. For example, an A-1-rated firm like GE Capital raises money on both the ABCP and the conventional CP markets. The discussion of ABCP and the fundamental multiseller ABCP scheme leads into a discussion of the FASB interpretation, Fin 46. Fin 46 has important implications for companies that have financial interests in special-purpose entities (SPEs). Since SPEs are central to securitization transactions, the implications of Fin 46 are significant for the securitization market. Fin 46 has forced financial institutions to consolidate the assets of many SPEs used in ABCP transactions and collateralized debt obligations in which they have a significant variable interest. Variable interests include, but are not limited to, the administration of the conduit and the supply of credit and liquidity enhancements.

Part Three, Securitization of Revolving Credit, discusses the structures used to securitize revolving credits. Chapter 7 examines how dealer floor plan loans are securitized, through a specific transaction sponsored by Chrysler Financial Corporation, and Chapter 8 focuses on credit card receivables, examining how MBNA, a credit card bank, uses securitization and how its securitization transactions are structured. Included in the analysis of the way the MBNA Credit Card Master Trust II, MBNA's most active credit card master trust, operates is a discussion of credit card master note programs, a recent financial innovation that credit card banks use to increase the efficiency of their securitization programs. One of the driving forces behind the introduction of the master note program was the constraints on retirement-plan investing in credit card ABSs imposed by ERISA. This chapter presents a brief discussion of how ERISA constrains investments in certain ABSs and how the credit card master note program releases the constraint.

In Part Four, Searching for Value in the Mortgage- and Asset-Backed Markets, Chapter 9 discusses the distribution of MBSs and ABSs across various segments of the capital and money markets. It examines how and why mutual funds, pension funds, banks, insurance companies, and real estate investment trusts (REITs) allocate capital to the MBS and ABS markets. One of the distinguishing features of these markets is the array of securities with differing risk profiles that are issued by a special-purpose vehicle when a pool of assets is securitized. For example, a CMO may be composed of twenty-five classes of securities, each with a risk profile that differs greatly or slightly from those of the other classes and that of the underlying mortgage pool. These differences depend on the extent to which the mortgage risk has been leveraged or deleveraged to or from the class. Securities that offer protection from mortgage prepayment risk are offered alongside securities that offer the opportunity to make leveraged bets on the direction or rate of payment.

The distillation and reallocation of the asset-pool risk is fundamental to the securitization process. When Ford Motor Credit securitizes retail automobile loans, the securities issued by the SPE are overall no more or less risky than the underlying loan pool, yet certain classes issued by the SPE are leveraged with respect to credit risk, interest-rate risk, or prepayment risk, whereas other classes will be deleveraged or less risky than the overall loan pool. Each point or section of the risk spectrum attracts different investors. Money market funds will buy the short-term securities issued by a securitization trust, while a hedge fund may purchase the subordinate or unrated class. We examine how the preferences of money managers for certain dimension of the MBS and ABS markets will change as their expectations about economic cycles change.

In the last chapter, we examine how certain classes of MBSs can be used to hedge the interest-rate risk of a fixed-income portfolio. The analysis builds on the tools developed in Chapter 3. Chapter 10 concludes with a discussion of the way credit risk embedded in asset pools is mitigated in the securitization process by internal and external forms of credit enhancements.

SECURITIZATION IS a broad, multifaceted subject. If we had traveled far down the accounting path and delved deeply into the accounting rules and bulletins that affect the supply and demand of ABSs, this book would be an in-depth treatment of the accounting issues but might then offer less coverage of cash-flow modeling, valuation, or the corporate finance dimension. Rather than take an exclusive path—whether that of accounting, finance, regulatory, or corporate finance—this book examines the subject of securitization from a comparatively wide perspective; but even from this vantage, there were subjects that fell, of necessity, outside the scope of the analysis. For example, we do not discuss the large and growing market for collateralized debt obligations. We have also passed to the side of the market for commercial MBSs. Home equity loans (HELs) structured as amortizing loans and lines of credit, while very important segments of the asset-backed market, are not specifically analyzed here. One interested in securities backed by HELs structured as revolving lines of credit will, however, benefit from the two chapters on the securitization of revolving credit lines and coverage on MBS issuance and valuation. Although home equity lines of credit have important distinctions from credit card receivables and dealer floor plan loans and from conforming first-lien fixed-rate mortgages, the chapters on these topics and on the valuation of an MBS will be useful to the reader who wants to specialize in the market for HELs. After our book the next logical step in the study of HELs would be to review the prospectus and prospectus supplement for the Advanta Revolving Home Equity Loan Trust 2000-A, for instance, or other home equity securitization transactions. *The Securitization Markets Handbook* can serve as a good complement to such filings.

Since we focus on the fundamentals of securitization, the subjects discussed lay important groundwork for the person who wants to pursue expertise in a segment or dimension of the market, such as the legal dimension of the CMO segment of the MBS market. Again, our objective has been to offer an in-depth analysis of selected portions of the MBS and ABS markets, so that, with this grounding, the reader can move into more in-depth study of any number of specific transactions, asset classes, laws, accounting statements, or other corners of the market.

THE
Securitization Markets Handbook

PART ONE

Key Structures and Cash Flow Dynamics

Chapter One

Mortgage-Backed Securities

I N THE UNITED STATES mortgage-backed securities (MBSs), created by securitizing mortgages, form the core of the secondary
mortgage market. Securitization, the process of pooling loans and
converting them into packages of securities, integrates the banking
market with the securities markets.

The process occurs as follows. Financial institutions (originators) sell pools of mortgages to government-sponsored enterprises
(GSEs)—the Federal Home Loan Mortgage Corporation (FHLMC,
or Freddie Mac), the Federal National Mortgage Association
(FNMA, or Fannie Mae), or the Government National Mortgage
Association (GNMA, or Ginnie Mae)—for cash or in exchange for
MBSs, or they sell pools of mortgages for cash to private-conduit-type
customers. The GSEs and private conduits finance their purchases
of the mortgage pools via vehicles called real estate mortgage investment conduits (REMICs) that then issue multiple short-, medium-,
and long-term positions (called tranches) of securities. The design
of these tranches of collateralized mortgage obligations (CMOs),
which are set up to pay different rates of interest depending on their
maturity, depends on the demand for the various elements within the
mortgage pool. Proceeds from the issues of CMOs are used to finance
the purchase of the mortgage pool from the conduit.

Mortgage-backed securities received in exchange for pools of
mortgages are either retained by the originator or refinanced through

REMICs. There is also an active forward market for mortgage loans in the United States. Originators sell their production of mortgage pools forward to conduits that warehouse the loans until the pool is large enough to be securitized. Conduits and originators hedge their risk exposures in the MBS and Treasury markets.

Origins of the Market

THE U.S. MBS market was kick-started and has been sustained by the activities of GNMA, FNMA, and Freddie Mac. The first GNMA-guaranteed MBS was issued in 1970. FNMA securitized its first pool in 1981, and Freddie Mac issued the first CMO, backed by thirty-year fixed-rate mortgages, in 1983. The pool was refinanced with the issue of three classes of securities that matured sequentially.

National mortgage conduits such as FNMA and Freddie Mac do not exist in Europe. Without the depth and liquidity of the mortgage- and asset-backed securities markets, securitization is not as valuable there nor as popular, especially where banks have alternative techniques of refinancing their mortgage portfolios. In the United Kingdom, the largest market in Europe for both mortgage- and asset-backed securities, only 6 percent of U.K. mortgages are securitized, according to the Council of Mortgage Lenders, while in the United States securitized mortgages constitute 60 percent of the market.[1]

Originating mortgage pools with the intent of liquidating them through whole loan sales or securitizations net of mortgage servicing is characteristic of the U.S. mortgage market. It is a model that has become ingrained in the housing finance system and is supported by the large mortgage conduits, such as General Motors Acceptance Corp. (GMAC), General Electric Capital Corporation (GE Capital), FNMA, Freddie Mac, and Countrywide Financial Corp., among others. It is a model that relies on a deep and liquid secondary mortgage market.

From the Primary to the Secondary Mortgage Market

THE PRIMARY mortgage market encompasses transactions between mortgagors and mortgagees. The secondary mortgage market is where mortgages are refinanced and distributed in the capital and money markets in the form of mortgage-backed securities.

Multifamily and single-family, fixed- and variable-rate, and level-pay and balloon mortgages are all securitized in the agency and private-label markets.

The Agency Market

Mortgage-backed securities issued by FNMA and Freddie Mac and guaranteed by GNMA are at the core of the secondary market for conforming mortgage loans. GNMA is a wholly owned corporate instrument of the United States within the Department of Housing and Urban Development. GNMA guarantees the full and timely payment of principal and interest on MBSs. The quality of the guarantee is that of "the full faith and credit of the United States."

A mortgage lender qualified to do business with GNMA originates a pool of mortgages and submits the mortgages to GNMA to create guaranteed MBSs. An institution acting as central paying and transfer agent registers the securities secured by a mortgage pool with a clearing agency registered with the Securities and Exchange Commission (the depository), which issues the MBSs through the book entry system. GNMA-guaranteed MBSs are backed by mortgages that are guaranteed by the following U.S. government agencies: the Federal Housing Administration (FHA), the Department of Agriculture's department of Rural Housing Service (RHS), the Department of Veterans Affairs (VA), and the Office of Public and Indian Housing (PIH).

As was noted earlier, FNMA and Freddie Mac are GSEs, chartered by the United States Congress. The equity of FNMA and Freddie Mac is owned by private investors. Shares of FNMA and Freddie Mac are listed on the New York Stock Exchange. Their congressional charters define their mission, which is to lower the cost of mortgage capital to low-, moderate-, and middle-income Americans by creating and sustaining a deep, liquid, and stable secondary mortgage market. They accomplish their mission by providing mortgage originators with an efficient way of liquidating their mortgage portfolios.

FNMA and Freddie Mac are able to offer continuous bid prices for mortgages at favorable rates because the market for agency MBSs and agency debt are efficiently priced. The market for agency-guaranteed MBSs is standard, deep, and liquid. In 2002 $721.2 billion of single-family residential mortgages were originated in the

United States. In 2002 $328.1 billion of federally related mortgage pools were securitized, and $100.4 billion of private mortgage pools were securitized. The principal value of federally related mortgage pools[2] outstanding at the end of the second quarter of 2002 was $3.04 trillion (approximately $2.995 trillion single-family residential mortgages and $86.1 billion multifamily mortgages). Debt of the U.S. federal government financed with Treasury securities at the same time was $3.42 trillion. Total household mortgage debt was $6.05 trillion.[3]

FNMA and Freddie Mac buy qualifying fixed- and variable-rate mortgages on the spot and forward markets net of servicing contracts from originators. The servicer is responsible for regularly collecting the mortgagors' payments. The servicer also collects payments on delinquent accounts, to foreclose properties if necessary, and to liquidate them with the goal of obtaining the maximum value. The servicer, typically the originator, retains a servicing fee (around 25 bps) which is a percentage of the outstanding balance in the previous period.

FNMA and Freddie Mac also exchange MBSs in the form of pass-through certificates and participation certificates (PCs), respectively, for pools of mortgages owned by financial institutions.[4] The two organizations guarantee the timely payment of interest and principal on the MBSs they issue.[5] MBSs that benefit from either the FNMA or Freddie Mac guarantee are not explicitly rated but trade like AAA or better credits.

The financial guarantees issued by FNMA and Freddie Mac are those of private companies and are primarily supported by, and traded on, the robustness of their financial strength. Senior unsecured debt of FNMA is rated AAA, and it has short-term ratings of A-1+/P-1. The capital adequacy of FNMA and Freddie Mac is regulated and monitored by the Office of Federal Housing Enterprise Oversight (OFHEO) within the department of Housing and Urban Development. Embedded in the overall strength of the FNMA and Freddie Mac MBS guarantees is their special status as GSEs with a public mission and their large asset bases and flows of funds.

The U.S. Treasury, at the discretion of the Secretary of the Treasury, has the option of buying up to $2.25 billion of FNMA obligations at any one time. While this option has not been exercised, its existence would increase the liquidity of FNMA should its capital become strained. If there ever were a case for the characterization "too big to fail," Freddie Mac and FNMA would both qualify. In 2001 Freddie Mac had a volume of mortgage purchases that was 41 percent of the volume executed by FNMA.

The Private-Label Market

The private-label market, also called the nonagency or nonconventional market, is securitized through trusts that generally elect REMIC status. Credit risk in private-label transactions is financed by subordinate and mezzanine classes of MBSs issued by the REMICs. The subordinate classes shield the senior classes issued by the trust from credit risk up to the principal amount of the subordination.

Financial institutions operating in the nonagency market, such as General Electric Capital, General Motors Acceptance Corp., Citicorp, and Wells Fargo to mention a few, also offer mortgage originators a source of liquid funds they can tap to refinance their mortgages in the money and capital markets. As discussed below in more detail, mortgage originators evaluate their refinancing options on a daily basis and sell their mortgage production to the entity offering the best terms.

So-called conforming mortgage loans are mortgages that conform to the underwriting standards and structural criteria of FNMA, Freddie Mac, and GNMA. A mortgage exceeding the FNMA or Freddie Mac limit on size or loan-to-value ratio, on the other hand, is nonconforming. On January 1, 2002, the maximum loan size for a mortgage on a single-family residence was increased from $275,000 to $300,700. Loans that are nonconforming cannot be used as collateral for an agency MBS, nor will the FNMA or Freddie Mac buy nonconforming loans on a cash basis. The private-label market is the route through which nonconforming mortgages are securitized.

Freddie Mac estimates that 64 percent of the $1.6 billion of single-family conventional mortgages originated in 2001 (conforming mortgages that are not guaranteed by U.S. government agencies such as the Federal Housing Administration or Office of Veterans Affairs) were sold to either FNMA or Freddie Mac.

Agency and Nonagency Market Segments Compared

COMMON TO BOTH the agency and private-label segments of the MBS market is the fact that mortgages are transformed from illiquid financial assets held by the originator of the loan into liquid, tradable securities that are distributed in the national and international money and capital markets. Although both private-label and agency MBSs compete for the same set of investors, the agencies have certain economic advantages due to their status as GSEs. Agency MBSs are exempt from registration with the SEC, have lower risk weightings than private-label MBSs, and are more liquid.

Credit Risk Considerations

Commercial banks and savings institutions are constrained by risk-based capital regulations, enforced by the Office of the Comptroller of the Currency (OCC). Each asset owned by a bank or savings institution and each off-balance-sheet commitment is assigned a risk weight. The risk weight is then multiplied by the principal value of the asset or commitment to determine the risk-weighted asset value. It is against the total of their risk-weighted assets that banks and savings institutions must allocate a minimum amount of capital to satisfy risk-based capital regulations.

what is
meant by
"capital"?

Credit losses that are embedded in private-label MBSs may be leveraged onto either a direct credit substitute or a recourse arrangement. Risk-based capital regulations issued by the agencies, the Federal Reserve Board, the OCC, and the Office of Thrift Supervision define direct credit substitutes as follows:

> an arrangement in which a bank assumes, in form or in substance, credit risk associated with an on- or off-balance-sheet asset or exposure that was not previously owned by the bank (third-party asset), and the risk assumed by the bank exceeds the pro rata share of the bank's interest in the third-party asset. If a bank has no claim on the third-party asset, then the bank's assumption of any credit risk is a direct credit substitute.

Two examples of direct credit substitutes are (1) a subordinate class of MBS bought by a bank that was issued to finance a pool of mortgages the bank did not originate, and (2) a standby letter of credit issued by a bank that finances the portion of an MBS's credit risk that exceeds the bank's financial interest in the MBS.

Leveraging of credit risk permits the concentration of risk onto securities and financial commitments to a degree that exceeds their proportionate interest in the underlying securities. For example, a subordinate class of securities finances a 10 percent interest in a pool of mortgages but finances the first $10 of pool losses before the senior class of securities—which finances a 90 percent interest in the mortgage pool—absorbs *any* losses. The subordinate class thus is financing a disproportionate share of the underlying risk embedded in the securitized mortgage pool. Another example of a direct credit substitute is a standby letter of credit issued by a bank to absorb the first $100 of losses experienced by a $1,000 mortgage pool that is expected to lose $110. Again, the bank that has issued the standby letter of credit—which serves as the direct credit substitute— is financing a share of the pool's credit risk that exceeds the bank's interest in the securitized assets.

The agencies define *recourse* as follows:

> a bank's retention, in form or in substance, of any credit risk directly or indirectly associated with an asset it has sold that exceeds a pro rata share of that bank's claim on the asset. If a bank has no claim on a sold asset, then the retention of any credit risk is recourse. A recourse obligation typically arises when a bank transfers assets and retains an explicit obligation to repurchase assets or to absorb losses due to a default on the payment of principal or interest or any other deficiency in the performance of the underlying obligor or some other party. Recourse may also exist implicitly if a bank provides credit enhancement beyond any contractual obligation to support assets it has sold.

Subordinate classes of MBSs associated with mortgages originated and securitized by the bank are an example of a bank's recourse positions.

Mortgage loans secured by first mortgage on one-to-four-family residential housing units are assigned a 50 percent risk weight. Private-label MBSs secured by residential mortgages that are assigned a risk weight of 50 percent also receive a maximum risk weight of 50 percent if the securities issued absorb their pro rata share of credit

---

EXHIBIT 1.1

Risk Weights as a Function of Asset Rating

LONG-TERM RATING CATEGORY	EXAMPLES	RISK WEIGHT (IN %)
Highest or second-highest investment grade	AAA, AA	20
Third-highest investment grade	A	50
Lowest investment grade	BBB	100
One category below investment grade	BB	200

Source: Stone/Zissu

---

losses. When the securities issued in the securitization of private-label MBSs are designed to absorb more (if subordinate classes and third-party guarantees) or less (if senior classes) than their pro rata share of credit losses, the risk weights assigned to each class of securities may range from as low as 20 percent to as high as 200 percent. The actual risk weight assigned to a class of mortgage- or asset-backed securities depends on the rating of the security, whether the security is externally rated by a nationally recognized statistical rating organization (Moody's, Standard & Poor's, and Fitch), and whether the security is traded. For example, a long-term position in a mortgage- or asset-backed security including recourse arrangements or direct credit substitutes that are rated and traded would be assigned risk weights as presented in EXHIBIT 1.1.

The maximum ratings are reduced to the 100 percent risk category if the bank relies on its own internal credit-risk metric system rather than an external rating. The bank's internal rating methodology must meet certain criteria spelled out in the regulations.[6]

MBSs guaranteed by FNMA, Freddie Mac, and GNMA have 20 percent risk weights. When private-label MBSs secured by first-lien mortgages are issued as a single class of securities that absorb all of the credit losses associated with the underlying assets, the risk weight assigned to the security is a maximum of 50 percent—the same as that of the underlying mortgages.

The primary difference between an MBS issued in the agency market and those in the private-label market is the way credit risk is managed. In the private-label market, credit risk embedded in the securitized mortgages is allocated between various classes of securities (senior, mezzanine, and subordinate) or funded by a third-party financial institution (such as Financial Guaranty Insurance Company or Ambac) that issues AAA-rated financial guarantees.

In the agency market, the credit risk is funded by FNMA, Freddie Mac, or GNMA.

Mortgage and Funds Flow in the Secondary Market

In EXHIBITS 1.2 and 1.3 are laid out the general mortgage and fund flows for the agency and nonagency mortgage markets. As has already been noted, the nonagency segment of the MBS market is also referred to as the private-label market. For example, when Wells Fargo Home Mortgage Inc. originates mortgages, sells them to a wholly owned subsidiary, and then through a trust securitizes the mortgages, the transaction is a private-label securitization. It is referred to as a private transaction because the MBSs are not guaranteed by the FNMA, Freddie Mac, or GNMA. Wells Fargo Home Mortgage Inc. taps both the private-label and agency markets for MBSs, it should be noted. In fact, Wells Fargo was the largest single seller of mortgages to Freddie Mac as recently as 2001.

The horizontal dotted line in each diagram is the separation between on- and off-balance-sheet financing. Mortgage originators have a choice between financing the mortgages they originate or selling them in the secondary market in return for cash or marketable mortgage-backed securities. Essentially all financial institutions that originate or buy mortgages now rely to some extent on refinancing their mortgage portfolios via the secondary mortgage market. Without the use of the secondary mortgage market the volume of mortgages an institution can originate is constrained by the funding capacity of its balance sheet. Without the use of the secondary mortgage market financial institutions with a surplus of mortgage capital would be unable to efficiently allocate these funds in mortgage assets. Both the private-label and agency sectors of the secondary mortgage market sever the constraint between origination capacity and financing capacity and give investors in all segments of the money and capital markets access to various dimensions of mortgage assets in the form of securities that can be priced off of the Treasury yield curve.

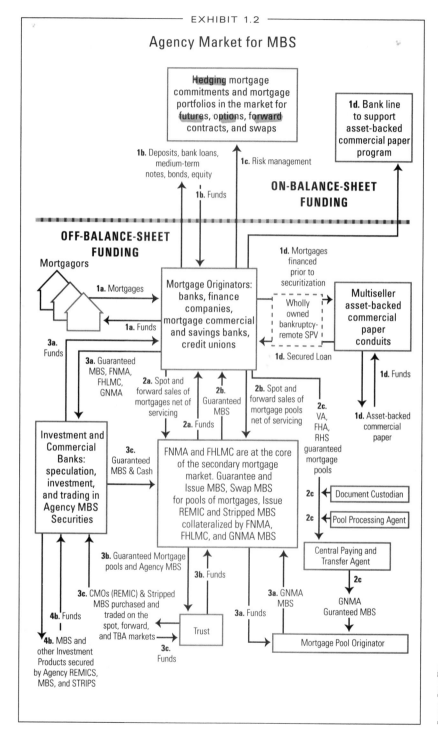

EXHIBIT 1.2

Agency Market for MBS

Source: Stone/Zissu

Agency market

Exhibit 1.2 is divided into three phases. Each phase encompasses multiple flows of mortgage assets and funds. Phase 1 is the origination and funding of mortgages by the mortgagee (the mortgage originator). Home buyers issue mortgages in return for funds (1a). The mortgage originator must raise the capital to finance the mortgages (1b). Interest-rate risk associated with making forward commitments to mortgagors and funding the mortgages are hedged (1c). In addition to raising funds by issuing deposits, debt, and equity and by taking out bank loans, the mortgage originator may tap an asset-backed commercial paper program to finance the accumulation of mortgages prior to their securitization (1d).

Phase 2 in the exhibit is the sale of mortgages either to financial institutions that will securitize the mortgages or directly to a securitization vehicle, such as a trust. One mortgage pool passes directly from the originator to the securitization trust, the other passes first to a financial institution and then to the securitization vehicle (2a). For example, Wells Fargo Home Mortgage Inc. originated and bought from other originators $675 million of thirty-year fixed-rate residential mortgages that it pooled and sold to its affiliate Wells Fargo Asset Securities Corporation. Wells Fargo Asset Securitization Corporation sold the mortgages to Wells Fargo Mortgage-Backed Securities 2001-4 Trust. The trust financed its purchase of the mortgages by issuing twenty-two classes of MBSs. Sixteen of the classes were senior (96.25 percent of the pool) and included a principal-only strip and a residual-interest strip, required because the trust elected to be treated as a REMIC for tax purposes. In this case, the two sets of arrows tell the story of the route of the mortgages from origination to securitization. Some of the mortgages were originated by Wells Fargo and securitized; others were originated by other institutions according to the underwriting standards of Wells Fargo, sold to Wells Fargo, and then securitized.

Very often, mortgage originators and purchasers of mortgages that are destined for securitization in the private market will use FNMA underwriting standards and analytics. Although mortgages may not conform to the size limits that constrain the guaranty business of FNMA and Freddie Mac, their credit quality will satisfy the agency standards. Investment and commercial banks that buy mortgages and MBSs to use as collateral for CMO issues or interest-only (IO) and principal-only (PO) securities use derivatives markets to hedge their exposure to the risks of the mortgage collateral between the time of the commitment to purchase the assets and the time the assets are sold to a securitization trust (2b).

Phase 3 in exhibit 1.2 is the sale of the mortgages to the securitization vehicle, which usually elects to be treated as a REMIC. The terms CMO and REMIC are often used interchangeably, but the two vehicles are not synonymous. A CMO is an MBS that reallocates principal and interest payments of underlying mortgages or mortgage pass-through securities across time and credit dimensions. As has been noted, a CMO is an issue of multiple classes of securities backed by a pool of mortgages or a portfolio of MBSs. Each class of security offers investors a claim on a different tranche of the mortgage collateral's amortizing principal.

In an example of a three-class CMO, tranche A has a claim on the first $1 million of principal that the trust receives beginning on January 1, 2004. Tranche B has a claim on the $2 million of principal that flows into the trust after tranche A has been paid off. Tranche C has a claim on $1 million of mortgage principal but will absorb all credit losses on the underlying principal before class A or B are written down due to defaults on the underlying mortgages. Class C only begins to receive principal after classes A and B have been retired. A tranche may be a zero-coupon security, or the interest rate may be fixed, float with an index, or float inversely to an index. Principal-only and interest-only classes are often issued as tranches of a CMO.

A REMIC, on the other hand, is essentially a creation of the federal tax code. Election of REMIC status is done so that the income of a trust that issues a CMO is not taxed at the issuer level. A REMIC is required to issue a single residual class that bears the burden of financing any tax liabilities of the issuer.

REMICs issue regular classes and must issue one, and only one, residual class. The residual class is designed to absorb all of the federal tax liabilities the trust may incur over its life, whereas the investors in the regular class treat their investments as debt for tax purposes. The REMIC tax rules are quite complex, and expert legal and accounting opinions are needed to evaluate the tax implications of investments in the residual class. Note that a REMIC *issues* CMOs—a REMIC is not a CMO.

In exhibit 1.3 is laid out the scheme for the agency market for MBSs. Here again, numbers designate the various stages of the process. For transactions that are connected within a stage we use the

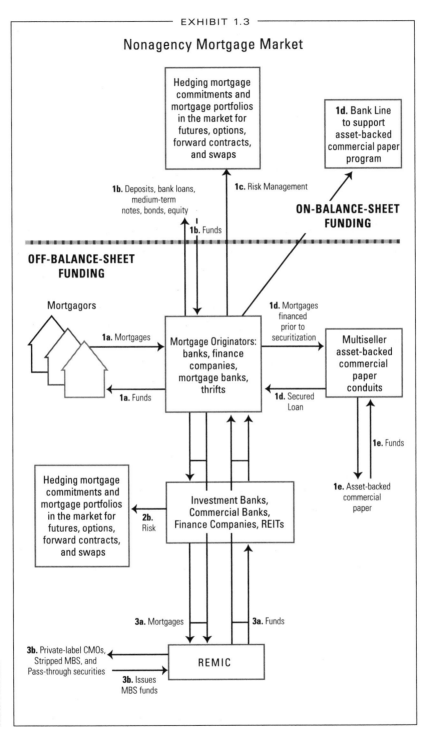

EXHIBIT 1.3

Nonagency Mortgage Market

Source: Stone/Zissu

same modifying letter. If the stage is composed of various disconnected transactions, then the phase number is modified with a different letter. For example, the management of the risk involved with originating and pooling mortgages is associated with the first stage of the market (1), but since risk management is distinct from origination (1a) and funding (1b), the risk-management transaction within stage 1 is labeled (1c).

In the second phase of exhibit 1.3, mortgages are sold to the agencies (Freddie Mac or FNMA) in the cash or forward markets (2a), pooled and swapped for Agency MBSs (2b), or pooled and securitized through the GNMA guaranty program (2c). A mortgage originator that issues GNMA MBSs will sell the MBSs directly to investors and to FNMA, Freddie Mac, and banks that will use the GNMA securities as collateral in CMO issues (3c). There are two entries for 2c because in this example, mortgage originators issue GNMA MBSs two times.

Mortgages that FNMA and Freddie Mac use as collateral for REMICs, IO, and PO securities structured by the agencies (3c) are acquired by investment and commercial banks, savings institutions, and other owners of FNMA, Freddie Mac, and GNMA MBSs (3a). Once FNMA and Freddie Mac have acquired the mortgages, they securitize them through trusts that elect to be treated as REMICs (3b). FNMA and Freddie Mac issue REMIC securities for MBSs in the spot and the "to be announced" (TBA) markets. The TBA market is for securities that have not yet been created. The securities are issued while the collateral is being accumulated. TBA transactions differ from forward transactions: a forward purchase or sale is for a security that already exists. Investment banks use agency CMOs and stripped securities as collateral for structured investment products that are issued through an off-balance-sheet special-purpose vehicle.

Industry Illustration

Here is an excerpt of a financial statement from Sovereign Bancorp, the parent of Sovereign Bank, a federally chartered savings institution, that illustrates how mortgage originators use both the private and the agency segments of the secondary mortgage markets to enhance their liquidity and manage risk.

As part of its mortgage banking strategy, Sovereign originates fixed-rate residential mortgages. It sells the majority of these loans to FHLMC, FNMA, and private investors. The loans are exchanged for cash or marketable fixed-rate mortgage-backed securities that are generally sold. This helps insulate Sovereign from the interest-rate risk associated with these fixed-rate assets. Sovereign uses forward sales, cash sales, and options on mortgage-backed securities as a means of hedging loans in the mortgage pipeline that are originated for sale. (Sovereign Bancorp, 10-K for fiscal year ended December 31, 2002)

Pricing of Newly Originated Mortgages

TYPICALLY, banks originate mortgages with the intention of selling them to FNMA, Freddie Mac, investment banks, or other financial institutions. Commercial banks seeking to do so are likely to receive quotations on the proffered purchasing price from several institutions at least once a day.

By way of example, EXHIBIT **1.4** presents Freddie Mac's description of Gold Cash, one of the mortgage origination programs it makes available to commercial banks.

Freddie Mac Sample Purchase Pricing

EXHIBIT **1.5** shows sample purchase pricing for fifteen-year fixed-rate mortgages. For example, Freddie Mac will pay for a fifteen-year 4.25 percent fixed-rate mortgage a price of 95.094 (ten-day commitment). This means that for a $100,000 mortgage with a 4.25 percent mortgage rate, Freddie Mac will pay $95,094. It will buy it at a discount because 4.25 percent is below current mortgage market rates. On the other hand, Freddie Mac will buy a fifteen-year 7.75 percent fixed-rate mortgage at $106.181. Because 7.75 percent is well above current mortgage market rates, Freddie Mac will buy the mortgage at a premium.

The longer the commitment, the lower the price offered by Freddie Mac. The prices take into account the servicing retained by the originating bank. Even though a bank sells its mortgages, it continues to service the loans and therefore retains 25 basis points as compensation per year.

EXHIBIT **1.7** plots the prices offered by Freddie Mac for fifteen-year (exhibit 1.5) and thirty-year (EXHIBIT **1.6**) fixed-rate mortgages,

---

EXHIBIT 1.4

Federal Home Loan Mortgage Corporation's Gold Cash Program for Commercial Banks

Gold Cash is **our premier cash execution,** giving you the benefits of a securities execution without the additional considerations of a swap. We base Gold Cash prices on actual securities market conditions, not formulas, so you receive competitive pricing for all your mortgages, including discount mortgages. Our Cash PC volume and our ability to buy mortgages nationwide work to your advantage.

You can sell both premium and discount mortgages when note rates are at or below our posted maximum eligible coupon. There is no par cap when you sell the entire mortgage yield (less your servicing spread) to us.

View live indication pricing, seller-specific pricing, and take out commitments with *Gold Connection for Cash* (GCC), our desktop software. Or, call our Cash Desk at 800-366-2353. Whether you use GCC or the commitment line, your loans can be funded within a few days of delivery.

---

with a ten-day commitment, over a range of mortgage rates. The top curve is for the fifteen-year fixed-rate mortgages. Prices offered for fifteen-year mortgages are always above prices offered for thirty-year fixed-rate mortgages. Both curves are steeper in the lower mortgage-rate range and flatter in the higher ranges. In the lower mortgage-rate range, the prepayment option is deeper in the money than it is in the middle range, and in the higher range the prepayment option goes out of the money. Because the prepayment option becomes deeper at a faster rate in the lower range, the prices offered by Freddie Mac or other institutions decrease at an increasing rate in the lower mortgage-rate range.

In general, prices offered for a forty-five-day commitment are always lower than those offered for thirty-day, fifteen-day, and ten-day commitments, the prices of the last being the highest.

EXHIBIT 1.5

Sample Purchase Pricing for 15-Year Fixed-Rate Mortgages

	GOLD CASH PROGRAMS 15-YEAR SFFR INDICATIONS					
	FOR MORE FREDDIE MAC NEWS, SEE OPTION 16					
					REDUCTION IN PRICE FOR USING:	
NOTE RATE	10-DAY	15-DAY	30-DAY	45-DAY	1ST TUES. REM.	3/8 SERVICING
4.250	95.094	94.895	94.807	94.561	0.150	0.750
4.375	95.844	95.653	95.561	95.323	0.150	0.750
4.500	96.594	96.411	96.313	96.083	0.150	0.750
4.625	97.344	97.168	97.063	96.840	0.150	0.750
4.750	98.094	97.926	97.813	97.598	0.150	0.750
4.875	98.844	98.684	98.563	98.356	0.150	0.750
5.000	99.474	99.320	99.193	98.988	0.100	0.630
5.125	99.974	99.824	99.693	99.484	0.100	0.500
5.250	100.474	100.328	100.193	99.980	0.100	0.500
5.375	100.974	100.832	100.693	100.476	0.100	0.500
5.500	101.437	101.304	101.161	100.946	0.084	0.463
5.625	101.859	101.741	101.595	101.388	0.085	0.422
5.750	102.281	102.179	102.028	101.829	0.085	0.422
5.875	102.703	102.616	102.462	102.270	0.085	0.422

					REDUCTION IN PRICE FOR USING:	
NOTE RATE	10-DAY	15-DAY	30-DAY	45-DAY	1ST TUES. REM.	3/8 SERVICING
6.000	103.040	102.968	102.808	102.639	0.049	0.337
6.125	103.286	103.225	103.058	102.928	0.049	0.246
6.250	103.532	103.483	103.308	103.217	0.049	0.246
6.375	103.778	103.741	103.558	103.506	0.049	0.246
6.500	104.004	103.969	103.779	103.739	0.041	0.226
6.625	104.207	104.164	103.971	103.911	0.041	0.203
6.750	104.410	104.359	104.162	104.083	0.041	0.203
6.875	104.613	104.555	104.354	104.254	0.040	0.203
7.000	104.850	104.788	104.583	104.473	0.055	0.237
7.125	105.123	105.061	104.852	104.743	0.054	0.273
7.250	105.397	105.334	105.122	105.012	0.055	0.274
7.375	105.670	105.608	105.391	105.282	0.054	0.273
7.500	105.884	105.821	105.599	105.489	0.030	0.214
7.625	106.032	105.970	105.739	105.630	0.029	0.148
7.750	106.181	106.118	105.880	105.771	0.030	0.149

INDICATION PRICES ASSUME 25 BASIS POINTS FOR SERVICING, AND USE OF THE GOLD

Source: Bloomberg

Mortgage Pricing from the Bank's Perspective

A commercial bank prices its mortgages according to the institution to which it plans to sell them. For instance, a bank selling its mortgages to Freddie Mac has to price its mortgages using columns (1) and (2) in EXHIBIT **1.8** (see also exhibit 1.6). The bank interested in making 1 percent revenue (R) up front when it originates a 4.75 percent thirty-year fixed-rate mortgage has to charge 7.719 points to the mortgagor in order to make up for the discount at which it can sell

EXHIBIT 1.6

Sample Purchase Pricing for 30-Year Fixed-Rate Mortgages

GOLD CASH PROGRAMS 30-YEAR SFFR INDICATIONS
FOR MORE FREDDIE MAC NEWS, SEE OPTION 16

					REDUCTION IN PRICE FOR USING:	
NOTE RATE	10-DAY	15-DAY	30-DAY	45-DAY	1ST TUES. REM.	3/8 SERVICING
4.750	93.281	93.234	93.117	92.875	0.085	0.758
4.875	94.039	93.992	93.871	93.633	0.085	0.758
5.000	94.797	94.750	94.625	94.391	0.085	0.758
5.125	95.555	95.504	95.375	95.145	0.085	0.758
5.250	96.313	96.258	96.125	95.898	0.085	0.758
5.375	97.070	97.012	96.875	96.652	0.085	0.757
5.500	97.828	97.766	97.625	97.406	0.085	0.758
5.625	98.488	98.426	98.281	98.066	0.074	0.660
5.750	99.148	99.086	98.938	98.727	0.073	0.660
5.875	99.809	99.746	99.594	99.387	0.074	0.661
6.000	100.469	100.406	100.250	100.047	0.074	0.660
6.125	100.969	100.906	100.742	100.543	0.056	0.500
6.250	101.469	101.406	101.234	101.039	0.056	0.500
6.375	101.969	101.906	101.727	101.535	0.056	0.500

					REDUCTION IN PRICE FOR USING:	
NOTE RATE	10-DAY	15-DAY	30-DAY	45-DAY	1ST TUES. REM.	3/8 SERVICING
6.500	102.469	102.406	102.219	102.031	0.056	0.500
6.625	102.805	102.742	102.547	102.402	0.038	0.336
6.750	103.141	103.078	102.875	102.773	0.038	0.336
6.875	103.477	103.414	103.203	103.145	0.038	0.336
7.000	103.813	103.750	103.531	103.516	0.038	0.336
7.125	104.094	104.027	103.809	103.777	0.032	0.281
7.250	104.375	104.305	104.086	104.039	0.031	0.281
7.375	104.656	104.582	104.363	104.301	0.031	0.281
7.500	104.938	104.859	104.641	104.563	0.032	0.282
7.625	105.266	105.188	104.961	104.883	0.037	0.328
7.750	105.594	105.516	105.281	105.203	0.037	0.328
7.875	105.922	105.844	105.602	105.523	0.037	0.328
8.000	106.250	106.172	105.922	105.844	0.037	0.328
8.125	106.469	106.391	106.137	106.055	0.025	0.219
8.250	106.688	106.609	106.352	106.266	0.025	0.219

INDICATION PRICES ASSUME 25 BASIS POINTS FOR SERVICING, AND USE OF THE GOLD

the mortgage (93.281) and to generate a 1 percent revenue. For the same mortgage rate, the bank interested in generating a 1.5 percent revenue up front will charge the mortgagor 8.219 points.

For a 6.25 percent mortgage rate, the bank can sell the mortgage to Freddie Mac at 101.469 percent. The bank interested in making only a 1 percent revenue at origination will charge 0 points to the mortgagor; to make 1.5 percent revenue, the bank will charge 0 .031 points; for 2 percent revenue, 0.531 points; and for 2.5 percent reve-

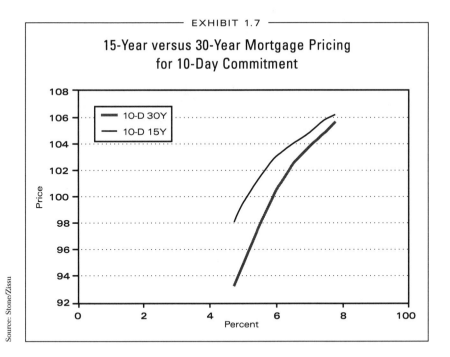

EXHIBIT 1.7

15-Year versus 30-Year Mortgage Pricing
for 10-Day Commitment

nue, 1.031 points. Note that the negative numbers in the highlighted area of exhibit 1.8 should actually be set to 0. A bank will never *pay* points to a mortgagor.

Here is the formula a bank uses to determine how many points to charge a mortgagor for a given mortgage rate. For discounted prices (Price_D) offered by Freddie Mac or other institutions:

$$\text{Points} = (100 - \text{Price}_D) + R \tag{1.1}$$

For **premium** prices (Price_P) offered by Freddie Mac or other institutions,

$$\text{if } (\text{Price}_P - 100) \geq R, \text{ then Points} = 0; \text{ and} \tag{1.2}$$

$$\text{if } (\text{Price}_P - 100) < R, \text{ then Points} = R - (\text{Price}_P - 100) \tag{1.3}$$

The above formulas are used to compute points in columns (3), (4), (5), and (6) of exhibit 1.8, on the following page.

— EXHIBIT 1.8 —

Mortgage Points: 30-Year Fixed-Rate

NOTE RATE	10-D 30Y	POINTS 1%	POINTS 1.5%	POINTS 2%	POINTS 2.5%
4.75000%	93.281	7.719	8.219	8.719	9.219
4.87500%	94.039	6.961	7.461	7.961	8.461
5.00000%	94.797	6.203	6.703	7.203	7.703
5.12500%	95.555	5.445	5.945	6.445	6.945
5.25000%	96.313	4.687	5.187	5.687	6.187
5.37500%	97.07	3.93	4.43	4.93	5.43
5.50000%	97.828	3.172	3.672	4.172	4.672
5.62500%	98.488	2.512	3.012	3.512	4.012
5.75000%	99.148	1.852	2.352	2.852	3.352
5.87500%	99.809	1.191	1.691	2.191	2.691
6.00000%	100.469	0.531	1.031	1.531	2.031
6.12500%	100.969	0.031	0.531	1.031	1.531
6.25000%	101.469	-0.469	0.031	0.531	1.031
6.37500%	101.969	-0.969	-0.469	0.031	0.531
6.50000%	102.469	-1.469	-0.969	-0.469	0.031
6.62500%	102.805	-1.805	-1.305	-0.805	-0.305
6.75000%	103.141	-2.141	-1.641	-1.141	-0.641
6.87500%	103.477	-2.477	-1.977	-1.477	-0.977
7.00000%	103.813	-2.813	-2.313	-1.813	-1.313
7.12500%	104.094	-3.094	-2.594	-2.094	-1.594
7.25000%	104.375	-3.375	-2.875	-2.375	-1.875
7.37500%	104.656	-3.656	-3.156	-2.656	-2.156
7.50000%	104.938	-3.938	-3.438	-2.938	-2.438
7.62500%	105.266	-4.266	-3.766	-3.266	-2.766
7.75000%	105.594	-4.594	-4.094	-3.594	-3.094
7.87500%	105.922	-4.922	-4.422	-3.922	-3.422
8.00000%	106.25	-5.25	-4.75	-4.25	-3.75
8.12500%	106.469	-5.469	-4.969	-4.469	-3.969
8.25000%	106.688	-5.688	-5.188	-4.688	-4.188

Source: PrivateRaise, LLC

One should understand, however, that a bank can sell mortgages originated in the past that have remained on its balance sheet. For example, a bank may hold a mortgage with a rate of 8 percent, originated a few years ago. At such a favorable rate, the bank can sell it to Freddie Mac at a premium of 6.25 percent (Price = 106.25 in exhibit 1.8). In fact, the high premium prices offered by Freddie Mac are not for new mortgages still to be originated but for outstanding mortgages that have not yet left the bank's balance sheet.

Chapter Notes

1. Council of Mortgage Lenders, www.cml.org.uk.

2. Federally related mortgage pools include GNMA, FNMA, Freddie Mac, and Farmers Home Administration pools. Also included are federally related pools that are used as collateral for federally related agency-issued CMOs and privately issued CMOs. Federally related mortgage pools exclude Federal Financing Bank holdings of pool securities, which are included with federal government mortgages and other loans and advances. (U.S. Flow of Funds)

3. Flow of Funds Accounts of the United States, September 9, 2003.

4. FNMA and Freddie Mac buy level-pay fixed-rate, variable-rate, and balloon mortgages and create MBSs from them. GNMA guarantees MBSs backed by mortgages that are insured by the Federal Housing Administration (FHA), the Department of Agriculture's department of Rural Housing Service (RHS), the Department of Veterans Affairs (VA), and the Office of Public and Indian Housing (PIH).

5. Freddie Mac guarantees the timely payment of interest and principal on its Gold participation certificates (PCs). On other PCs backed by variable-rate mortgages and fixed mortgages not issued in its Gold program, Freddie Mac guarantees the timely payment and ultimate payment of principal no later than one month after the final maturity date of the security. (Freddie Mac Mortgage Participation Certificates Offering circular, February 1, 2001)

6. On November 29, 2001, the OCC and FRB, FDIC, and OTS published a final rule, "Risk-Based Capital Guidelines; Capital Adequacy Guidelines; Capital Maintenance: Capital Treatment of Recourse, Direct Credit Substitutes, and Residual Interests in Asset Securitizations" (66 FR 59614). The effective date was January 1, 2002. The final rule amended Section 3.4 of Part 3 and Appendix A. It did not amend Appendix B.

Chapter Two

Price Dynamics of
Mortages and Cash Flows

INVESTORS CONSIDERING an allocation of funds to the mortgage-backed security (MBS) market—no matter in what segment, whether private or agency; or in what form of security, whether interest-only (IO) strip, Federal National Mortgage Association (FNMA) pass-through, or inverse-floater class of a collateralized mortgage obligation (CMO) secured by Government National Mortgage Association (GNMA) MBS—must understand the price dynamics of mortgages and cash flows. To participate, fixed-income investors must be tempted away from the Treasury market, which offers liquid streams of certain cash flows over an uncertain interest-rate environment. The MBS market offers streams of uncertain cash flows over an uncertain interest-rate environment. Is the additional yield available in the MBS market sufficient compensation for the additional risks, including those of prepayment, interest rate, liquidity, and credit?

To explore this question, we first must consider how the yield of noncallable fixed-income securities reacts to changes in market interest rates. After presenting the price/yield relationship for the fixed-rate Treasury debt market, we analyze the price/yield relationship for a mortgage that has no embedded prepayment option. Prepayment risk is the main factor that distinguishes the risk profile of an MBS from the risk profiles of other types of fixed-income debt. This chapter discusses how the prepayment option embedded in fixed-rate mortgages affects the price/yield relationship of pools of such mortgages.

Investors must be able to compare investments in various segments of the fixed-income market. In this context, we first describe the characteristics of a fixed-rate bond and those of a fixed-rate mortgage, along with the basic approach to valuing a bond and a mortgage and developing the price/yield relationship of each. We explain how *duration* and *convexity* are measured both for noncallable fixed-income securities and for pools of fixed-rate mortgages that give the mortgagor the right to prepay. *Duration* measures interest-rate risk, and *convexity* measures how duration changes as interest rates change. Convexity reflects the sensitivity of a security's interest-rate risk to movements in market rates.

Via duration and convexity we can compare a fixed-rate bond's sensitivity to yield changes with a fixed-rate mortgage's sensitivity to mortgage-rate changes. These concepts provide a foundation for the following chapter, which develops a valuation model for asset- and mortgage-backed securities.

Bond and Mortgage Basics

A BOND IS a security representing a corporate, municipal, or government debt. For example, say firm XYZ needs to raise $10 million. It could go to bank A and ask to borrow that amount, but bank A may be unwilling to take such a risk. Firm XYZ could then go to bank B, bank C, and so on, but the firm will soon discover that no single bank is willing to assume the entire risk. Firm XYZ then may decide to borrow small amounts, such as $1,000, from many people, enough to come up with the original $10 million. The approach used to borrow $1,000 from many individuals is to issue bonds. Individual investors buy bonds—which pay coupons, or interest, yearly, semiannually, or quarterly—with a set maturity, or date when they receive their principal back. When investors buy bonds, they are lending money to the issuer, whether government, municipality, or corporation. At maturity, when the investors receive their principal back (the face value of the bond), the debt is paid off.

Bond Valuation

The price an investor is willing to pay for such a security is a function of the coupon rate (Cr), which is a percentage of the face value of the bond; the maturity of the bond (n), which represents the length of time during which the debt is outstanding; and the yield to maturity (y), which corresponds to rates of comparable investments, or market rates. In general, the approach to valuing a security is to list the known or expected cash flows (CF) of the security, paid over time, and discount each one at the appropriate rate (yield). In the case of a bond, the cash flows paid over time are the coupons (coupon rate times face value), plus the face value paid at maturity.

Example: Bond XYZ

Firm XYZ issued a bond with the following characteristics:

$Cr = 8\%$/year
Face value = $\$1,000$
$y = 10\%$
$n = 30$

We can quickly calculate the coupon (c) by multiplying the coupon rate by the face value:

$$c = (\text{Face value})(Cr), \text{ or}$$
$$c = (\$1,000)(.08) = \$80$$

The stream of cash flows an investor receives is shown below:

Time	0	1	2	3	4 ...	29	30
CF		80	80	80	80 ...	80	1,080

Notice that the coupons are paid at the end, and not at the beginning, of each period. This scheme corresponds to that of an ordinary annuity.

Discounting each cash flow to the present, we obtain the price of the bond (P):

$$P = c/(1+y)^1 + c/(1+y)^2 + c/(1+y)^3 + \dots + c/(1+y)^{n-1}$$
$$+ (\text{Face} + c)/(1+y)^n \tag{2.1}$$

The market value that firm XYZ can obtain for the bonds it issues when the yield is 10 percent is calculated as follows:

EXHIBIT 2.1

Price/Yield Relationship for Bond XYZ

YIELD (y)	PRICE (P)
0.02	$2,343.79
0.04	$1,691.68
0.06	$1,275.30
0.08	$1,000.00
0.10	$811.46
0.12	$677.79
0.14	$579.84
0.16	$505.82
0.18	$448.32
0.20	$402.53

Source: Stone/Zissu

$$P = 80/(1+0.1)^1 + 80/(1+0.1)^2 + 80/(1+0.1)^3 + \ldots$$
$$+ 80/(1+0.1)^{n-1} + (1{,}000+80)/(1+0.1)^n \qquad (2.2)$$

EXHIBIT 2.1 lists the different bond prices for different yields.

Price/Yield Relationship

EXHIBIT 2.2 at right shows the price/yield relationship for a bond. As yield increases, the value of the bond decreases. When the yield is equal to the coupon rate of 8 percent, the bond trades at face value, or $1,000. When the yield is above the coupon rate, the bond trades at discount, because investors realize that the market rate pays better than the coupon rate, and the only way for them to invest to advantage in such bonds is to buy them at discount ($y > 8\%$). On the other hand, when the market rate is below the coupon rate, this means that the bond is more attractive and investors are willing to pay a premium ($y < 8\%$).

Fixed-Rate Mortgages

A fixed-rate mortgage is a loan made by a bank (the mortgagee) to an individual borrower (the mortgagor), for the purchase of a house. The mortgage typically amortizes over a period of thirty years, although it can be over a period of fifteen years. The mortgagor

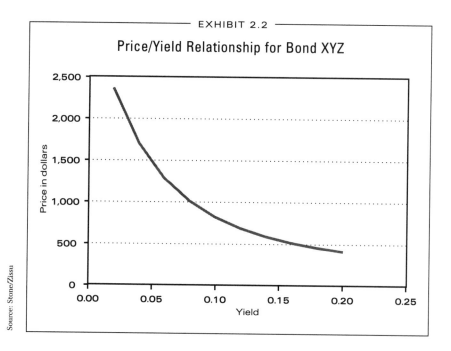

EXHIBIT 2.2

Price/Yield Relationship for Bond XYZ

makes fixed monthly payments (PMT), until the loan is fully amortized (end of year thirty). A mortgage payment has two components:
the principal component (Princ) and the interest component (Int).
The following example shows how the payments are calculated, and
then how the principal and interest components of each payment
are calculated. For simplicity, assume that payments are made at the
end of each year, rather than at the end of each month; this will
facilitate the comparison with the example used for the thirty-year
fixed-rate bond.

Using the example of a mortgage with an initial balance (B_0)
of \$100,000, a fixed rate (r) of 8 percent, over a period of thirty
years (n):

$B_0 = \$100,000$
$r = 8\%$
$n = 30$

Time	0	1	2	3	4......	29	30
	100,000	PMT	PMT	PMT	PMT......	PMT	PMT

The initial balance of $100,000 corresponds to the present value of each payment discounted at the mortgage rate of 8 percent:

$$B_0 = PMT/(1+r)^1 + PMT/(1+r)^2 + PMT/(1+r)^3 + \dots$$
$$+ PMT/(1+r)^{n-1} + (PMT)/(1+r)^n \qquad (3)$$

or

$$100,000 = PMT \left[1/(1+r)^1 + 1/(1+r)^2 + 1/(1+r)^3 + \dots \right.$$
$$\left. + 1/(1+r)^{n-1} + (1)/(1+r)^n \right] \qquad (4)$$

Using the closed formula for the present value interest factor of an annuity (PVIFA) inside the square bracket, PMT is solved as:

$$PMT = 100,000/\left[1/r - 1/r(1+r)^n \right] \qquad (5)$$

$$PMT = \$8,882.74$$

Therefore the mortgagor will make thirty equal payments of $8,882.74 each. Company XYZ only makes interest payments (the coupons) at the end of each year, and it is only when the bond matures that the entire principal amount (Face value) is paid. Bond XYZ, contrary to the fixed-rate mortgage, is a nonamortizing loan.

A mortgage amortizes over time, and this means that the outstanding balance decreases over time. From equation (3), the balance at time zero (B_0) corresponds to the present value of the thirty scheduled payments. In the same manner, the balance at time t (B_t) is the present value of the remaining payments (n-t).

$$B_t = PMT\left[1/r - 1/r(1+r)^{n-t} \right] \qquad (6)$$

For example, the outstanding balance of the mortgage after the sixteenth payment has just been made is:

$$B_{16} = \$8,882.74\left[1/.08 - 1/.08(1+.08)^{30-16} \right] = \$73,231.44$$

Using equation (6), the mortgage outstanding balance can be calculated from year zero to year thirty. The results are in EXHIBIT 2.3.

EXHIBIT 2.3

Mortgage Outstanding Balance over Time

TIME	BALANCE (t)	TIME	BALANCE (t)
0	$100,000.00	16	$73,231.44
1	$99,117.26	17	$70,207.21
2	$98,163.89	18	$66,941.05
3	$97,134.26	19	$63,413.59
4	$96,022.26	20	$59,603.93
5	$94,821.30	21	$55,489.50
6	$93,524.26	22	$51,045.92
7	$92,123.45	23	$46,246.85
8	$90,610.59	24	$41,063.85
9	$88,976.69	25	$35,466.22
10	$87,212.08	26	$29,420.77
11	$85,306.31	27	$22,891.69
12	$83,248.07	28	$15,840.28
13	$81,025.17	29	$8,224.76
14	$78,624.44	30	$0.00
15	$76,031.65		

The mortgage outstanding balance over time is graphed in EXHIBIT 2.4 on the following page.

As explained earlier, each payment is made of an interest component and a principal component. The interest component at time t corresponds to the interest rate (mortgage rate) times the outstanding balance in the previous period:

$$\text{Int}(t) = rB_{t-1} \tag{7}$$

For example, of the yearly fixed payment of $8,882.74, the interest component in year seventeen is equal to the mortgage rate of 8 percent times the outstanding balance in year sixteen of $73,231.44:

$$\text{Int }(17) = .08(73,231.44) = \$5,858.52 \tag{8}$$

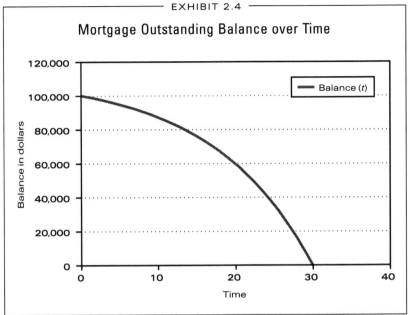

EXHIBIT 2.4

Mortgage Outstanding Balance over Time

and the principal component for the same year is simply the difference between the fixed yearly payment and the interest-rate component for that year:

$$Princ(t) = PMT - Int(t) \qquad (9)$$

for year seventeen:

$$Princ(17) = \$8,882.74 - \$5,858.52 = \$3,024.23$$

EXHIBIT 2.5 shows the principal and interest components over time.

The valuation of a fixed-rate mortgage V(M) is obtained by taking the present value of each fixed payment, using the market mortgage rate r_m as discount:

$$V(M) = PMT[1/r_m - 1/r_m(1 + r_m)^{30}]$$

Therefore, a bank having on its balance sheet a thirty-year fixed-rate mortgage with a contract mortgage rate of 8 percent, while market rates are at 6 percent, could sell it at $122,269, at a premium. On

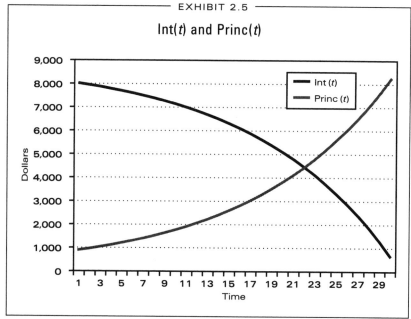

EXHIBIT 2.5

Int(*t*) and Princ(*t*)

EXHIBIT 2.6

Value of Fixed-Rate Mortgages

MORTGAGE RATE r_m	PRICE
0.00	$266,482.30
0.02	$198,941.97
0.04	$153,600.69
0.06	$122,269.46
0.08	$100,000.00
0.10	$83,736.86
0.12	$71,552.13
0.14	$62,202.87
0.16	$54,870.47
0.18	$49,004.37
0.20	$44,226.61

the other hand, had the market mortgage rates been at 12 percent, the bank would have had an asset worth $71,552.

The value of such asset is shown in EXHIBIT **2.6** and graphed in

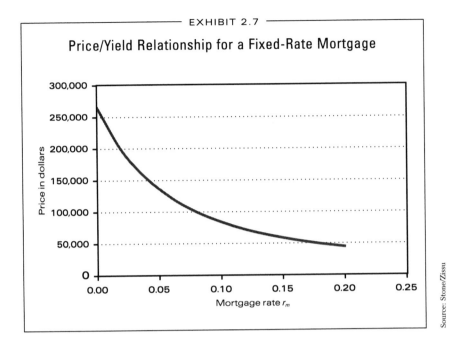

EXHIBIT 2.7
Price/Yield Relationship for a Fixed-Rate Mortgage

Source: Stone/Zissu

EXHIBIT 2.7. Notice the similarity of exhibits 2.7 and 2.2. This relationship is only for mortgages with no prepayment option.

Prepayment Option

Typically, in a thirty-year fixed-rate mortgage, the mortgagor has the option of refinancing a mortgage at a lower market rate. For example, let's say the mortgagor has a thirty-year 8 percent mortgage rate contract. If rates increase in the market, our mortgagor will feel good about the contract, while the bank will incur an opportunity cost, having its funds tied up at 8 percent. If, on the other hand, mortgage rates drop to 6 percent, our mortgagor may go to the bank and refinance the mortgage's outstanding balance at 6 percent.

There are two main measures of prepayment rates. The first is the constant prepayment rate (CPR), which simply assumes a constant prepayment rate for each period of the entire life of the loan. The second is the Public Security Association (PSA). A 100 PSA assumes a 0.2 percent prepayment rate in the first month of origination, and increases every month by an additional 0.2 percent. At the end of thirty months, the prepayment rate has reached a 6 percent rate $(0.2\% \times 30 = 6\%)$ and is assumed to remain at that

--- EXHIBIT 2.8 ---

Value of Pool of Fixed-Rate Mortgages
with Prepayment Option

CPR (%) (1)	MORTGAGE RATE r_m AT $t = 8$ (2)	VALUE OF 100 MORTGAGES (3)
100	0.00	$10,000,000.00
80	0.02	$10,715,762.50
60	0.04	$10,815,913.22
40	0.06	$10,530,058.62
10	0.08	$10,000,000.00
8	0.10	$9,368,986.08
6	0.12	$8,846,912.11
4	0.14	$8,406,954.87
2	0.16	$8,029,680.04
1	0.18	$7,723,832.86
0	0.20	$7,460,661.80

level for the remaining life of the loan. A 200 PSA simply starts at a 0.4 percent prepayment rate in the first month, and increases every month by an additional 0.4 percent until it reaches a 12 percent prepayment rate in the thirtieth month $(0.4\% \times 30 = 12\%)$. A 500 PSA will reach a prepayment level of 30 percent in the thirtieth month $(1\% \times 30 = 30\%)$.

Both measurements of prepayment rates—CPR and PSA—will be used throughout the book.

The prepayment option changes the price/yield relationship for a fixed-rate mortgage. **EXHIBIT 2.8** shows the value of one hundred thirty-year 8 percent mortgages, with a market mortgage rate of 8 percent for the first eight years, after which it changes to the rates shown in column (2). When mortgage rates drop from 8 percent to 6 percent, 40 percent of mortgagors prepay, as shown in column (1); when rates drop to 4 percent, 60 percent of mortgagors prepay, and so on. When rates increase, note that there still is a positive prepayment rate, which is independent of the market rates; we call this the *natural prepayment* level.

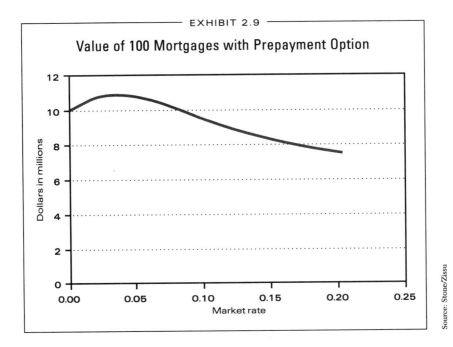

EXHIBIT 2.9 graphs the value of the one hundred mortgages given changes in market rates and the corresponding prepayment rates shown in exhibit 2.8.

Macaulay and Modified Duration

The price/yield relationship for bond XYZ in exhibit 2.2 shows that there is a negative relationship between the price of a fixed-rate bond and its yield: as yield increases, the value of the bond decreases. Given a change in yield, the percentage change in value of the bond is not constant. In the low yield range, the price sensitivity is greater than in the high yield range. This price sensitivity to changes in yield can be measured with what is called the *Macaulay duration*. The Macaulay duration (D_{Mac}) measures the percentage change in price given a percentage change in yield. Where "*dP*" corresponds to "change in price" and "*dy*" to "change in yield,"

$$D_{Mac} = \%dP/\%dy \qquad (2.3)$$

Equation (2.3) measures the slope of the tangent to a given point on the price/yield curve depicted in exhibit 2.2. Equation (2.3) becomes more explicit when rewritten as

$$D_{\text{Mac}} = (dP/P\,/(y/dy))\qquad(2.4)$$

and after rearranging some of the terms we have

$$D_{\text{Mac}} = (dP/dy)(y/P)\qquad(2.5)$$

Now note the introduction of a slight modification to the second term of equation (2.5), which results in the following instead:

$$D_{\text{Mac}} = (dP/dy)[(1+y)/P]\qquad(2.6)$$

The first term of equation (2.6) represents the first derivative of the price function, shown in equation (2.1), with respect to a change in yield (dy). We now calculate the first derivative:

$$dP/dy = -c\{[(1)(1+y)^0/(1+y)^2] + [(2)(1+y)^1/(1+y)^4]$$
$$+ [(3)(1+y)^2/(1+y)^6] + \ldots + [(n)(1+y)^{n-1}/(1+y)^{2n}]\}$$
$$- [\text{Face}(n)(1+y)^{n-1}/(1+y)^{2n}]\qquad(2.7)$$

The first term of equation (2.6) is developed in equation (2.7). To complete equation (2.6), we multiply equation (2.7) by the second term, $[(1+y)/P]$:

$$(dP/dy)[(1+y)/P] = \{-c[(1)/(1+y)^1 + (2)/(1+y)^2 + \ldots + (n)/(1+y)^n]$$
$$- \text{Face}(n)/(1+y)^n\}/P\qquad(2.8)$$

We can deduce from equation (2.8) that the Macaulay duration of a security is equal to the sum of the present value of each cash flow to be received (known or expected) multiplied by the time at which it is received, the whole then divided by the initial price of the security:

$$D_{\text{Mac}} = [\Sigma_{t=1\ldots n}CF_t(t)/(1+y)^t]/P\qquad(2.9)$$

Equation (2.9), the Macaulay duration, measures the percentage change in price of a security, given a percentage change in yield—see equation (2.6). It is, however, impractical to calculate a percentage change in yield. Traders and investors prefer to use a measurement of "the percentage change in price given a change in yield" instead of a percentage change in yield. This measurement is called *modified duration* (D_{mod}):

$$D_{mod} = \%dP/dy \qquad (2.10)$$

We calculate the modified duration in equation (2.10) by dividing the Macaulay duration by the term $(1 + y)$:

$$D_{mod} = D_{Mac}/(1 + y) \qquad (2.11)$$

From equation (2.10) one can compute the security's percentage change in price given a change in yield as:

$$\%dP = dy D_{mod} \qquad (2.12)$$

And the new price due to modified duration is computed as:

$$P_N (D_{mod}) = P_0[1 \pm \%dP] \qquad (2.13)$$

Columns (1) and (2) of EXHIBIT **2.10** are the same as in exhibit 2.1, for a bond with thirty years left to maturity, a yearly coupon of $80, and a face value of $1,000. Columns (3) and (4) represent the Macaulay duration and the modified duration given the corresponding initial yields and prices in columns (1) and (2), respectively. For example, when yield to maturity is 12 percent, the corresponding price is $677.79, the Macaulay duration is 9.37, and the modified duration is 8.37.

Notice that duration is higher in the low yield range, and lower in the higher yield range. This can be seen in the price/yield relationship already graphed in exhibit 2.1. What this means is that the price sensitivity of a bond to changes in yield is higher in the low yield range, and weaker in the high yield range.

Columns (5) and (6) are based on an initial yield of 10 percent, with a corresponding initial price of $811.46. For example, for a negative change in yield of 200 basis points (from 10 percent to 8 percent), using equations (2.12) and (2.13) respectively, we have in column (5),

--- EXHIBIT 2.10 ---

Duration and Bond Valuation

YIELD (y) (1)	P_0 (2)	D_{mac} (3)	D_{mod} (4)	%dP (5)	$P_N D_{mod}$ (6)
0.00	3400.00	19.76	19.76	0.97	1597.10
0.02	2343.79	17.79	17.44	0.77	1439.98
0.04	1691.68	15.79	15.18	0.58	1282.85
0.06	1275.30	13.89	13.10	0.39	1125.72
0.08	1000.00	12.16	11.26	0.19	968.59
0.10	811.46	10.65	9.68	0.00	811.46
0.12	677.79	9.37	8.37	-0.19	654.33
0.14	579.84	8.30	7.28	-0.39	497.20
0.16	505.82	7.43	6.41	-0.58	340.08
0.18	448.32	6.71	5.69	-0.77	182.95
0.20	402.53	6.13	5.11	-0.97	25.82

a positive percentage change in price of 19 percent, and in column (6), a corresponding new price of $968.59.

EXHIBIT **2.11** on the following page illustrates the bond's price/yield relationship, from columns (1) and (2) of exhibit 2.10, and the new price, $P_N(Dur)$, from column (6), which is represented as the straight line tangent to the curve. The point at which the straight line is tangent to the curve is where the initial price and yield are, respectively, $811.46 and 10 percent. As yield changes up or down, the true price of the bond is found by moving along the curve. Measuring by means of duration, however, the new price given a change in yield is found by moving along the straight line.

Convexity

For small changes in yield, the difference in the price found on the curve versus the price on the tangent is very small, but as the change (positive or negative) in yield increases, the difference between the true price and that calculated using duration increases significantly. This is due to the convexity, or the curvature of the price/yield relationship, of a bond. In fact, whether yield increases or decreases, the price found along the straight line is always below the true price on the curve. To correct for

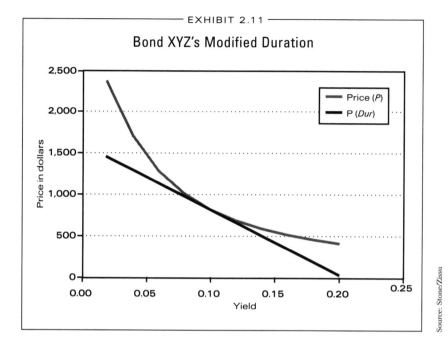

this underpricing, the percentage change in price due to *convexity* must be added back to the percentage change in price due to duration.

Convexity is found by taking the second derivative of equation (2.1) with respect to change in yield, and the percentage change in price due to convexity ($\%dP_{\text{conv}}$) is computed as:

$$\%dP_{\text{conv}} = (1/2)(\text{convexity})(dy)^2 \qquad (2.14)$$

For an increase in yield, the new true price (on the curve) is equal to

$$P_T = P_0[1 - dyD_{\text{mod}} + (1/2)(\text{convexity})(dy)^2] \qquad (2.15)$$

and for a decrease in yield, the new true price is equal to

$$P_T = P_0[1 + dyD_{\text{mod}} + (1/2)(\text{convexity})(dy)^2] \qquad (2.16)$$

The duration and convexity of a fixed-rate mortgage without prepayment option are similar to those of a bond, as shown in exhibit 2.6. The effect of a prepayment option is demonstrated in EXHIBIT **2.12**,

——————— EXHIBIT 2.12 ———————

Effect of Prepayment Option on Mortgage Values

CPR (%) (1)	MORTGAGE RATE r AT $t = 8$ (2)	VALUE OF 100 MORTGAGES WITH PREPAYMENT OPTION (3)	VALUE OF 100 MORTGAGES WITHOUT PREPAYMENT OPTION (4)
80	0.02	$10,715,762.50	$19,894,196.64
60	0.04	$10,815,913.22	$15,360,069.36
40	0.06	$10,530,058.62	$12,226,946.22
10	0.08	$10,000,000.00	$10,000,000.00
0	0.10	$8,373,686.17	$8,373,686.17
0	0.12	$7,155,213.17	$7,155,213.17
0	0.14	$6,220,286.80	$6,220,286.80
0	0.16	$5,487,046.88	$5,487,046.88
0	0.18	$4,900,437.13	$4,900,437.13
0	0.20	$4,422,661.41	$4,422,661.41

which compares the value of a pool of one hundred mortgages with no prepayment option to a pool of one hundred mortgages with a prepayment option for a range of yields. All mortgages are 8 percent thirty-year fixed rate. The initial yield of 8 percent changes at the end of year eight to the different yields shown in column (2). As yield decreases, prepayment rates increase, as shown in column (1). A 0 percent prepayment rate is assumed for yields above the initial mortgage rate of 8 percent. The values from exhibit 2.7 are graphed in EXHIBIT **2.13** on the following page.

At lower yields, the curve of the price/yield relationship of the pool of mortgages with prepayment option differs from that of bonds or of mortgages with no prepayment option. This curve represents a *negative convexity*: as yields decrease, the value of the pool of mortgages increases at a decreasing rate. Mortgages with no prepayment option, like noncallable bonds, have a positive convexity: as yields decrease, their value increases at an increasing rate.

The area between the two curves in exhibit 2.13 represents the expected value of the prepayment option. This is because the prepayment rates in column (1) of exhibit 2.12 are expected, rather than actual, rates.

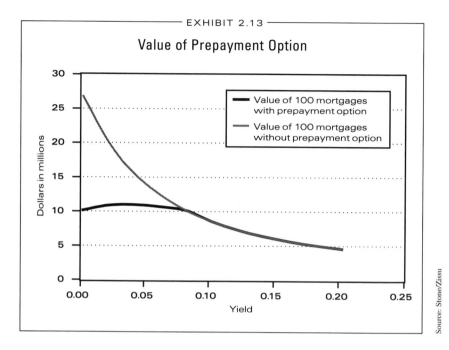

EXHIBIT 2.13

Value of Prepayment Option

Source: Stone/Zissu

Risk Exposures

Both fixed-rate bonds and fixed-rate mortgages are subject to three areas of risk: credit, interest-rate, and prepayment risk. Credit risk is the possibility that a bond issuer—for example, a corporation or a municipality—may default on its payment, in which case a bondholder may not receive the scheduled interest or principal (the face value, for a classic nonamortizing bond) payment. Likewise, a mortgagor may default on its loan and the mortgagee (the lending bank) will not receive the scheduled interest and principal payment.

Bonds and mortgages also face interest-rate risk. The risk can be determined by the duration and convexity. A high duration means that for a small change in yield, the percentage change in price, for a bond or a mortgage, is significant. A high convexity means that for a decrease in yield, price increases at an increasing rate, while for an increase in yield, price decreases at a decreasing rate.

Prepayment risk also exists for certain categories of bonds and mortgages. Mortgagors have the option to refinance their mortgage loans at a lower market yield (the prepayment option), and certain bonds are callable (the issuer has the option to refinance its outstanding bonds at a lower market yield). The prepayment option causes the convexity to be negative. This means that as yield decreases, the value of the mortgage or callable bond increases at a decreasing rate.

Chapter Three

Valuation of Mortgage- and Asset-Backed Securities

THE TYPICAL mortgage securitization process is presented in EXHIBIT 3.1. Arrow (1) corresponds to the fixed payments made by mortgagors to the bank, based on a 10 percent thirty-year fixed-rate mortgage. The bank receives the mortgage payments, and even though it sold its mortgages to Federal Home Loan Mortgage Corporation (Freddie Mac), Federal National Mortgage Association (FNMA), or an investment bank, it retains a servicing fee, typically about 0.25 percent of the outstanding balance of the mortgage in the previous year. The servicing fee is compensation for the bank's still collecting the mortgage payments, taking care of payment delays, and, if necessary, foreclosing the property.

After deducting the servicing fee, the commercial bank passes the 10 percent mortgage payment, minus the 0.25 percent servicing fee,

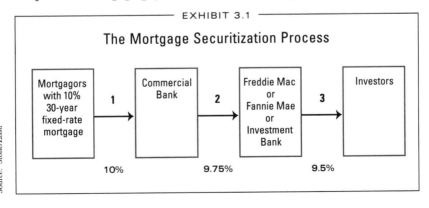

EXHIBIT 3.1

The Mortgage Securitization Process

45

to the purchaser of the mortgage, as shown by arrow (2). The purchaser of the mortgages pools them together and sells shares of the
pool of these *pass-through securities* to investors. If the purchaser is
Freddie Mac or FNMA, it will retain a 0.25 percent guarantee fee
to protect investors against credit risk and guarantee them timely
receipt of interest and principal payment, the so-called pass-through.
The pass-through rate cannot exceed 9.5 percent in the example
depicted in exhibit 3.1 (in other words, Freddie Mac receives payments based on 9.75 percent, and after deducting its guarantee fee
of 0.25 percent, it can pass a maximum of 9.5 percent to investors).
If the purchaser of the pool of mortgages is an investment bank, the
credit enhancement is provided not by Freddie Mac or FNMA but by
a different third party (referred to as external credit enhancement) or
alternatively is provided internally as part of the securitization structure itself (*internal credit enhancement*). There is a cost associated
with credit enhancement, whether internally or externally provided,
which is deducted from what is passed to investors.

Instead of pass-through securities, interest-only (IO) and principal-
only (PO) securities can be created by stripping apart the interest from
the principal mortgage payment, and after deducting servicing and cost
of credit enhancement, passing the former portion to IO investors and
the latter to PO investors.

Modeling Cash Flows of Pass-Through, PO, and IO Securities

THE FOLLOWING section builds a spreadsheet that can be used to
model and evaluate the cash flows due to the owners of mortgage-
backed securities (MBSs) collateralized by a pool of one hundred
thirty-year conventional fixed-rate mortgages. The structures of the
MBSs considered here are pass-through securities (the classic MBS
structure), PO strips, and IO strips. The pool of mortgages prepays at
a constant rate. The cash flows of the MBSs, POs, and IOs are analyzed across an array of constant prepayment rates (CPRs).

The prices of the securities are calculated by discounting their
cash flows at the zero-coupon U.S. Treasury note rate that corresponds most closely to the weighted average maturity of the MBS.
The weighted average maturity of the MBS depends on the rate at

which the securitized mortgages are expected to prepay. In the analysis, the CPR depends only on the difference between the coupon on the securitized mortgages and the rate at which the mortgages can be refinanced. It is assumed that the spread above the Treasury yield curve is constant across maturities.

Yield to maturity is calculated by using a prepayment model that links current mortgage rates to CPR. Based on the prepayment rates, the cash, consisting of principal and interest from the securitized mortgages net of a guarantee fee and servicing charge, that flows into the special-purpose vehicle (SPV) is then calculated.

A few words of background on the role of the SPV in a securitization transaction: the assets to be securitized are sold from the originator's balance sheet, which is general purpose, since it may be used to fund a broad array of assets with diverse terms, to a funding vehicle that is highly constrained with respect to the type of assets it may fund (e.g., thirty-year fixed-rate mortgages or credit card receivables originated by bank X) and that are generated by a set of designated accounts. This "special-purpose" funding entity may be a corporation, a limited liability company, a partnership, or a trust. Whatever its legal form, it is referred to as a special-purpose vehicle (SPV) or special-purpose entity (SPE). Its special purpose is to fund a narrowly defined pool of assets or flow of assets.

IO and PO strips are derived from pass-through certificates or pools of mortgages. IOs are leveraged with respect to the rate at which the underlying mortgages prepay. An SPV may in turn issue IO and PO strips to fund the purchase of pass-through certificates or pools of mortgages. The SPV that issues POs and IOs must allocate the principal it receives to the owners of the PO certificates, and the interest it receives to the owners of the IO certificates.

Unlike most fixed-income securities, IOs can decrease in value with falling interest rates. Lower interest rates increase the value of the mortgagor's prepayment option at the expense of the IO class of securities. The amount of interest that is received by the SPV and available to the investors in IOs depends on the amount of mortgage principal that remains to be amortized. When mortgage rates decline and prepayment rates increase, the amount of interest available to the SPV is diminished (what is termed the prepayment effect).

Higher interest rates cause prepayment rates to decline, extending the period over which the mortgages underlying the pass-through certificates will be amortized. When interest rates increase, the short position in the prepayment option declines in value. The decline in the value of the prepayment option (the prepayment effect) is captured by the investors in IOs. Beyond a certain level of interest rates, the decline in the value of the option is relatively small compared to the effect of higher discount rates. The value of the prepayment option is less sensitive to changes in interest rates the farther out of the money it is, and the higher discount rates begin to decrease the value of the IO (termed the discount effect). Because the value of an IO is positively correlated with interest rates, IO strips are valuable instruments for hedging.

As was noted above, PO strips are claims to the principal received by the SPV. The value of the PO is positively correlated with the value of the mortgagor's prepayment option. When the probability of prepayment increases, the PO strip increases in value. Faster prepayment of the underlying mortgages increases the rate at which the accrual of the discount on the PO is realized. PO strips are leveraged with respect to prepayment risk. Relatively small deviations from expected prepayment rates lead to larger changes in the value of a PO than would result for a pass-through certificate backed by the same mortgage principal.

The following exercise will assist you in becoming familiar with the mechanical side of securitization as well as gaining insight into the sources of value that can be derived from the process of securitization.

Information Set

A bank originates one hundred conventional thirty-year fixed-rate mortgages. The contract rate on each mortgage is r percent. Mortgagors make annual payments of interest and principal (PMT). The bank securitizes the pool of one hundred mortgages. The bank that originates the mortgages services them after they are securitized. The yearly servicing fee is s percent of the outstanding mortgage balance at the beginning of each year. A third party guarantees (in the form of credit enhancement) the timely interest and principal payments due to the owners of the MBSs for an annual fee of g percent per year of the pool of mortgages that are outstanding at the beginning of each year.

Mortgagors have the option to call their mortgages from the mortgagee at any time prior to maturity. The mortgagor prepays the mortgage by paying the bank the book value of the principal of the outstanding loan. We assume a constant annual prepayment rate (CPR) for the pool of one hundred mortgages. Cash flows received at time t are discounted back to the present at the expected risk-free cost of capital between time 0 and time t. The risk-free rate is used because the guarantee ensures that all principal and interest payments are paid on time.

Model

The following equations compose the spreadsheet. $Pool_0$ is a pool of mortgages at time 0, m_0 is the number of mortgages in $Pool_0$ at time 0, and B_0 is the original balance of individual mortgages at time 0.

$$Pool_0 = m_0 B_0$$

Each mortgage is a thirty-year fixed-rate mortgage with a coupon rate r. CPR is the constant prepayment rate,[1] and $Pool_t$ is the pool at time t. The number of mortgages left in the pool at time t is $m_0(1-CPR)^t$.

$$Pool_t = m_0(1-CPR)^t B_t$$

The outstanding pool principal at time t is equal to the number of outstanding mortgages (not prepaid) multiplied by their outstanding balance at time t. B_t is the outstanding balance of individual mortgages at time t; s is the servicing rate; and g is the guaranty rate. The pass-through rate on the MBS $\leq (r-s-g)$. The cash flow passed through to the owners of the MBS (the investor) at the end of the first year, at time 1, is PT_1:

$$PT_1 = m_0 PMT + (CPR)m_0 B_1 - (s+g)m_0 B_0$$

At the end of year 1 we are left with $Pool_1 = m_0(1-CPR)B_1$. The cash flow passed through to the owners of the MBS at the end of the second year, at time 2, is PT_2:

$$PT_2 = m_0(1-CPR)^1 PMT + CPR m_0(1-CPR)^1 B_2 - (s+g)\, m_1 B_1$$

And we are left with $Pool_2 = m_0(1-CPR)^2 B_2$. The cash flow passed through to the owners of the MBS at the end of the third year, at time 3, is PT_3:

$$PT_3 = m_0(1-CPR)^2 PMT + CPR m_0(1-CPR)^2 B_3 - (s+g) m_2 B_2$$

And we are left with $Pool_3 = m_0(1-CPR)^3 B_3$. From PT_1, PT_2, and PT_3, we can deduct PT_t, the pass-through at time t:

$$PT_t = m_0(1-CPR)^{t-1} PMT + CPR m_0(1-CPR)^{t-1} B_t - (s+g) m_{t-1} B_{t-1}$$

After factoring the term $m_0(1-CPR)^{t-1}$ we have:

$$PT_t = m_0(1-CPR)^{t-1}[PMT + CPR B_t - (s+g)B_{t-1}] \qquad (3.1)$$

The formula for cash flows of IO and PO strips is as follows. IO at time t is equal to the pass-through rate times the outstanding pool in the previous period:

$$IO_t = (r-s-g)m_0(1-CPR)^{t-1} B_{t-1} \qquad (3.2)$$

The PO at time t is the pass-through at time t minus the IO at time t:

$$PO_t = PT_t - IO_t \qquad (3.3)$$

EXHIBITS **3.2**, **3.3**, and **3.4** illustrate simulations, using the formulas developed above, of the cash flow received over time by investors in pass-through securities and in IO and PO securities under three prepayment scenarios. Of course, the outstanding balance of an individual mortgage over time B_t is independent of prepayment rates, and therefore column B_t remains the same in the three exhibits. Column m_t represents the number of mortgages left in the pool over time. In exhibit 3.2 we assume a 0 percent prepayment rate, and consequently the number of mortgages in the pool does not change. In exhibit 3.3, prepayment is assumed to be 15 percent per year, and in exhibit 3.4

—————— EXHIBIT 3.2 ——————

Cash Flows Received at CPR of 0 Percent

t	Bt	mt	PTt	$IO(t)$	$PO(t)$
0	$100,000.00	100			
1	$99,392.08	100	$1,010,792.48	$950,000.00	$60,792.48
2	$98,723.36	100	$1,011,096.44	$944,224.71	$66,871.73
3	$97,987.77	100	$1,011,430.80	$937,871.90	$73,558.90
4	$97,178.62	100	$1,011,798.60	$930,883.80	$80,914.79
5	$96,288.56	100	$1,012,203.17	$923,196.90	$89,006.27
6	$95,309.49	100	$1,012,648.20	$914,741.30	$97,906.90
7	$94,232.51	100	$1,013,137.74	$905,440.15	$107,697.59
8	$93,047.84	100	$1,013,676.23	$895,208.88	$118,467.35
9	$91,744.70	100	$1,014,268.56	$883,954.48	$130,314.09
10	$90,311.24	100	$1,014,920.13	$871,574.64	$143,345.49
11	$88,734.44	100	$1,015,636.86	$857,956.82	$157,680.04
12	$86,999.96	100	$1,016,425.26	$842,977.21	$173,448.05
13	$85,092.03	100	$1,017,292.50	$826,499.65	$190,792.85
14	$82,993.31	100	$1,018,246.47	$808,374.33	$209,872.14
15	$80,684.72	100	$1,019,295.83	$788,436.47	$230,859.35
16	$78,145.27	100	$1,020,450.12	$766,504.84	$253,945.29
17	$75,351.87	100	$1,021,719.85	$742,380.03	$279,339.81
18	$72,279.13	100	$1,023,116.55	$715,842.75	$307,273.80
19	$68,899.12	100	$1,024,652.92	$686,651.74	$338,001.18
20	$65,181.11	100	$1,026,342.92	$654,541.63	$371,801.29
21	$61,091.29	100	$1,028,201.93	$619,220.51	$408,981.42
22	$56,592.50	100	$1,030,246.84	$580,367.27	$449,879.57
23	$51,643.82	100	$1,032,496.23	$537,628.71	$494,867.52
24	$46,200.28	100	$1,034,970.57	$490,616.30	$544,354.27
25	$40,212.38	100	$1,037,692.34	$438,902.64	$598,789.70
26	$33,625.69	100	$1,040,686.29	$382,017.62	$658,668.67
27	$26,380.34	100	$1,043,979.64	$319,444.10	$724,535.54
28	$18,410.45	100	$1,047,602.31	$250,613.22	$796,989.09
29	$9,643.57	100	$1,051,587.26	$174,899.26	$876,688.00
30	$0.00	100	$1,055,970.70	$91,613.90	$964,356.80

Source: Stone/Zissu

─── EXHIBIT 3.3 ───

Cash Flows Received at CPR of 15 Percent

t	Bt	mt	PTt	IO(t)	PO(t)
0	$100,000.00	100			
1	$99,392.08	85	$2,501,673.61	$950,000.00	$1,551,673.61
2	$98,723.36	72.25	$2,118,154.79	$802,591.01	$1,315,563.78
3	$97,987.77	61.4125	$1,792,701.20	$677,612.45	$1,115,088.75
4	$97,178.62	52.20063	$1,516,568.12	$571,679.02	$944,889.11
5	$96,288.56	44.37053	$1,282,324.82	$481,914.55	$800,410.27
6	$95,309.49	37.71495	$1,083,657.29	$405,875.58	$677,781.71
7	$94,232.51	32.05771	$915,200.61	$341,486.31	$573,714.30
8	$93,047.84	27.24905	$772,396.46	$286,983.45	$485,413.00
9	$91,744.70	23.16169	$651,371.99	$240,869.22	$410,502.77
10	$90,311.24	19.68744	$548,836.92	$201,871.46	$346,965.46
11	$88,734.44	16.73432	$461,996.01	$168,909.74	$293,086.28
12	$86,999.96	14.22418	$388,474.74	$141,066.54	$247,408.20
13	$85,092.03	12.09055	$326,256.08	$117,562.76	$208,693.32
14	$82,993.31	10.27697	$273,626.80	$97,736.90	$175,889.91
15	$80,684.72	8.735422	$229,131.82	$81,027.36	$148,104.47
16	$78,145.27	7.425109	$191,535.40	$66,957.43	$124,577.97
17	$75,351.87	6.311342	$159,788.18	$55,122.52	$104,665.66
18	$72,279.13	5.364641	$132,999.14	$45,179.29	$87,819.85
19	$68,899.12	4.559945	$110,411.81	$36,836.40	$73,575.41
20	$65,181.11	3.875953	$91,384.01	$29,846.74	$61,537.27
21	$61,091.29	3.29456	$75,370.67	$24,000.70	$51,369.98
22	$56,592.50	2.800376	$61,909.21	$19,120.55	$42,788.66
23	$51,643.82	2.38032	$50,607.10	$15,055.63	$35,551.47
24	$46,200.28	2.023272	$41,131.32	$11,678.24	$29,453.09
25	$40,212.38	1.719781	$33,199.42	$8,880.19	$24,319.23
26	$33,625.69	1.461814	$26,571.85	$6,569.87	$20,001.98
27	$26,380.34	1.242542	$21,045.51	$4,669.68	$16,375.83
28	$18,410.45	1.05616	$16,448.26	$3,113.97	$13,334.28
29	$9,643.57	0.897736	$12,634.22	$1,847.22	$10,787.01
30	$0.00	0.763076	$9,479.83	$822.45	$8,657.38

Source: Stone/Zissu

─── EXHIBIT 3.4 ───

Cash Flows Received at CPR of 30 Percent

t	Bt	mt	PTt	IO(t)	PO(t)
0	$100,000.00	100			
1	$99,392.08	70	$3,992,554.74	$950,000.00	$3,042,554.74
2	$98,723.36	49	$2,780,958.03	$660,957.30	$2,120,000.73
3	$97,987.77	34.3	$1,936,021.30	$459,557.23	$1,476,464.06
4	$97,178.62	24.01	$1,347,014.93	$319,293.14	$1,027,721.78
5	$96,288.56	16.807	$936,596.47	$221,659.58	$714,936.89
6	$95,309.49	11.7649	$650,755.76	$153,740.57	$497,015.19
7	$94,232.51	8.23543	$451,785.47	$106,524.13	$345,261.34
8	$93,047.84	5.764801	$313,367.29	$73,724.30	$239,642.99
9	$91,744.70	4.035361	$217,137.54	$50,958.22	$166,179.33
10	$90,311.24	2.824752	$150,287.22	$35,171.18	$115,116.04
11	$88,734.44	1.977327	$103,885.08	$24,235.16	$79,649.92
12	$86,999.96	1.384129	$71,706.25	$16,668.41	$55,037.84
13	$85,092.03	0.96889	$49,414.14	$11,439.82	$37,974.32
14	$82,993.31	0.678223	$33,989.11	$7,832.26	$26,156.85
15	$80,684.72	0.474756	$23,329.77	$5,347.36	$17,982.41
16	$78,145.27	0.332329	$15,974.63	$3,639.03	$12,335.60
17	$75,351.87	0.232631	$10,907.96	$2,467.15	$8,440.82
18	$72,279.13	0.162841	$7,424.38	$1,665.27	$5,759.11
19	$68,899.12	0.113989	$5,034.45	$1,118.15	$3,916.29
20	$65,181.11	0.079792	$3,398.90	$746.11	$2,652.79
21	$61,091.29	0.055855	$2,282.81	$494.09	$1,788.72
22	$56,592.50	0.039098	$1,523.73	$324.16	$1,199.56
23	$51,643.82	0.027369	$1,009.44	$210.20	$799.24
24	$46,200.28	0.019158	$662.59	$134.28	$528.32
25	$40,212.38	0.013411	$429.92	$84.09	$345.83
26	$33,625.69	0.009387	$274.85	$51.23	$223.62
27	$26,380.34	0.006571	$172.30	$29.99	$142.31
28	$18,410.45	0.0046	$105.13	$16.47	$88.67
29	$9,643.57	0.00322	$61.68	$8.05	$53.63
30	$0.00	0.002254	$34.00	$2.95	$31.05

it is assumed to be 30 percent. Clearly, the number of mortgages left in the pool over time decreases faster in exhibit 3.4.

Cash Flow over Time

EXHIBIT **3.5** shows the pass-through over time for three prepayment scenarios. Notice that under the 0 percent prepayment rate, we have an almost straight line. It would be perfectly horizontal were the servicing fee and guarantee fee equal to zero. In such case, the cash flow going to investors at each period would be exactly $100 \times 10{,}607.92$. However, the servicing and guarantee fees are each 0.25 percent of the outstanding pool, and the outstanding pool decreases over time due to the natural amortization of fixed-rate mortgages; therefore, the dollar amount of servicing and guarantee fee decreases over time, so that less is deducted from the cash flow to be passed to investors over time. This explains why the pass-through over time is almost flat but goes slightly higher over time for a 0 percent prepayment rate.

When the prepayment rate is high (CPR = 30 percent), the pass-through is very high early on, because more people prepay their outstanding balance, and decreases rapidly toward zero within a few

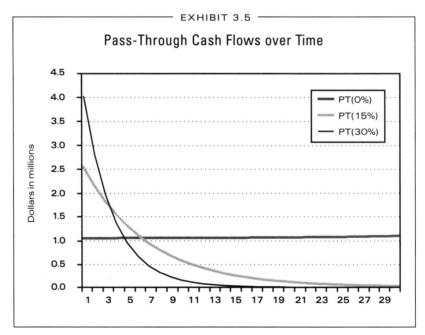

EXHIBIT 3.5

Pass-Through Cash Flows over Time

Source: Stone/Zissu

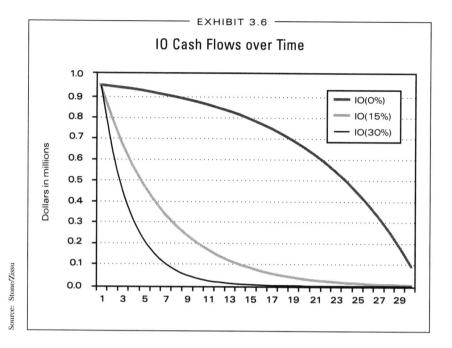

EXHIBIT 3.6

IO Cash Flows over Time

years only. With a low prepayment rate, the pass-through starts at a much lower level and decreases slowly over a longer period of time.

EXHIBIT 3.6 shows the cash flow of an IO security under three prepayment scenarios. One can easily see that the amount of cash flow received over time is severely reduced for an elevated prepayment rate, because the principal outstanding decreases fast, and interest, which is linked with principal, has been reduced. The 0 percent prepayment scenario, optimal for an IO investor, exhibits a concave curve for the cash flows to be paid over time. As soon as some prepayment occurs, the curve becomes convex and is below the curve corresponding to the 0 percent prepayment scenario. Convexity of the curve increases with prepayment rate.

EXHIBIT 3.7 shows the cash flows of PO securities over time under different prepayment scenarios. Notice that the area under any of the curves in exhibit 3.7 is always the same, independent of the prepayment rate. In the simulations, we used a pool of one hundred mortgages with an initial balance of $100,000 each; therefore the total principal to be repaid to a group of PO investors is $10 million. The $10 million will be repaid over a short period if the prepayment rate is high and over many years if the prepayment rate is low. The

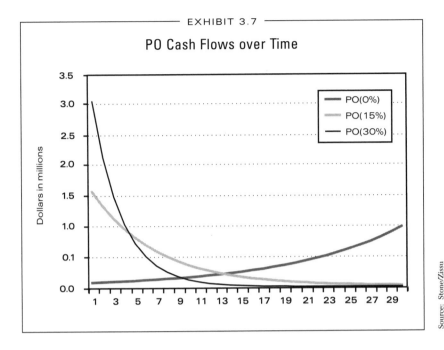

EXHIBIT 3.7

PO Cash Flows over Time

sooner principal is repaid, the better it is for investors, who can then reinvest the principal.

EXHIBIT 3.8 shows the values of a pass-through security, an IO security, and a PO security obtained by adding the discounted cash flows for each security derived under the different prepayment rates from column (1) at the corresponding discount rate (k) in column (2) of exhibit 3.8. Columns (3), (4), and (5) are computed as follows:

$$V(PT) = \sum_{t=1}^{n} PT_t/(1 + k)^t \qquad (3.4)$$

$$V(IO) = \sum_{t=1}^{n} IO_t/(1 + k)^t \qquad (3.5)$$

$$V(PO) = \sum_{t=1}^{n} PO_t/(1 + k)^t \qquad (3.6)$$

The values of the three securities are graphed in **EXHIBIT 3.9**. The horizontal axis represents the discount rates (market rates) from column (2) of exhibit 3.8.

The values (price) of the pass-through, PO, and IO securities are a function of the discount effect and the prepayment effect. As market rates increase, the cash flows of securities are discounted at a higher

--- EXHIBIT 3.8 ---

Valuation of PT, IO, and PO Securities under Different CPR Discounting Scenarios

CPR	k	V(PT)	V(IO)	V(PO)
0%	15%	6661656	5766230	895425
0%	14%	7106920	6107613	999307
0%	13%	7609888	6487446	1122442
1%	12%	8289428	6500172	1789256
5%	11%	9132169	5496260	3635909
7%	10%	9725030	5224437	4500592
10%	9%	10249562	4741685	5507877
15%	8%	10629240	3985186	6644054
20%	7%	10902292	3428711	7473581
25%	6%	11107139	3005091	8102048
30%	5%	11266176	2673037	8593138
35%	4%	11393110	2406281	8986829
40%	3%	11496726	2187522	9309203
45%	2%	11582888	2004991	9577897
50%	1%	11655654	1850436	9805217

Source: Stone/Zissu

level (divided by a bigger number), which in turn lowers the present value of the securities. As discussed in Chapter 2, the value of a bond decreases with yields increasing. This price/yield relationship is illustrated in exhibit 2.2. The same phenomenon occurs with the PT, PO, and IO securities, but some of the discount effect may be offset by the prepayment effect.

When market rates increase, prepayment rates decrease. Lower prepayment rates have a positive effect on IO securities, as less of the cash flow to be paid over time is reduced. Higher prepayment rates reduce the pool's outstanding balance faster, and because the interest payment is a percentage of the pool's outstanding balance, less of it is included in the cash flows paid to IO investors.

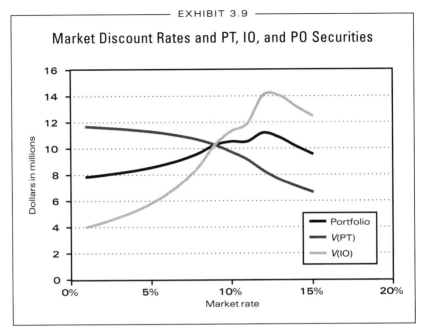

EXHIBIT 3.9

Market Discount Rates and PT, IO, and PO Securities

IO investors are therefore confronted with both the prepayment effect and the discount effect. As market rates increase, prepayment rates decrease, and that has a positive effect that more than offsets the discount effect over a range of market rates, as exhibits 3.8 and 3.9 illustrate. The value of the IO security rises as market rates increase up to 12 percent, after which the value starts to decrease due to the discount effect taking over. This is the case because, at some point, the prepayment rate reaches a minimum level below which it will not go, even though market rates continue to increase. Of course, the example modeled here is based on expected prepayment rates linked to changes in market rates, and this is what determines the shape of the upside-down-parabola price/yield relationship of the IO security. Note, however, that one can never be sure of the yield at which the parabola will reach its maximum point (turnover point).

PO investors benefit from a decrease in market rates (a lower discount rate), which in turn increases prepayment rates. Higher prepayment rates increase the speed at which PO investors receive their principal back. Discount effect and prepayment effect go in the same direction when determining the value of a PO security. You can see in exhibit 3.9 how the value of the PO security decreases as market rates increase. This is due to the higher discount (negative effect on price) and lower prepayment (negative effect on price) linked to higher market rates.

The value of the pass-through security represents a kind of combination of the IO and PO securities. Notice, however, that contrary to the price/yield relationship observed in a noncallable bond (see exhibit 2.2) or in a mortgage with no prepayment option (see exhibit 2.7), for the pass-through security a negative convexity exists in the low yield range. This is due to the prepayment effect. When market rates decrease, mortgagors refinance their mortgages, and investors receive their principal earlier and are forced to reinvest it at the lower market rate. In a conventional bond, price increases as yield decreases (positive convexity). Exhibit 2.13 displays the positive and negative convexities for a pool of mortgages without prepayment option and for a pool with prepayment option.

Effective Duration

WHEN COMPUTING the modified duration (the percentage price change of a security for a given change in yield) of an MBS, in order to evaluate the security's price sensitivity to changes in interest rate, one has to take into account the change in cash flows due to prepayment. When taking the changes in cash flows into account, we then can obtain the *effective duration*—in other words, the security's price sensitivity for a given shift in the underlying yield curve.

The effective duration is computed by taking the difference between the new price obtained with a decrease in yield by 100 bp (P_{-100}) with a corresponding PSA or CPR, and the new price obtained with an increase in yield by 100 bp (P_{+100}) with a corresponding PSA or CPR. We must then divide the difference between the two prices $[(P_{-100})-(P_{+100})]$ by the current price before any change in yield (P_0), multiplied by the difference between the current yield plus 100 bp and the current yield minus 100 bp $(Y_{0+100}-Y_{0-100})$, which means multiplied by twice the change in yield $(2 \times 100 \text{ bp})$.

$$\text{Effective duration} = [(P_{-100})-(P_{+100})/P_0(Y_{0+100}-Y_{0-100}) \qquad (3.7)$$

Equation (3.7) can be rewritten as:

$$\text{Effective duration} = [(P_{-100}) - (P_{+100}) / [P_0(2 \times 100 \text{ bp})] \qquad (3.8)$$

Let's compute the effective duration of the pass-through security from exhibit 3.8, using as base case a yield of 9 percent with the corresponding price of \$10,249,562:

$$\begin{aligned} \text{Effective duration (PT)} &= [10,629,240 - 9,725,030]/10,249,562(0.1-.08) \\ &= 4.41096 \end{aligned}$$

The effective duration for the IO security is:

$$\begin{aligned} \text{Effective duration (IO)} &= [3,985,186 - 5,224,437]/4,741,685\,(0.1-.08) \\ &= -13.06762 \end{aligned}$$

The effective duration for the PO security is:

$$\begin{aligned} \text{Effective duration (PO)} &= [6,644,054 - 4,500,592]/5,507,877\,(0.1-.08) \\ &= 19.45815 \end{aligned}$$

Effective Convexity

THE EFFECTIVE CONVEXITY, that is, the second derivative of the effective duration, can be approximated by the following formula:

$$\begin{aligned} \text{Effective convexity} &= [(P_{+100}) + (P_{-100}) - 2\,(P_0)] \\ &\quad / (P_0)[0.05\,(Y_{0+100} - Y_{0-100})^2] \qquad (3.9) \end{aligned}$$

Equation (3.9) can be rewritten as:

$$\text{Effective convexity} = [(P_{+100}) + (P_{-100}) - 2\,(P_0)]/(P_0)(100 \text{ bp})^2 \qquad (3.10)$$

Let's compute the effective convexity of the pass-through security from exhibit 3.8, using as base case a yield of 9 percent with the corresponding price of \$10,249,562:

Effective convexity (PT) = $[9,725,030 + 10,629,240 - 2(10,249,562)]$
$/10,249,562 (.01)^2 = -141.32$

The effective convexity for the IO security is:

Effective convexity (IO) = $[5,224,437 + 3,985,186 - 2(4,741,685)]$
$/4,741,685 (.01)^2 = -577.32$

The effective convexity for the PO security is:

Effective convexity (PO) = $[4,500,592 + 6,644,054 - 2(5,507,877)]$
$/5,507,877(.01)^2 = 234.01$

To connect these concepts to actual market practice, presented below are the characteristics of a pass-through security issued by Federal National Mortgage Association (FNMA).

Case Study: A Pass-Through Security Issued by FNMA

EXHIBIT **3.10**, illustrating a Bloomberg Professional Service screen, describes a pass-through security issued by FNMA. The top portion describes a generic 8 percent coupon FNMA pass-through, whereas the bottom portion describes a specific 8 percent coupon FNMA pass-through pool: FN 50000 FNCL. FN 50000 was issued May 1, 1987, and expected to mature May 1, 2017. Its original amount was $191.179 million, backed by 128 thirty-year fixed-rate mortgages possessing an original weighted average coupon (WAC) of 8.78 percent with a maximum mortgage rate of 9.38 percent and a minimum of 8.5 percent; a weighted average loan age (WALA) of fifteen years and eight months, with a weighted average remaining maturity (WARM) of twelve years and eight months as of December 2002; and an original weighted average maturity (WAM) of twenty-nine years and eleven months.

FN 50000 has an outstanding balance of $6.379 million (3.3368 percent of the original amount), and its current WAC is 8.776 percent.

Mortgages from sixteen states comprise the pool of FN 50000, with New York representing the highest percentage of the current balance, at 21.69 percent; Texas coming in second, at 14.74 percent; and Kansas coming in last, with only 0.45 percent of the outstanding pool balance.

```
─────────────────── EXHIBIT 3.10 ───────────────────

        Pass-Through Security Issued by FNMA, May 1, 1987


                    SECURITY DISPLAY
                    GENERIC INFORMATION
                                                      LATEST CPR
   TICKER    FNCL     BID PRICE 107-6   ORIG AMT ($MM)    119,623    1 MON 45.0
   COUPON    8.000    ASK PRICE 107-8   CURR AMT ($MM)      9,693    3 MON 43.1
                      AS OF     12/09   "FACTOR"        0.08102977   6 MON 38.5
   WAC       8.535    SEASONED          POOLS               21522   12 MON 40.2
   REM WAM   19Y 7M                                                 ISSUE 25.2
                    CONVENTIONAL LOAN  POOL INFO
   65) Personal Notes                    [ GEO <GO> FOR GEOGRAPHIC REPORT ]
                                                       DELAY DAYS 54(24)
   TICKER    FN       MAT'Y DATE  5/ 1/17  ORIG AMT191,179,079.00  LATEST PSA CPR
   POOL      50000    ISSUE DATE  5/ 1/87  CURR AMT  6,379,263.51   3 MON 696 41.7
   TYPE (CL) FNCL                          Dec02 FACT  0.03336800   6 MON 556 33.3
   COUPON    8.000    Dec02 WALA  15Y 8M   CUSIP       313614RV3   12 MON 538 32.3
   Curtailed 20 mos   Dec02 WARM  12Y 8M   Orig WAC         8.7870  ISSUE 321 18.0
   CURR WAC  8.7760                         Orig WAM      29Y 11M   LOANS       128
   MULTIPLE POOL                                    8.78  152  188   358   79,459
                                                    WAC  WARM WALA  WADLT   AOLS
                                           MAX      9.38  174   189   360  153,100
                             00000         75%      8.88  173   188   360  121,850
                                           MED      8.75  172   188   360   93,800
                                           25%      8.63  150   187   360   63,600
                                           MIN      8.50    8   187   300   30,000
```

Prepayment Standard Assumption Levels

EXHIBIT 3.11 is a summary of FN 50000's expected prepayment standard assumption (PSA) for shifts in the yield curve by ±50 bps, ±100 bps, ±200 bps, and ±300 bps, as submitted by ten different investment banks. It is fascinating to observe the divergence in expected PSA among the different banks. For example, for a 300 bps decrease in market rates, Lehman Brothers expects a PSA of 1136, while UBS expects a PSA of 538, half of that expected by Lehman Brothers.

Of course, the divergence in expected PSA is much narrower for positive shifts in the yield curve. For example, for an increase of 300 bps, Lehman Brothers expects a 170 PSA, while UBS expects a 161 PSA. That is because as market rates increase, prepayment decreases, until it reaches some minimum level that is independent of market rates. People move for different reasons, people default, people die, people get divorced, people get promoted with a higher salary; these are all causes for prepayment that are independent of market rates.

S-Curve Prepayment Function

EXHIBIT 3.12 plots, for different changes in yield, the corresponding expected PSA level for each investment bank that submitted information to Bloomberg. The changes in yield are represented on the

——————— EXHIBIT 3.11 ———————

Dealer Prepayment Forecasts

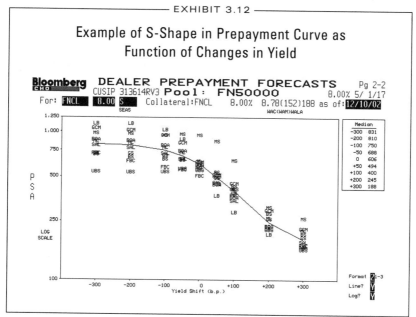

Bloomberg CMO **DEALER PREPAYMENT FORECASTS** Pg 1-2
CUSIP 313614RV3 **Pool: FN50000**   8.00% 5/ 1/17
For: FNCL 8.00 S   Collateral:FNCL   8.00% 8.78(152)188 as of: 12/10/02
SEAS   WAC(WAM)WALA

	OBP	WAM		--------- basis point shift ---------								
Firm	PSA	Yr Mo	WAC	-300	-200	-100	-50	+0	+50	+100	+200	+300
FBC	503		8.78	708	633	575	555	503	445	373	230	173
UBS	548		8.78	538	533	541	565	548	500	411	219	161
BS	617		8.78	701	672	655	646	617	533	431	282	206
ML	630		8.78	858	842	786	724	630	528	412	263	217
LB	618		8.78	1136	1132	1037	891	618	370	288	204	170
SAL	562		8.78	804	777	714	652	562	456	346	225	181
GCM	624		8.78	1055	1026	943	845	624	513	449	295	223
MS	948		8.78	977	970	948	961	948	857	642	309	261
BOA	595		8.78	880	867	811	743	595	439	361	231	166
GS	579		8.78	714	711	687	650	579	487	388	259	195
Avg	622			837	816	770	723	622	513	410	252	195
MED	606			831	810	750	688	606	494	400	245	188

Bloomberg MEDIAN PREPAYMENTS

Source: Bloomberg

——————— EXHIBIT 3.12 ———————

Example of S-Shape in Prepayment Curve as
Function of Changes in Yield

Bloomberg CMO **DEALER PREPAYMENT FORECASTS** Pg 2-2
CUSIP 313614RV3 **Pool: FN50000**   8.00% 5/ 1/17
For: FNCL 8.00 S   Collateral:FNCL   8.00% 8.78(152)188 as of: 12/10/02
SEAS   WAC(WAM)WALA

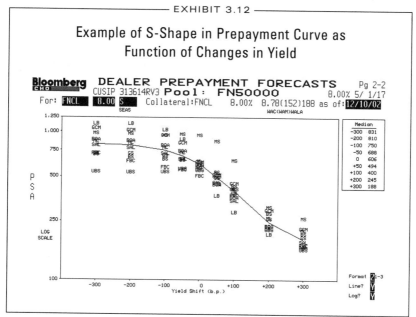

Source: Bloomberg

horizontal axis, with the corresponding expected PSA levels on the
vertical axis. The curve represents the median for the ten banks. One
can see that the prepayment curve as a function of changes in yield
has an S-shape. This is true not only for the median in exhibit 3.12 but

also for the expected PSA levels supplied by each individual investment bank.

The S-shape prepayment function of each bank can be observed in
EXHIBITS **3.13** and **3.14**, which graph separately the composite information contained in exhibit 3.11. Investment banks have their own
proprietary prepayment model, but all have in common the S-curve
prepayment function. The S-curve shows a steeper slope around the
initial market rate (at 0 percent change in yield), with the prepayment
rate increasing as market rates continue to drop, until a so-called
burnout effect is reached, and the curve flattens. Prepayment burnout
happens when some mortgagors have a greater propensity to prepay
than others. Once these mortgagors have left the pool of mortgages,
the remaining ones will have a slower propensity to prepay. At that
point, the prepayment rate no longer increases as it did in the middle
range of the market rate's decrease.

The S-curve also flattens in the high range of market rates. What
happens is that the prepayment rate decreases with an increase in market rates until it reaches a minimum beyond which no further decrease
in prepayment rates is observed. In other words, the natural level of prepayment rate (that is, the prepayment rate that is independent of mar-

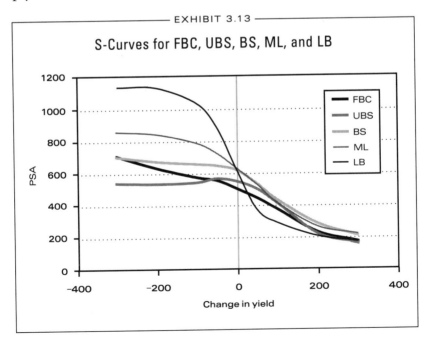

EXHIBIT 3.13

S-Curves for FBC, UBS, BS, ML, and LB

Source: Stone/Zissu using data from Bloomberg

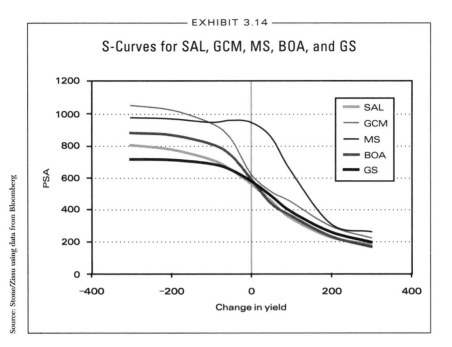

EXHIBIT 3.14

S-Curves for SAL, GCM, MS, BOA, and GS

ket rates) is reached, but is a function of mortgagors' personal events.

The S-shaped prepayment curves of five of the ten banks are graphed together in exhibit 3.13, and the remaining five in exhibit 3.14. In exhibit 3.13, one curve sticks out: that of Lehman Brother (LB). LB expects a much higher PSA rate for large negative changes in yields than the remaining four banks in that group.

In exhibit 3.14, Morgan Stanley (MS) is the one differentiating itself. MS consistently has a higher PSA rate for the period covered than the other four banks, for each change in yield, positive or negative, except for Greenwich Capital's curve, which crosses the MS curve for high negative changes in yields, achieving the highest expected PSA rate.

Weighted Average Life and Different Spreads Measurements

EXHIBIT 3.15 represents the median of the expected PSA and the corresponding weighted average life (WAL) for FN 50000, given a change in yield. The WAL is computed as follows:

$$WAL = \{\textstyle\sum_{t=1}^{n} (t)\, \text{Princ}_t\} / \sum_{t=1}^{n} \text{Princ}_t \qquad (3.11)$$

EXHIBIT 3.15

Weighted Average Life for FN 50000

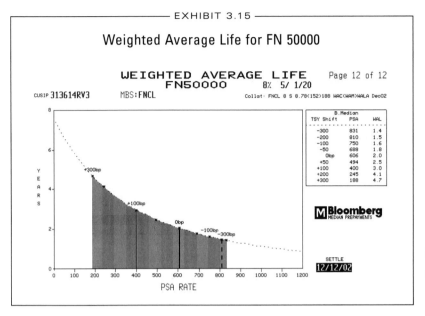

The principal portion received at each point in time is multiplied by the time at which it is received; it is then added to all other principal amounts multiplied by the time at which they are received, the total being divided by the total initial principal of the security.

From the pass-through security used as an example in the beginning of this chapter, using the simulated cash flows under the three prepayment scenarios in exhibits 3.2, 3.3, and 3.4, the following WAL were derived:

CPR=0 percent	WAL=21.82 years
CPR=15 percent	WAL=6.21 years
CPR=30 percent	WAL=3.27 years

For example, the WAL of 21.82 years was computed using the principal amount (PO) paid at each period as shown in exhibit 3.2:

$$WAL = [(1)60,792.48 + (2)66,871.73 + (3)73,558.9 + \ldots + (30)964,356.8] / 10,000,000$$

Naturally, the WAL of a security decreases with increases in prepayment rates.

Spread I, Static Spread (Spread Z), and Spread S

It is standard in the market to compare an asset-backed security (ABS) to a Treasury with a maturity close to the ABS's WAL. For example, investors may look at a pass-through security priced at "twenty over Treasury." What that means is that the Treasury security with a maturity close to the WAL of the pass-through security, based on a given prepayment speed, is the one used as a benchmark to compute the spread. This is shown under Spread I in EXHIBIT **3.16**.

FN 50000's median weighted average lives for different change in yields and corresponding PSA from the submissions of different investment banks to Bloomberg on January 30, 2003, are shown in exhibit 3.16.

The highlighted line corresponds to the base case with no change in yield. The spreads are defined by Bloomberg as follows: Spread I, conventional yield spread to interpolated yield curve; Spread Z, cash flow spread to implied spot curve; and Spread S, cash flow spread to actual U.S. strip curve.

The first three columns from exhibit 3.16 are graphed in exhibit 3.15. The change in yield is represented on the horizontal axis; the WAL on the vertical axis, in years; and the corresponding PSA levels are shown along the curve.

The disadvantage in using Spread I is that it assumes the MBS has

---

EXHIBIT 3.16

Median Weighted Average Lives for FN 50000

CHANGE IN YIELD (1)	PSA (2)	WAL (3)	PRICE (4)	SPREAD I (5)	SPREAD Z (6)	SPREAD S (7)
−300	832	1.42	105–19	+196.2	+148.8	+143.3
−200	813	1.46	105–24+	+194.7	+146.2	+140.5
−100	766	1.57	106–06+	+190.7	+139.4	+133.1
0	611	2.01	108–00	+174.2	+114.2	+105.5
100	439	2.73	110–27+	+141.7	+81.1	+69.1
200	270	3.87	115–06+	+90.0	+43.9	+27.3
300	200	4.53	117–22+	+61.1	+27.6	+8.8

a maturity equal to its WAL and that principal is paid at maturity (as with a regular bond), rather than being paid over time as a function of the prepayment speed.

Bloomberg uses Spread Z, or the static spread. The static spread is based on the Treasury spot-rate curve and discounts the cash flow of the MBS, assuming that investors hold the security until maturity, so that the present value is equal to the price of the MBS. Its computation is shown in equation (3.12), where n is the maturity of the MBS, CF_t is the cash flow of the MBS at time t, R_{TSt} is the Treasury spot rate at time t, and s is the static spread.

$$\text{Price (MBS)} = PV = \sum_{t=1}^{n} \left[CF_t / (1 + R_{TSt} + s)^t \right] \qquad (3.12)$$

The problem with the static spread is that once prepayment speed is determined, based on an initial shift in the yield curve, the model will not allow it to change over time, meaning the model has a zero volatility (i.e., the standard deviation is equal to zero).

EXHIBIT **3.17** compares the different spread calculations from exhibit 3.16. Columns (1) and (2) are for Spread I, columns (3) and (4) are for Spread Z, and columns (5) and (6) are for Spread S.

Option-Adjusted Spread

Finally, the most widely used spread is the option-adjusted spread (OAS), which reflects the value of mortgagors' option of refinancing at lower mortgage rates.

In using OAS, a few hundred paths of the term structure of interest rates and the spot rates (the theoretical yields on a zero-coupon Treasury) are created via Monte Carlo simulations. Each path will generate specific cash flows over time for the MBS, based on proprietary prepayment models, allowing prepayment speed to change as a function of the spot rates.

Then, after adding a spread, the OAS, to the spot rate at each point in time, the cash flows of the MBS are discounted to the present at a rate equal to the spot rate plus the OAS. Using the same spread, the present value is computed for all simulated paths of spot rates. The average of all present values is computed and compared to the actual price of the MBS. If the average present value of all paths is equal to the price, the OAS is correct; otherwise a different spread is

──────── EXHIBIT 3.17 ────────

Treasury Curves

TREASURY CURVE (1)	(2)	TREASURY SPOT CURVE (3)	(4)	TREASURY STRIP CURVE (5)	(6)
3 mos	1.16%	3 mos	1.14%		
6 mos	1.19%	6 mos	1.18%		
		1	1.38%	1	1.30%
2	1.75%	2	1.76%	2	1.76%
		3	2.19%	3	2.29%
5	3.00%	5	3.18%	5	3.08%
				7	3.81%
10	4.04%	10	4.29%	10	4.48%
				15	5.20%
				25	5.48%
30	4.92%	30	5.83%		

Source: Bloomberg

used until the average present value of the discounted cash flows for each simulated term structure of interest rates is equal to the current price of the MBS. In equation 3.13, g is the number of simulated paths of term structure of interest rates; h is path h; and PV_h is the present value of the cash flows for path h.

$$AvgPV(MBS) = \Sigma_{h=1}^{g}\ PV_h/g \qquad (3.13)$$

where PV_h is defined in equation (3.14) below and corresponds to the present value of the cash flows of the MBS based on path h with its corresponding prepayment speeds. CF_{ht} is the cash flow of path h at time t, and R_{hTSt} is the Treasury spot rate at time t for path h.

$$PV_h = \Sigma_{t=1}^{n}\ CF_{ht}/(1 + R_{hTSt} + OAS)^t \qquad (3.14)$$

Clearly, the OAS of an MBS will differ among the different institutions supplying the calculation. There are two main reasons for the divergence. The first is that simulations of future interest rate paths are random and cannot coincide from one institution to another. Second, the prepayment models used to estimate future cash flows linked to the Treasury spot rates vary among institutions.

The OAS provided by Bloomberg for FN 50000 on January 30, 2003, is 146.6. The option cost, which is calculated by taking the difference between the static spread—Spread Z, or column (6) of exhibit 3.16 at the level of the base case—and the OAS, is 114.2 minus 146.6, or –25.4.

One could interpret the OAS as the spread above Treasury after stripping away the cost of the prepayment option from the static spread. Once that prepayment-option cost is removed, the OAS represents the true spread left above Treasury.

Negative Option Cost

Notice that FN 50000 has a negative option cost. A negative option cost arises when investors benefit from high-speed prepayments. This can be explained by the fact that FN 50000 was issued in 1987 and will soon mature. It is now similar to a PO security, because the payments are now mostly principal and very little interest. As was discussed previously, a PO security benefits from high-speed prepayment and therefore has a negative option cost. EXHIBITS 3.18 through 3.20 graph the cash flows of FN 50000 for, starting from the bottom, the scheduled principal, the prepaid principal, the interest portion, and the servicing amount, over time for different expected PSA scenarios corresponding to changes in yield, as provided by First Boston. As was noted earlier, each investment bank has its own expected PSA scenarios for similar changes in yield, which are a function of a bank's proprietary prepayment model. Notice that the servicing amount is similar to an IO security and can actually be traded. The servicing is negatively affected by high prepayment levels.

The PSA levels provided by First Boston, for changes in yield going from –300 bps to +300 bps, range from 708 PSA (a CPR of about 42 percent) to 173 PSA (a CPR of 10.38 percent).

Whether the prepayment rate is high (as in exhibit 3.19) or low (as in exhibit 3.18), the total area of scheduled and prepaid principal is always the same. The shape of it changes and stretches over time for low prepayment rate, while it is concentrated over a shorter period of time for high prepayment rate, with the area under the

EXHIBIT 3.18

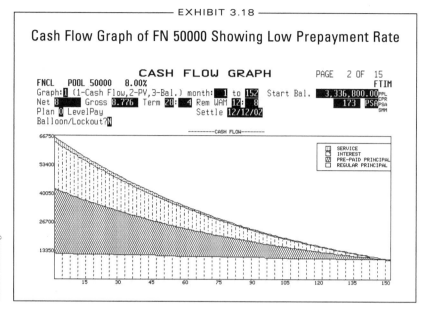

Cash Flow Graph of FN 50000 Showing Low Prepayment Rate

EXHIBIT 3.19

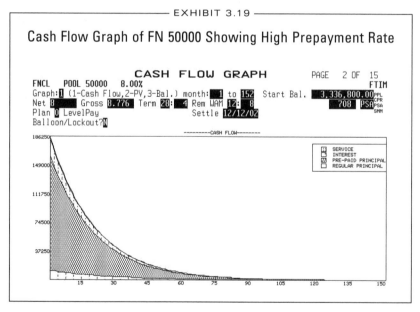

Cash Flow Graph of FN 50000 Showing High Prepayment Rate

curve unchanged. On the other hand, the area of the servicing or that of the interest payments over time is considerably reduced for elevated prepayment rates. This is due to the fact that elevated prepayment rates reduce the amount of outstanding balance in the

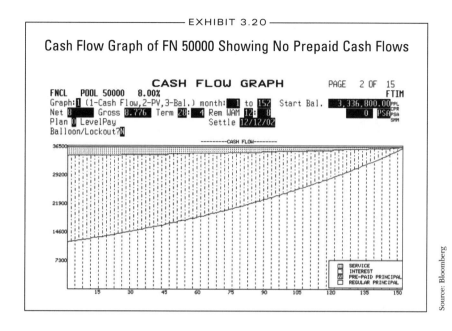

EXHIBIT 3.20

Cash Flow Graph of FN 50000 Showing No Prepaid Cash Flows

Source: Bloomberg

pool, and servicing and interest are computed as a percentage of the outstanding balance.

Exhibit 3.20 has only three components: scheduled principal cash flows, interest cash flows, and servicing cash flows over time. There is no prepaid cash flows category as we are in a zero-PSA scenario. This is akin to exhibit 1.5, in which the cash flows of the principal and interest portion are graphed for a traditional amortizing fixed-rate mortgage. As of December 9, 2002, FN 50000 was priced at 108-23+, according to the Bloomberg data. It is priced at premium because its pass-through rate of 8 percent is above the market rate. Keep in mind that at a 0 percent change in yield (as seen in exhibit 3.11), the median PSA is 606 (a CPR of about 36 percent). This means that even though FN 50000 has a pass-through rate better than the market rate, because it is backed by mortgages with a WAC of 8.78 percent, which is above current mortgage rates, investors are exposed to a significant prepayment risk. Note, however, that having existed since 1987, FN 50000 now acts like a PO security, with a negative option cost. This means that investors would benefit if prepayment speed increased.

Case Study: Principal-Only and Interest-Only Securities

OUR CASE STUDY continues with a look at PO and IO securities based on the same pool of mortgages, using as an example first the FHS 3 Freddie Mac strip, a PO strip, and later, FHS 3 Class B, an IO strip. The original amount of the pool was $33,728,000. Class A is a PO strip, with an original weighted average life of 8.72 years, and Class B is an IO strip with a 9 percent coupon rate. Both classes are expected to mature June 1, 2017.

Classes A and B were issued October 20, 1989. They were collateralized by mortgages with a WAC of 9.9007 percent, a weighted average maturity (WAM) of twenty-seven years and three months, and seasoning of two years and nine months. As of November 1, 2002, the WAC of the remaining mortgages in the pool was 9.9331 percent, the WAM was thirteen years and eleven months, and seasoning was fifteen years and seven months. The securities were originally priced based on an expected 179 PSA.

PO Strip

The CPRs for Class A, the PO strip, for January, February, March, April, May, June, and July 2002, were respectively 1.6, 1.5, 77.2, 2.2, 14.8, 1.6, and 71.8 percent. For the same months, the corresponding PSAs were 26; 26; 1,286; 36; 247; 27; and 1,197.

EXHIBITS **3.21** through **3.24** represent the projected cash flow for the FH3 PO strip over time for four different prepayment scenarios. Keep in mind that PO investors receive the same total amount of principal, independent of prepayment rates. They simply will receive the principal faster, over a shorter period, for higher prepayment rates, and over a longer period for lower prepayment rates. The value of the PO security or its yield (holding the price constant) goes up with an increase in expected prepayment rates, and down with a decrease in expected prepayment rates. Exhibits 3.21 through 3.24 reflect the following data:

PRICE = 89-20

0%	1.2958
20%	3.1776
40%	6.0319
80%	15.9829

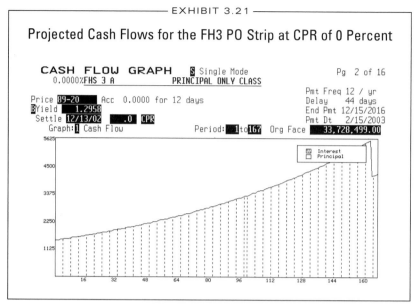

EXHIBIT 3.21

Projected Cash Flows for the FH3 PO Strip at CPR of 0 Percent

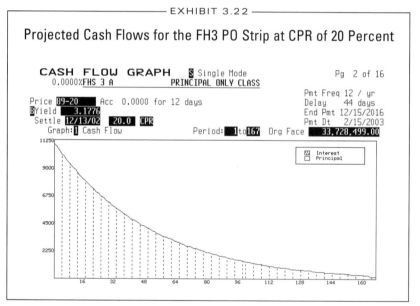

EXHIBIT 3.22

Projected Cash Flows for the FH3 PO Strip at CPR of 20 Percent

Source: Bloomberg

Clearly, the yield to maturity increases when expected prepayment increases, and price is held constant at 89-20.

EXHIBITS 3.25 and **3.26** show the weighted average life (WAL) and PSA for the different changes in yields, supplied by Lehman

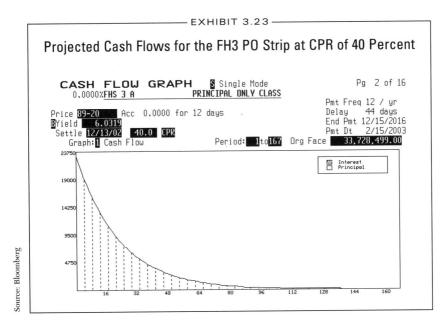

EXHIBIT 3.23

Projected Cash Flows for the FH3 PO Strip at CPR of 40 Percent

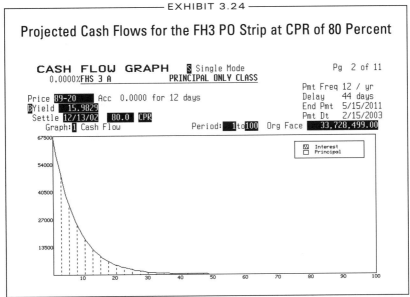

EXHIBIT 3.24

Projected Cash Flows for the FH3 PO Strip at CPR of 80 Percent

Brothers and Salomon Brothers, respectively. **EXHIBIT 3.27** provides information including Macaulay duration, modified duration, effective duration, effective convexity, and WAL.

———— EXHIBIT 3.25 ————

Weight Average Life and PSA for Lehman Brothers

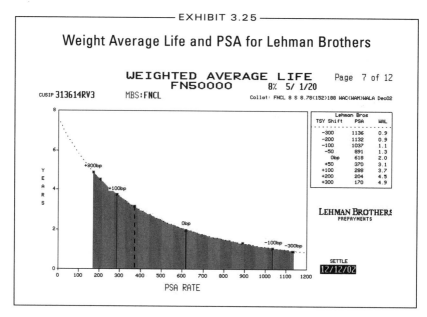

———— EXHIBIT 3.26 ————

Weight Average Life and PSA for Salomon Brothers

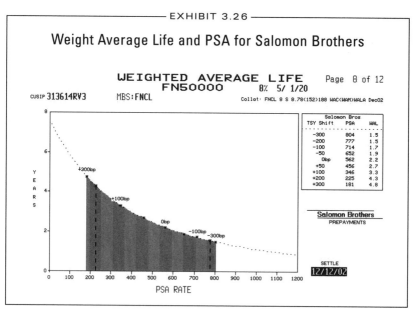

Interpretation of the information provided under "Effective values for 100 bp shift" (in the upper right side of exhibit 3.27) reveals the following: the effective duration is 5.736, the effective convexity is –0.35 (negative convexity), and dP/dy is 5.225.

——————————————— EXHIBIT 3.27 ———————————————

Quick Yield Analysis

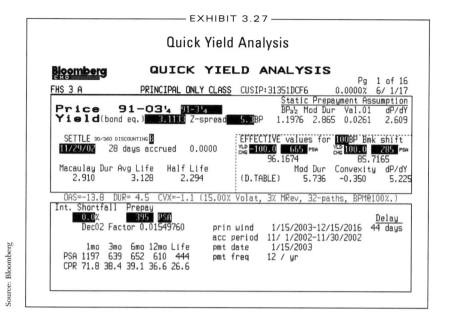

For a –100 bps yield change, the expected PSA is 665 with a corresponding new price of 96.1674, and for a +100 bps yield change, the expected PSA is 285 with a corresponding price of 85.7165 (see the upper right quadrant of exhibit 3.27).

Based on the posted price of 91-3¼ and the above information, one can easily calculate the new prices corresponding to a positive or negative 100 bps change in yield.

As was discussed in Chapter 2, replacing modified duration with effective duration, and convexity with effective convexity, has the following effects. For an increase in yield, the new true price (on the curve) is equal to:

$$P_T = P_0[1 - dyD_{\text{effective}} - (1/2)(\text{convexity}_{\text{effective}})(dy)^2]$$

and for a decrease in yield:

$$P_T = P_0[1 + dyD_{\text{effective}} - (1/2)(\text{convexity}_{\text{effective}})(dy)^2]$$

Note that, contrary to a noncallable bond, when calculating the new price along the curve given a change in yield, we deduct rather than add back the percentage change in price due to convexity, from the new price computed by incorporating the *percentage change in price due to duration* only. The reader should refer back to the PO price/yield relationship in exhibit 3.9 to visualize the negative convexity.

Using the effective duration and convexity, we can find the new price of 96.16 for a decrease in yield by 100 bps, and a new price of 85.71 for an increase in yield by 100 bps as follows:

Decrease in yield by 100 bps = 96.16
$$= 91\text{-}3\frac{1}{4}\,[1+5.736(.01)-(1/2)(0.35)(.01)^2]$$

Increase in yield by 100 bps = 85.71
$$= 91\text{-}3\frac{1}{4}\,[1-5.736(.01)-(1/2)(0.35)(.01)^2]$$

Exhibit 3.27 presents a bond equivalent yield of 3.1133. This corresponds to the cash-flow yield, or the yield that will equate the present value of the projected cash flows (adjusted for monthly payment) to the actual price 91-3¼ of the PO security.

Spread I (Spread/WAL) and Spread Z (static spread) are represented in EXHIBITS **3.28** and **3.29**, respectively. The OAS supplied by the Bloomberg Professional service as of February 25, 2003, for FHS 3A is 114.3, with a cost of option equal to +20.

IO Strip

With respect to the FHS Class B, an IO strip, EXHIBITS **3.30** and **3.31** graph the projected cash flows investors would receive for a 0 PSA and for multiple PSAs, respectively. Clearly a 0 PSA is the best possible scenario for an IO investor. One can see the difference in the areas under the curves. The higher the prepayment speed, the higher the cash-flow truncation for investors and the smaller the area under the curve of cash flows to be paid.

The pass-through security is the simplest structure in securitization, often referred to as a "plain-vanilla" structure. The IOs and POs are derivatives of pass-through securities, and investors choose to invest in one or the other as a function of their expectations about interest rates and prepayment rates. These securities can also be used as hedging tools (see Chapter 9). In the next chapter we describe the CMO (collateralized mortgage obligation), the PAC (planned amortization class), and the floater/inverse floater structures. The financial

——— EXHIBIT 3.28 ———

Spread I (Spread/WAL) for FHS Class A

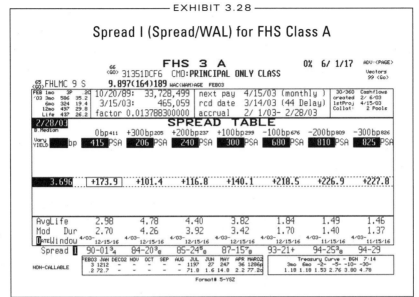

——— EXHIBIT 3.29 ———

Spread Z (Static Spread) for FHS Class A

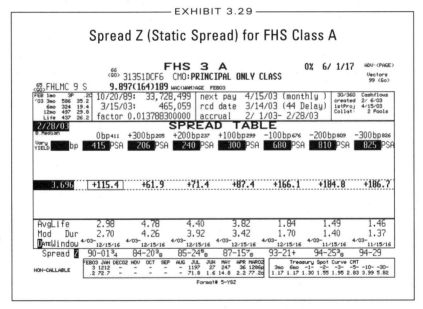

engineer starts with a plain-vanilla structure, the pass-through security, and by "slicing and dicing" it, creates securities with different
structures, each to satisfy specific investors' needs.

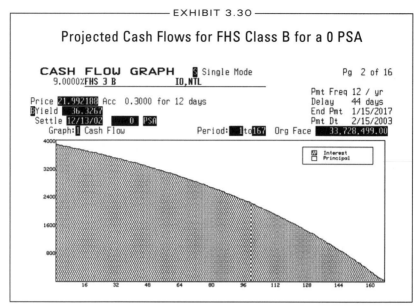

EXHIBIT 3.30

Projected Cash Flows for FHS Class B for a 0 PSA

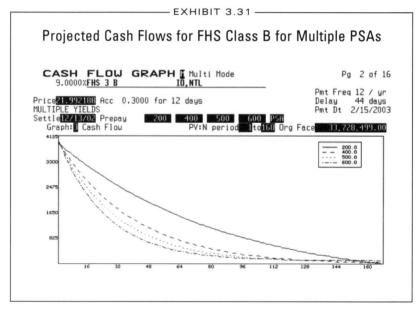

EXHIBIT 3.31

Projected Cash Flows for FHS Class B for Multiple PSAs

Chapter Notes

1. A CPR of 5 percent indicates that mortgage principal is being prepaid at an annual rate of 5 percent. A prepayment model developed by the Public Securities Association (PSA) is also widely used for quoting prices on MBSs.

Chapter Four

Other Structures in Asset-Backed Securities: CMOs, PACs, Floaters, and Inverse Floaters

CHAPTER 3 introduced the basic structure of asset-backed securities: the pass-through structure and its derivatives, interest-only (IO) and principal-only (PO) structures. This chapter explains other securities structures derived from the plain-vanilla pass-through security.

Collateralized Mortgage Obligations

WHEN A special-purpose vehicle (SPV) finances the purchase of pass-through certificates or pools of mortgages with multiple classes of debt that differ with respect to amortization and accrual schedules, the securities are referred to as collateralized mortgage obligations (CMOs). The important distinction between the CMO structure and the pass-through structure is that CMOs enable the issuer to obtain a finer separation of risks that are associated with thirty-year fixed-rate mortgages. The pass-through structure does not issue securities with different stated maturity dates and amortization schedules but instead distributes principal and interest to the different classes of securities as it is received by the SPV. Investors receive a pro rata share of the distributions based on their interest in the SPV's assets. An SPV that issues CMOs must allocate the cash flows it receives from the servicer of the underlying mortgages to each class of securities according to detailed amortization and accrual schedules. Each class of CMOs issued by an SPV will have different coupon or accrual rates depending on the type and quantity of risk it funds, on its respective anticipated maturity profile, and on the anticipated term structure of interest rates at the time the securities are structured.

In the following example, we simulate an SPV that issues four classes of CMOs (classes A, B, C, and D) to fund a portfolio of 9.5 percent Federal National Mortgage Association (FNMA) pass-through certificates for a total amount of $10 million. Each class of securities finances 25 percent of the portfolio of pass-through. Class A has an 8.25 percent coupon, class B an 8.50 percent coupon, class C a 9 percent coupon, and class D a 9.25 percent coupon. Class A must be amortized before class B begins to receive any principal payments (its last payment may overlap with class B's first payment); class B must be amortized before class C begins to receive principal; and class C must be amortized before class D begins to receive principal. While principal is being distributed to class A, classes B, C, and D receive interest payments computed as their respective coupon rate times their respective outstanding balance. Each class's outstanding balance does not start the amortization process until the previous class has been fully paid, so until then, its interest payment is constant.

EXHIBITS **4.1** through **4.4** list the principal cash flow of each class under four prepayment scenarios (0 percent, 15 percent, 30 percent, and 45 percent) with their respective graphs represented in EXHIBITS **4.5** through **4.8**. Looking at each graph, one can notice the similarities to the cash flows of a PO security. The difference is that in the sequential classes, the prepayment risk is reallocated among the four classes, rather than in one class of PO investors.

Under a 0 percent prepayment scenario, it takes eighteen years for class A to be fully paid; class B starts to receive principal payment in year eighteen and is fully retired in year twenty-four; class C starts to receive principal in year twenty-four and is fully amortized in year twenty-eight; and finally, class D receives its principal between year twenty-eight and year thirty.

EXHIBIT **4.9** summarizes the results from exhibits 4.1 through 4.4. It shows when a class starts to receive principal payment, and when it is fully retired, under the four different prepayment scenarios. Clearly class D is the most exposed to prepayment risk. It has the highest variation in windows during which the class receives principal payment.

——— EXHIBIT 4.1 ———

Principal Cash Flows at CPR of 0 Percent

t	CLASS A	CLASS B	CLASS C	CLASS D
0				
1	60792.48253	0	0	0
2	66871.73078	0	0	0
3	73558.90386	0	0	0
4	80914.79424	0	0	0
5	89006.27367	0	0	0
6	97906.90103	0	0	0
7	107697.5911	0	0	0
8	118467.3503	0	0	0
9	130314.0853	0	0	0
10	143345.4938	0	0	0
11	157680.0432	0	0	0
12	173448.0475	0	0	0
13	190792.8523	0	0	0
14	209872.1375	0	0	0
15	230859.3512	0	0	0
16	253945.2863	0	0	0
17	279339.815	0	0	0
18	$35,186.86	$272,086.94	0	0
19	0	338001.1761	0	0
20	0	371801.2937	0	0
21	0	408981.4231	0	0
22	0	449879.5654	0	0
23	0	494867.522	0	0
24	0	$164,382.08	$379,972.19	0
25	0	0	598789.702	0
26	0	0	658668.672	0
27	0	0	724535.539	0
28	0	0	$138,033.90	$658,955.20
29	0	0	0	$876,688.00
30	0	0	0	$964,356.80

Source: Stone/Zissu

--- EXHIBIT 4.2 ---

Principal Cash Flows at CPR of 15 Percent

t	CLASS A	CLASS B	CLASS C	CLASS D
0				
1	1551673.61	0	0	
2	948326.3899	$367,237.39	0	
3	0	1115088.753	0	
4	0	944889.1063	0	
5	0	$72,784.75	$727,625.52	
6	0	0	677781.7121	
7	0	0	573714.2951	
8	0	0	485413.0011	
9	0	0	$35,465.47	$375,037.30
10	0	0	0	$346,965.46
11	0	0	0	$293,086.28
12	0	0	0	$247,408.20
13	0	0	0	$208,693.32
14	0	0	0	$175,889.91
15	0	0	0	$148,104.47
16	0	0	0	$124,577.97
17	0	0	0	$104,665.66
18	0	0	0	$87,819.85
19	0	0	0	$73,575.41
20	0	0	0	$61,537.27
21	0	0	0	$51,369.98
22	0	0	0	$42,788.66
23	0	0	0	$35,551.47
24	0	0	0	$29,453.09
25	0	0	0	$24,319.23
26	0	0	0	$20,001.98
27	0	0	0	$16,375.83
28	0	0	0	$13,334.28
29	0	0	0	$10,787.01
30	0	0	0	$8,657.38

EXHIBIT 4.3

Principal Cash Flows at CPR of 30 Percent

t	CLASS A	CLASS B	CLASS C	CLASS D
0				
1	2500000	$542,554.74	0	0
2	0	$1,957,445.26	$162,555.47	$0.00
3	0	$0.00	$1,476,464.06	0
4	0	$0.00	$860,980.47	$166,741.31
5	0	$0.00	$0.00	$714,936.89
6	0	$0.00	$0.00	$497,015.19
7	0	$0.00	$0.00	$345,261.34
8	0	$0.00	$0.00	$239,642.99
9	0	$0.00	$0.00	$166,179.33
10	0	$0.00	$0.00	$115,116.04
11	0	$0.00	$0.00	$79,649.92
12	0	$0.00	$0.00	$55,037.84
13	0	$0.00	$0.00	$37,974.32
14	0	$0.00	$0.00	$26,156.85
15	0	$0.00	$0.00	$17,982.41
16	0	$0.00	$0.00	$12,335.60
17	0	$0.00	$0.00	$8,440.82
18	0	$0.00	$0.00	$5,759.11
19	0	$0.00	$0.00	$3,916.29
20	0	$0.00	$0.00	$2,652.79
21	0	$0.00	$0.00	$1,788.72
22	0	$0.00	$0.00	$1,199.56
23	0	$0.00	$0.00	$799.24
24	0	$0.00	$0.00	$528.32
25	0	$0.00	$0.00	$345.83
26	0	$0.00	$0.00	$223.62
27	0	$0.00	$0.00	$142.31
28	0	$0.00	$0.00	$88.67
29	0	$0.00	$0.00	$53.63
30	0	$0.00	$0.00	$31.05

——— EXHIBIT 4.4 ———

Principal Cash Flows at CPR of 45 Percent

t	CLASS A	CLASS B	CLASS C	CLASS D
0				
1	2500000	$2,033,435.87	0	0
2	0	$466,564.13	$2,013,618.42	$0.00
3	0	$0.00	$486,381.58	$869,728.50
4	0	$0.00	$0.00	$741,026.39
5	0	$0.00	$0.00	$404,639.85
6	0	$0.00	$0.00	$220,782.50
7	0	$0.00	$0.00	$120,359.87
8	0	$0.00	$0.00	$65,550.28
9	0	$0.00	$0.00	$35,660.82
10	0	$0.00	$0.00	$19,376.40
11	0	$0.00	$0.00	$10,513.60
12	0	$0.00	$0.00	$5,695.71
13	0	$0.00	$0.00	$3,080.15
14	0	$0.00	$0.00	$1,662.32
15	0	$0.00	$0.00	$895.06
16	0	$0.00	$0.00	$480.66
17	0	$0.00	$0.00	$257.33
18	0	$0.00	$0.00	$137.28
19	0	$0.00	$0.00	$72.93
20	0	$0.00	$0.00	$38.55
21	0	$0.00	$0.00	$20.26
22	0	$0.00	$0.00	$10.57
23	0	$0.00	$0.00	$5.47
24	0	$0.00	$0.00	$2.80
25	0	$0.00	$0.00	$1.41
26	0	$0.00	$0.00	$0.70
27	0	$0.00	$0.00	$0.34
28	0	$0.00	$0.00	$0.16
29	0	$0.00	$0.00	$0.07
30	0	$0.00	$0.00	$0.03

Source: Stone/Zissu

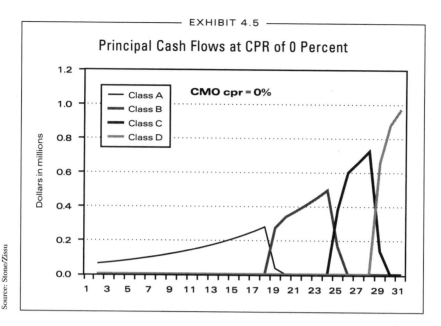

Source: Stone/Zissu

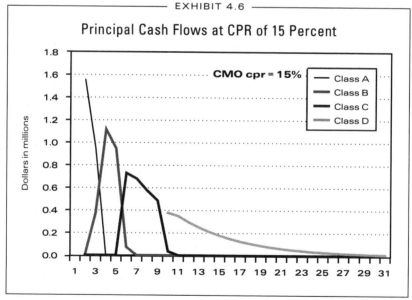

Source: Stone/Zissu

EXHIBIT 4.10 represents the first page of an eighty-two-class mortgage-based security (MBS) issued by FNMA in 2003. The first five classes are sequential notes assigned to three different groups. Class B will not receive any principal until class A, class AG, class AR, and class AT are fully amortized.

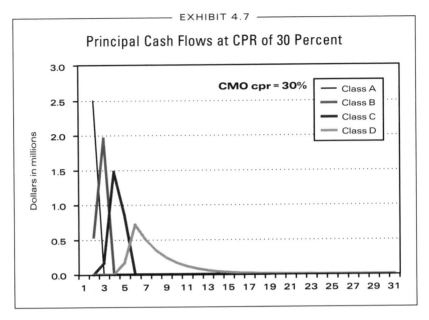

EXHIBIT 4.7

Principal Cash Flows at CPR of 30 Percent

Source: Stone/Zissu

EXHIBIT 4.8

Principal Cash Flows at CPR of 45 Percent

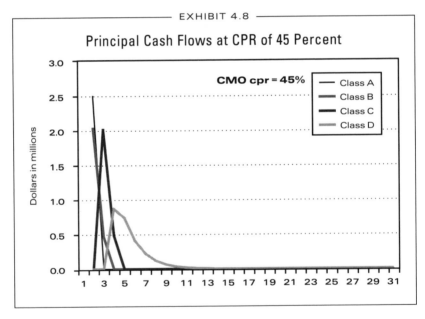

Source: Stone/Zissu

EXHIBITS **4.11** through **4.15** graph the projected cash flows (interest and principal) for each of the five classes under four different prepayment standard assumption (PSA) scenarios—0 PSA, 25 PSA, 267 PSA, and 450 PSA. The first four classes are paid pari passu (simultaneously),

Source: Stone/Zissu

EXHIBIT 4.9

Summary of Principal Cash Flows at Different CPRs

	CPR = 0%	CPR = 15%	CPR = 30%	CPR = 45%
Class A	1–18	1–2	1	1
Class B	18–24	2–5	1–2	1–2
Class C	24–28	5–9	2–4	2–3
Class D	28–30	9–30	4–30	3–30

Source: Bloomberg

EXHIBIT 4.10

Class Structure of MBS Issued by FNMA in 2003

CMO/ABS SECURITIES   Pg 1 of 5
All Classes for **FNR 2003-1** FANNIE MAE

	Class	Orig Amt (000s)	Coupon	Orig WAL	Orig Maturity	CUSIP	GRADE	Description
*	1) A	30,000	5.50	4.10	8/25/30	31392HSG9	1ED	SEQ
*	2) AG	151,250	5.00	4.10	8/25/30	31392HSH7	2ED	SEQ
*	3) AR	33,750	7.00	4.10	8/25/30	31392HSJ3	--	SEQ
*	4) AT	25,000	6.50	4.10	8/25/30	31392HSK0	0ED	SEQ
*	5) B	60,000	5.50	14.00	2/25/33	31392HSL8	9EE	SEQ
*	6) BB	11,444	5.50	11.40	2/25/33	31392HSM6	14EE	SUP,RTL
*	7) DC	8,421	5.50	3.00	2/25/33	31392HSN4	1DC	AD,TAC(22)
*	8) FG	14,735	2.74	5.20	2/25/33	31392HSP9	-	FLT,DLY,SUP
*	9) FJ	7,868	2.24	3.10	1/25/32	31392HSQ7	-	FLT,SUP
*	10) GC	13,067	5.50	2.80	10/25/32	31392HSR5	1DC	SCH(22)
*	11) GD	3,119	5.50	6.00	11/25/32	31392HSS3	3ED	SCH(22)
*	12) GE	2,275	5.50	8.00	12/25/32	31392HST1	5ED	SCH(22)
*	13) GJ	5,031	5.50	11.20	2/25/33	31392HSU8	7EE	SCH(22)
*	14) GK	2,349	5.50	13.70	2/25/33	31392HSV6	8EE	SCH(22)
*	15) GL	28,605	5.50	1.80	8/25/31	31392HSW4	2EE	SUP
*	16) GM	4,876	5.50	3.20	10/25/31	31392HSX2	10EE	SUP
*	17) GO	356	0.00	9.90	2/25/33	31392HSY0	z59EE	PO,SUP
*	18) GP	8,214	5.50	3.70	2/25/32	31392HSZ7	12EE	SUP

as they belong to different groups. The fifth class, class B, only receives interest payment as long as the four other classes are still outstanding. Once they are fully retired, class B starts to receive its principal as well. Exhibit 4.15, contrary to exhibits 4.11 through 4.14, displays a horizontal line at the beginning of each PSA scenario. That line represents the interest payment that is computed by multiplying the monthly coupon rate of class B times its outstanding balance:

$$\text{Interest Payment} = (1/12)(5.5\%)\$60,000,000 = \$275,000$$

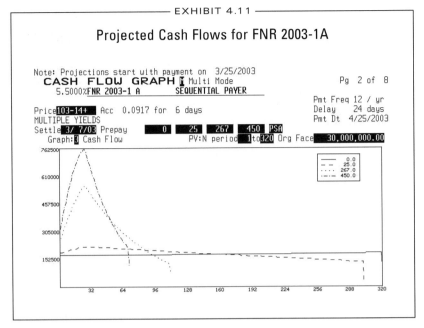

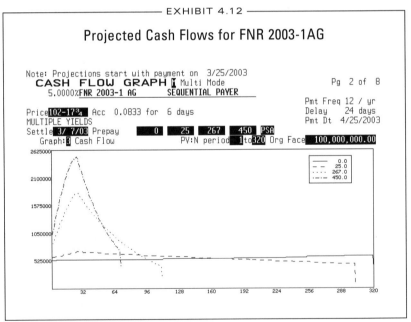

When the line starts to rise, it means that class B starts amortizing, and the first four classes are fully amortized. Under a 0 percent CPR, class B starts to receive principal in 2029, whereas under a 60

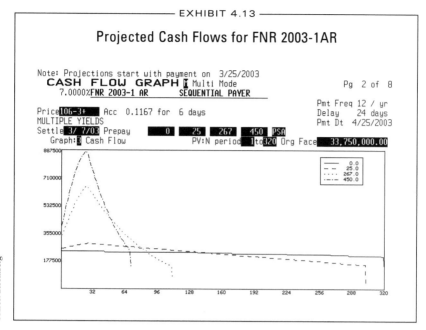

Source: Bloomberg

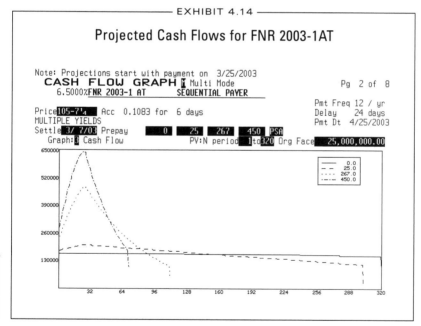

Source: Bloomberg

percent CPR, it starts receiving principal in 2004. Most prepayment risk has been shifted away from the first four classes of FNR 2003-1 to class B.

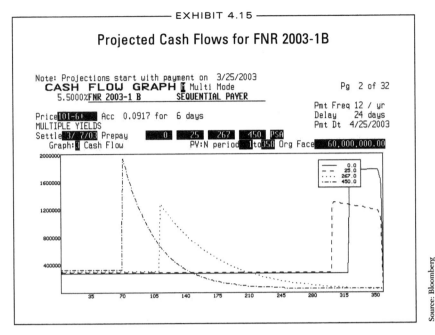

EXHIBIT 4.15

Projected Cash Flows for FNR 2003-1B

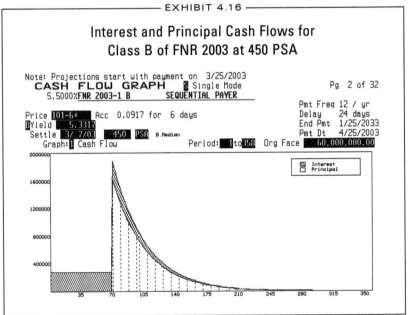

EXHIBIT 4.16

Interest and Principal Cash Flows for Class B of FNR 2003 at 450 PSA

EXHIBIT 4.16 shows one specific scenario for class B, that of a 450 PSA. It graphs the interest and principal cash flows over time. It takes about seventy months before class B receives any principal payment, meaning that the other four classes are taking that long before being fully retired.

Planned Amortization Class

SEQUENTIAL CLASSES do not satisfy all investors with respect to prepayment risk reallocation. Some investors want to know exactly how much and when they will receive interest and principal cash flows. There exists a structure that can meet the needs of such a group of investors; it is called a planned amortization class (PAC).

Creating a PAC for a given pass-through security involves establishing a prepayment rate band, such as a CPR between 15 percent and 30 percent. One then plots the principal only (PO) under the lower prepayment (a CPR of 15 percent), and on the same graph, the PO under the higher prepayment (a CPR of 30 percent).

As long as the prepayment rate is between 15 percent and 30 percent, it will always be possible to replicate the area under the two curves in EXHIBIT **4.17**. That area corresponds to the portion of the area under the PO curve that is common to both a 15 percent CPR and a 30 percent CPR.

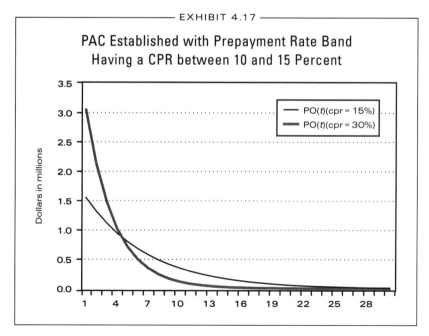

EXHIBIT 4.17

PAC Established with Prepayment Rate Band
Having a CPR between 10 and 15 Percent

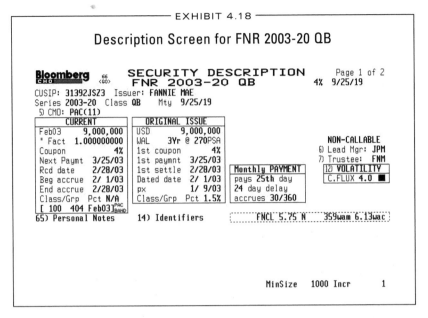

EXHIBIT 4.18

Description Screen for FNR 2003-20 QB

This gives the PAC class greater certainty with regard to amortization, albeit at the expense of the other securities (companion classes or support classes) issued by the SPV. The amortization schedule of a PAC is determined by calculating the principal that will be received by the SPV under two prepayment scenarios, in this example 15 percent and 30 percent per annum. Choosing an amortization window that can be adhered to for all prepayment rates between 15 percent and 30 percent determines the principal funded by the PAC. The remainder of the principal is funded by the companion classes.

As an example, in **EXHIBIT 4.18** consider the following FNMA mortgage-backed security in which a PAC class was structured. The FNR 2003-20 QB is a PAC class with a prepayment band comprised between a 100 PSA and a 404 PSA.

As long as the PSA remains between 100 and 404, the investors receive the cash flow shown in **EXHIBIT 4.19**, which has a 200 PSA. On the other hand, if the PSA is below 100, as in **EXHIBIT 4.20**, the PAC breaks, and not enough cash flow is received from the underlying security to be paid to the investors. Similarly, in **EXHIBIT 4.21**, with a 600 PSA, there is enough cash flow early on to satisfy the PAC investors, but later, because of high prepayment and payment to the companion class, there is a shortfall of cash flow to be paid to the PAC

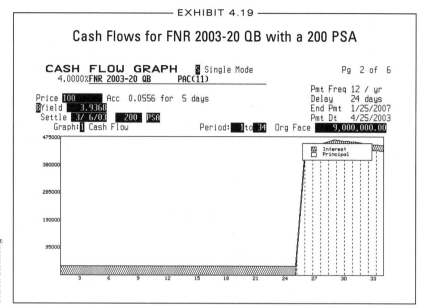

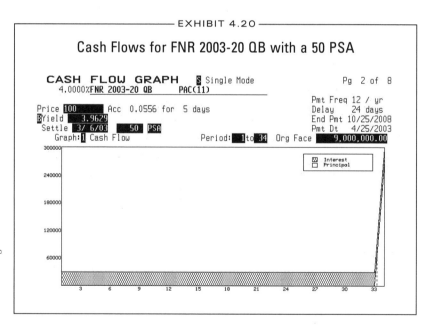

investors. **EXHIBIT 4.22** graphs the projected cash flows to be paid under four different PSA scenarios (100 PSA, 150 PSA, 250 PSA, and 400 PSA) to show how the cash flows are exactly the same.

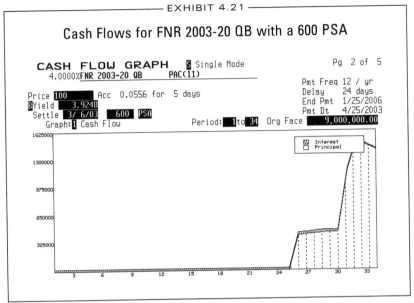

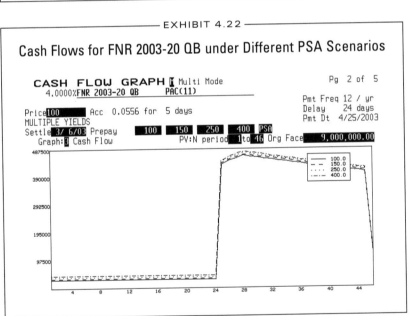

Cash flows (interest and principal payment) allocated to PAC investors appear in EXHIBIT **4.23** under three different PSA scenarios, so the reader can better visualize when the PSA is below, above, or in the established PSA band (100 to 404). The interest payments under the three PSA scenarios are graphed in EXHIBIT **4.24**, and the principal payment under those same three scenarios appears in EXHIBIT **4.25**.

Floaters and Inverse Floaters

WHEN AN SPV issues a floating-rate security to finance fixed-rate assets, an inverse-floating-rate security must also be issued. The two certificates—floater and inverse floater—must have a WAC less than or equal to the coupon of the underlying collateral. In EXHIBIT **4.27**, on page 103, a floating-rate and inverse-floating-rate security issued to fund a portfolio of 10 percent FNMA pass-through certificates is constructed and analyzed. The securities are constructed according to the following parameters:

1 The floater finances 95 percent of the fixed-rate pass-through certificates purchased by the SPV, for a Wf of 0.95.

2 The inverse floater finances the remaining 5 percent of the portfolio of pass-throughs, for a Wif of 0.05.

3 The floater has a coupon equal to the one-month Libor (London interbank offer rate) plus 50 basis points (bp), and cannot exceed 9.5 percent. Capping the coupon on the floater is necessary to insure a minimum coupon on the inverse floater of 0 percent.

4 The mortgages backing the floater and the inverse floater have a 10 percent weighted average coupon, and the maximum weighted average coupon (WAC) for the two certificates (floater and inverse floater) issued by the SPV, after deducting servicing and costs associated with credit enhancement, is 9.5 percent.

Equation (4.1) is the constraint that ties the coupons of the floater (Cf) and inverse floater (Cif) to the weighted average coupon that will be paid by the SPV.

$$Wf \times Cf + Wif \times Cif = \text{WAC} = 9.5\% \qquad (4.1)$$

The coupon on the inverse floater is set to satisfy equation (4.1). Next is an illustration of how the coupon on the inverse floater is calculated.

$$Cif = (\text{WAC} - Wf \times Cf)/Wif \qquad (4.2)$$

EXHIBIT 4.23

Cash Flows Allocated to Investors for FNR 2003-20 QB

NO.	DATE	COUP	INT (50 PSA)	INT (200 PSA)	INT (600 PSA)	PRINC (50 PSA)	PRINC (200 PSA)	PRINC (600 PSA)
1	4/25/03	4	30000	30000	30000	0	0	0
2	5/25/03	4	30000	30000	30000	0	0	0
3	6/25/03	4	30000	30000	30000	0	0	0
4	7/25/03	4	30000	30000	30000	0	0	0
5	8/25/03	4	30000	30000	30000	0	0	0
6	9/25/03	4	30000	30000	30000	0	0	0
7	10/25/03	4	30000	30000	30000	0	0	0
8	11/25/03	4	30000	30000	30000	0	0	0
9	12/25/03	4	30000	30000	30000	0	0	0
10	1/25/04	4	30000	30000	30000	0	0	0
11	2/25/04	4	30000	30000	30000	0	0	0
12	3/25/04	4	30000	30000	30000	0	0	0
13	4/25/04	4	30000	30000	30000	0	0	0
14	5/25/04	4	30000	30000	30000	0	0	0
15	6/25/04	4	30000	30000	30000	0	0	0
16	7/25/04	4	30000	30000	30000	0	0	0
17	8/25/04	4	30000	30000	30000	0	0	0
18	9/25/04	4	30000	30000	30000	0	0	0
19	10/25/04	4	30000	30000	30000	0	0	0
20	11/25/04	4	30000	30000	30000	0	0	0
21	12/25/04	4	30000	30000	30000	0	0	0
22	1/25/05	4	30000	30000	30000	0	0	0
23	2/25/05	4	30000	30000	30000	0	0	0
24	3/25/05	4	30000	30000	30000	0	0	0
25	4/25/05	4	30000	30000	30000	0	407801	407801
26	5/25/05	4	30000	28641	28641	0	421117	421117
27	6/25/05	4	30000	27237	27237	0	431366	431366
28	7/25/05	4	30000	25799	25799	0	441427	441427
29	8/25/05	4	30000	24328	24328	0	439228	439228
30	9/25/05	4	30000	22864	22864	0	437042	1168538
31	10/25/05	4	30000	21407	18968	0	434866	1521144
32	11/25/05	4	30000	19957	13898	0	432702	1464487
33	12/25/05	4	30000	18515	9016	269435	430550	1409944
34	1/25/06	4	29102	17080	4316	269230	428409	1294948

NO.	DATE	COUP	INT (50 PSA)	INT (200 PSA)	INT (600 PSA)	PRINC (50 PSA)	PRINC (200 PSA)	PRINC (600 PSA)
			28204	15652		268820	426279	
			27308	14231		268413	424161	
			26414	12817		268008	422055	
			25520	11410		267604	419958	
			24628	10010		267202	417875	
			23738	8617		266801	415800	
			22848	7231		266404	413739	
			21960	5852		266008	411687	
			21074	4480		265613	409646	
			20188	3114		265221	407617	
			19304	1756		264830	405599	
			18421	404		264441	121076	
			17540			264054		
			16660			263668		
			15781			263286		
			14903			262904		
			14027			262524		
			13152			262147		
			12278			261770		
			11405			261397		
			10534			261024		
			9664			260653		
			8795			260285		
			7928			259918		
			7061			259553		
			6196			259190		
			5332			258828		
			4469			258469		
			3608			258112		
			2747			257755		
			1888			257401		
			1030			257049		
			173			51983		

Source: Bloomberg

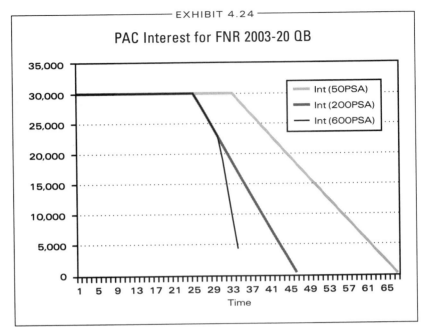

EXHIBIT 4.24

PAC Interest for FNR 2003-20 QB

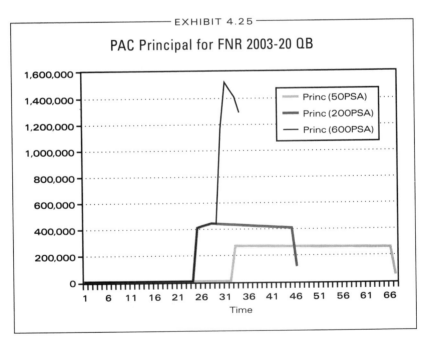

EXHIBIT 4.25

PAC Principal for FNR 2003-20 QB

Source: Stone/Zissu using data from Bloomberg

Source: Stone/Zissu using data from Bloomberg

Replacing *Cf* with (Libor + 50 bp) gives the following:

$$Cif = 1.9 - 19 \times (\text{Libor} + 50 \text{ bp}) \tag{4.3}$$

The factor by which the term (Libor + 50 bp) is multiplied is the leverage ratio of the inverse floater. In equation (4.3) the leverage ratio is 19. For every 100 bp change in Libor, the coupon on the inverse floater will change in the opposite direction by 1,900 bp.

The leverage ratio depends on the percent of the SPV's assets financed by the inverse floater. As the percentage financed by the inverse floater declines relative to the amount funded by the floater, the leverage ratio increases. The leverage ratio is computed as follows:

$$L = Wf / Wif \tag{4.4}$$

Exhibit **4.26** shows how the leverage ratio increases at an increasing rate as the weight of the floater increases and that of the inverse floater decreases.

Exhibit 4.27 illustrates how the coupon on an inverse floater depends on both the leverage ratio and the Libor. The cap on the floater must be adjusted for different leverage ratios so that the inverse floater will not have a zero or negative coupon. In the case of an inverse floater with a 5 percent weight, the cap on the floater has to be 9.5 percent. Paying anything above 9.5 percent to the investors in the floater would create a negative coupon for the inverse floater (see the highlighted column in exhibit 4.27).

Exhibit 4.27 is constructed assuming the WAC of the floater and inverse floater is constant at 9.5 percent. The exhibit indicates that if the inverse floater issued by the SPV funds 1 percent of the assets ($L = 99$) and the Libor is 3 percent, the coupon is 603.5 percent, and the floater's coupon is 3.5 percent. As the leverage ratio decreases, the range of coupons paid to the inverse floater across Libor decreases. This is another way of saying that the uncertainty of the coupon paid to the inverse floater is negatively correlated with the leverage ratio. For a leverage ratio of 99, the coupon on the inverse floater takes on values between 0 percent (a negative coupon cannot be paid) and 801.5 percent, while the range of coupons for a leverage ratio of 4 is 5.5 percent to 41.5 percent.

EXHIBIT 4.26

Leverage Ratio

Wf	L
50%	1
55%	1.22222222
60%	1.5
65%	1.85714286
70%	2.33333333
75%	3
80%	4
85%	5.66666667
90%	9
95%	19
96%	24
97%	32.3333333
98%	49
99%	99

The following excerpt from the Bear Stearns Prospectus Supplement dated May 21, 1992, for Mortgage Pass-Through Certificates Series 1992-4 illustrates a typical characterization of floaters and inverse floaters:

The Class 2AF Certificates will bear interest at a rate of 4.35% per annum during their first 12 Interest Accrual Periods (as defined herein). During each Interest Accrual Period thereafter, the Class 2AF Certificates will bear interest, subject to a maximum rate of 10.0% per annum and a minimum rate of 0.70% per annum, at a rate per annum equal to 0.70% in excess of the London interbank offered rate for one-month U.S. dollar deposits ("LIBOR"), as more fully described herein.

The Class 2AS Certificates will bear interest at a rate of 5644.3497% per annum during their first 12 Interest Accrual Periods. During each

——— EXHIBIT 4.27 ———

Coupon on Inverse Floaters with Different Leverage Ratios and Libors

LIBOR	*Wif* 1%	*Wif* 2%	*Wif* 5%	*Wif* 10%	*Wif* 20%
	L = 99	L = 49	L = 19	L = 9	L = 4
0.01	8.015	4.015	1.615	0.815	0.415
0.02	7.025	3.525	1.425	0.725	0.375
0.03	6.035	3.035	1.235	0.635	0.335
0.04	5.045	2.545	1.045	0.545	0.295
0.05	4.055	2.055	0.855	0.455	0.255
0.06	3.065	1.565	0.665	0.365	0.215
0.07	2.075	1.075	0.475	0.275	0.175
0.08	1.085	0.585	0.285	0.185	0.135
0.09	0.095	0.095	0.095	0.095	0.095
0.095	−0.4	−0.15	0	0.05	0.075
0.1	−0.895	−0.395	−0.095	0.005	0.055

*All cell entries are percentages in hundreds, i.e., 7.015 = 701.5%.

Source: Stone/Zissu

Interest Accrual Period thereafter, the Class 2AS Certificates will bear interest, subject to a maximum rate of 9290.6997% per annum and a minimum rate of 0% per annum, at a rate per annum equal to $9290.6997\% - (999.0 \times \text{LIBOR})$.

The Class 2AF and the Class 2AS have an initial principal of $29,571,087 and $29,600 respectively. The weight of the Class 2AF (the floater) is computed as follows:

$$Wf = [29{,}571{,}087 / (29{,}571.087 + 29{,}600)] = 99.9000023\%$$

The weight of the Class 2AS (the inverse floater) is computed as:

$$Wif = [29{,}600 / (29{,}571.087 + 29{,}600)] = 0.0999976\%$$

EXHIBIT 4.28

Bear Stearns Inverse Floater Example

LIBOR	Cf	Cif	WAC
0.01	0.017	82.917	0.0999
0.02	0.027	72.927	0.0999
0.03	0.037	62.937	0.0999
0.04	0.047	52.947	0.0999
0.05	0.057	42.957	0.0999
0.06	0.067	32.967	0.0999
0.07	0.077	22.977	0.0999
0.08	0.087	12.987	0.0999
0.09	0.097	2.99699	0.0999
0.1	0.1	0	0.0999

Source: Stone/Zissu

The information provided in the above prospectus is sufficient to compute the coupon on the floater, the coupon on the inverse floater, and the WAC sought by Bear Sterns using equations (4.1) and (4.2). These values are charted in EXHIBIT **4.28**.

Whether Libor increases or decreases, the WAC for Class 2AF and Class 2AS is 0.999 percent. As Libor increases, the coupon on the inverse floater decreases, causing a reduction in the amount of the future cash flows to be received by the certificate holder, and a decrease in the value of the inverse floater due to a higher discount rate.

In summary, the following three effects determine the price dynamics of an inverse floater:

1 as Libor increases, the inverse floater receives a lower coupon (the coupon effect);

2 the magnitude of expected interest payments increases due to a decline in the prepayment rate (the prepayment effect); and

3 the cash flows are discounted at a higher rate (the discount effect).

PART TWO

Corporate Debt
and the
Securitization Markets

C h a p t e r   F i v e

How Ford Motor Credit Corporation Has Used Securitization

THIS CHAPTER illustrates how a company can use the securitization market to raise capital. A discussion of the Ford Motor Credit Corporation (FMCC) serves to explain the specifics of automobile loan securitization. After a description of FMCC's basic business model, the securitization market is compared to the corporate debt market, especially as concerns credit rating and cost. Then we demonstrate how an entity that is designed to function with the sole purpose of funding a defined pool of financial assets or a flow of finance receivables known as a special-purpose vehicle (SPV) is positioned and capitalized to separate the credit rating of the corporation, in this case FMCC, from the credit rating of the asset-backed security. This is what allows one to achieve a better credit rating for asset-backed securities than corporate debt. Next, we show how to establish the credit ratings of asset-backed securities. We compare FMCC's cost of funding for on-balance-sheet and off-balance-sheet transactions. We explain the allocation of different kinds of risk to different classes of securities. The chapter concludes with a case study of asset-backed securities issued by FMCC on March 23, 2000, in the amount of $2.891 million. In this context are discussed the specifics of credit enhancement and ratings parameters.

The Case of Ford Motor Credit

FMCC'S PRIMARY business is to supply Ford Motor–affiliated new car dealers with capital. The dealers use this capital to finance their inventories of unsold vehicles and make loans and extend leases to their retail and corporate customers. FMCC buys the loans dealers make to their customers at the negotiated purchase price of the vehicle net of any trade-in value and down payment received by the dealer. These loans then compose FMCC's retail loan portfolio.

FMCC also extends revolving credit to its dealers. This is known as dealer floor plan financing and composes the wholesale segment of FMCC's receivable portfolio. In addition, through its Primus division, FMCC offers wholesale financing to dealers of vehicles sold under the Jaguar, Land Rover, Aston Martin, and Mazda brands and buys loans extended by these dealers. FMCC also has subsidiaries that specialize in financing used cars and have a clientele that is considered high-risk or "non-prime-credit." Other subsidiaries offer financial services to vehicle leasing companies and fleet purchasers. These services include underwriting auto insurance.

Securitized Receivables

FMCC HAS USED securitization since 1988 to refinance portions of its wholesale and retail receivable portfolio. In addition to the term-securitization programs through which it refinances dealer floor plan loans, retail installment loans, and leases, FMCC sponsors a single-seller, asset-backed commercial paper program called FCAR Owner Trust. FCAR issues commercial paper to fund purchases of asset-backed securities from bankruptcy-remote, wholly owned, special-purpose subsidiaries of FMCC and business trusts sponsored by FMCC.

FMCC has also established an asset-backed notes program, the "Motown Notes Program," which is used to refinance interests in pools of dealer floor plan loans. The Motown Notes are issued out of the securitization vehicle Ford Credit Floor Plan Master Owner Trust A. Dealer floor plan loans are collateralized by the dealer's inventory of unsold cars. According to the Federal Reserve, of $65 billion of such wholesale motor vehicle credit extended by finance companies as of June 30, 2000, 40 percent was securitized.

Through its European banking subsidiary, FCE Bank, FMCC has established a $5 billion European securitization program called Globaldrive. Globaldrive B.V. is a Dutch SPV that makes secured loans to securitization vehicles established by subsidiaries of FCE Bank. Globaldrive finances these secured loans by issuing asset-backed notes. The loans are secured by the asset-backed securities issued by special-purpose securitization vehicles established by FCE subsidiaries. The asset-backed securities are issued by bankruptcy-remote SPVs that have bought the loans from the FCE subsidiary that originated the credit. Each series of notes issued by Globaldrive is secured by a separate pool of financial receivables or series of asset-backed securities.

Globaldrive is a "compartmentalized" securitization vehicle—the credit quality of one series is isolated from the credit quality of other series issued by Globaldrive B.V. Investors who purchase asset-backed securities issued by Globaldrive are exposing themselves to the risk of a single compartment. Series issued by each compartment may be tranched along credit risk—in other words, subordinate, mezzanine, or senior classes. Globaldrive offers FCE Bank an efficient and alternative outlet to the capital markets through which it can refinance its retail and wholesale portfolios of receivables. Between 1997 and July 2003, the Globaldrive program issued five series of asset-backed notes to refinance approximately €2.5 billion of receivables.

In autumn 2003 FMCC sold about $3 billion of retail receivables directly to Bear Stearns Asset Backed Funding Inc., a Bear, Stearns & Co. Inc. affiliate. Bear Stearns Asset Backed Funding Inc. pooled a portion of the receivables purchased from FMCC with portfolios of receivables purchased from DaimlerChrysler Services North America LLC and Volvo Finance North America Inc. and securitized the receivables through a qualifying special-purchase vehicle, Whole Auto Loan Trust 2002-1. Ford is using sales of receivables such as this one to further diversify its sources of liquidity and to protect itself from a premium that the markets may charge in the future for asset-backed securities issued by Ford-sponsored trusts. Sources of this premium might be saturation of the market for securities coming out of the Ford programs or a perception in the market that stresses on Ford's balance sheet would filter through to the asset-backed securities issued by Ford securitization programs.

Such perceptions can have an effect in the market, even though they would be ignoring the fundamental strength of asset-backed securities, and the isolation and separation of receivable risk from transferor risk. Perception drives prices in the short run, and the short run is exactly when liquidity problems often become critical. By combining receivable pools from different originators into a single issue, Bear, Stearns is internalizing the diversification process for investors and offering the originators a new path to the securitization markets.

Advantages of Securitization

SINCE THE late 1990s, securitization has gone from being a marginal funding source for the captive finance companies of automobile manufacturers to one of these manufacturers' core sources of liquidity. Securitization is an effective way to tap the capital and money markets because the hundreds and thousands of transactions launched by the large, captive finance companies of the car manufacturers are stable, predictable, and transparent. A company like FMCC must pay rates corresponding to a BBB/P-2 (Standard & Poor's) corporate credit risk when issuing senior unsecured debt from its balance sheet. But securitization offers FMCC a way of refinancing a portfolio of receivables at a rate that is an average of AAA/BBB/BB/P-1 rated debt and a cost corresponding to FMCC's cost of capital. (Factoring in FMCC's capital cost is necessary to account for the residual interest in the asset pool that is retained by FMCC.) The advantage of securitization increases as this average diminishes, but even when the average equals the cost of BBB debt, securitization still offers advantages. Securitization alleviates balance sheet pressures caused by excessive leverage ratios, low asset performance ratios, or strained credit agreements.

EXHIBIT 5.1 shows the cost of refinancing receivables via securitization relative to the cost of funding the receivables with debt issued from FMCC's own balance sheet. The advantage of securitized funding increases as the credit rating of FMCC declines, from A+ at 12/13/99 to BBB at 10/25/02 (rating by Moody's Investors Service). In January 2002 Moody's lowered Ford Motor Credit's short-term credit rating from P-1 to P-2.

Source: Ford Motor Credit Annual Report, Form 10-K for the year ending December 2001

EXHIBIT 5.1

Ford Motor Credit Funding Spreads

	31-DEC	30-SEP	30-JUN	31-MAR	2000	1999
Unsecured debt funding	264	217	131	160	157	86
Securitized funding	99	87	91	85	93	70
Unsecured over (under) securitized	165	130	40	75	64	16

*The spreads listed are indicative only and do not reflect specific trades.

As FMCC's specific cost of funds increased due to deterioration in its balance sheet, the general level of credit spreads also increased. **EXHIBIT 5.2** illustrates the yield spread between A2-rated paper issued by finance companies over the Treasury strip curve. In response to the decline in its own credit quality and the overall increase in credit spreads, FMCC shifted funding from the corporate debt markets to the securitization markets. **EXHIBIT 5.3** shows the extent of this swing in funding from on-balance-sheet obligations to off-balance-sheet transactions.

As FMCC's ratings have deteriorated, its cost of funding from its general balance sheet has increased relative to the cost of funding by means of securitization. In September 2001, Standard & Poor's lowered Ford Motor Credit's unsecured rating from A to BBB. On April 14, 2000, Moody's lowered FMCC's rating from A1 to A2. On January 16, 2002, Moody's lowered FMCC's senior unsecured rating from A2 to A3 and FMCC's short-term rating from P-1 to P-2. As FMCC's specific cost of funds has increased due to deterioration in its balance sheet, the general level of credit spreads has also increased.

EXHIBIT 5.2

Spreads of Debt Issued by A-2-Rated Finance Companies over Two-Year Treasury Strips

10/4/02	108 bp	10/2/98	71 bp
10/4/01	102 bp	10/3/97	38 bp
10/4/00	95 bp	10/2/96	41 bp
10/4/99	88 bp		

Source: Bloomberg

EXHIBIT 5.3

Securitized Funding as a Percent of Total Debt

	2001	2000	1999	1998	1997
Total securitized funding (billions of dollars)	$46.2	$24.7	$16.0	$12.2	$9.0
Total balance-sheet debt	$146.3	$146.3	$133.1	$115.0	$100.7
Total securitized funding as a percent of total balance-sheet debt	31.5%	16.8%	12.02	10.60%	8.9%

Source: Ford Motor Credit Annual Report, Form 10-K for year ending December 2001

Ford's management values the stability that securitization has offered as other sources of funds have become more costly and more uncertain. It bears noting, however, that securitization is just one part of a funding program. Companies that have relied too heavily on securitization have been squeezed and have experienced severe liquidity problems when the market for subordinate tranches of asset-backed securities has become inaccessible. FMCC explicitly states how securitization fits into its overall funding program:

> Maintaining liquidity through access to diversified sources of funds has always been a key factor in our funding strategy. We define liquidity as our ability to meet our funding needs, which includes purchasing retail installment sale and lease contracts, funding other financing programs, and repayment of our debt obligations as they become due. In December 1988, we began selling a portion of our receivables in securitization transactions to fund our operations, and we have been a regular participant in the securitization market since then. Securitization represents an additional source of funding that has been less susceptible to changing market conditions. (2001, 10-K Ford Motor Credit)

An active issuer like FMCC can tap the market at a relatively low cost, because rating agencies and investors are familiar with its offerings, the underlying documentation, and, most important, the receivables that are being securitized and the quality of the servicer. Successful shelf registrations demand this type of consistency between series.

Special-Purpose Structure

FORD CREDIT Auto Receivables Two LLP is a wholly owned special-purpose vehicle (SPV) that is structured as a Delaware limited partnership. The general partner is Ford Credit Auto Receivables Two, Inc., which is a wholly owned limited-purpose subsidiary of Ford Motor Credit. The special or limited purpose of Ford Credit Auto Receivables Two LLP is to buy pools of retail installment contracts from Ford Motor Credit and to sell these pools to Ford Credit Auto Owner Trusts, one of which is 2000-A.

Trust 2000-A finances its purchase of the receivables by issuing asset-backed notes and asset-backed certificates. The property of Trust 2000-A includes the receivables and the collections on the receivables, security interests in the vehicles financed by the receivables, bank accounts, rights to proceeds under insurance policies that cover the obligors under the receivables or the vehicles financed by the receivables, remedies for breaches of representations and warranties made by the dealers that originated the receivables, and other rights under documents relating to the receivables.

The asset-backed notes and certificates issued by Trust 2000-A are publicly underwritten, privately placed, or retained by the seller. Asset-backed notes are also sold to asset-backed commercial paper conduits such as FCAR, FMCC's asset-backed commercial paper program, or one of the many bank-sponsored asset-backed commercial paper conduits.

For investors in asset-backed securities to be willing to differentiate between the credit quality of the transferor—in this case FMCC (rated BBB by Standard & Poor's)—and the credit quality of the asset-backed securities issued by the trust, a defensible barrier between the transferor's credit risk and the credit risk embedded in the securitized receivable pool must be erected. The three pillars of the defense are (1) a "true sale" for bankruptcy purposes of the receivable pool to a (2) "special- or limited-purpose vehicle" that is (3) "bankruptcy remote" from the transferor. A true sale is necessary so that a bankruptcy court does not judge the transfer to be a secured loan.

A secured loan from the transferor to the SPV means that in a bankruptcy of the transferor, the SPV becomes a creditor of the transferor. Its assets—the securitized receivables—can be consolidated with the assets of the bankrupt transferor, and the secured loan can then be placed in a subordinate position with respect to debtor-in-possession financing. Bankruptcy remoteness is necessary so that the securitized receivables are beyond the reach of the transferor and can be isolated from the bankruptcy estate of the transferor.

If the SPV were not designed to be bankruptcy remote, then the true sale could be neutralized, since the substantive consolidation of the SPV into the transferor would become a more likely outcome in a bankruptcy proceeding. Should this happen, investors in the asset-backed securities would become creditors of the transferor. A true sale to a subsidiary that is not bankruptcy remote exposes the investor in the asset-backed security to the bankruptcy risk of the transferor, as does a transfer to a bankruptcy-remote subsidiary that is a secured loan rather than a true sale.

The "special purpose" designation is necessary to eliminate the possibility that the transferee voluntarily or involuntarily files for bankruptcy protection. If the transferee were not designed as a "special-purpose" vehicle, it could issue debt to finance acquisitions of risky assets or engage in other activities that would increase the risk of the asset-backed securities and therefore the yield required by investors, which translates into a higher cost of financing for the transferor.

Allocating and Funding Credit Risk: Subordinate Classes and Residual Interests

THE ECONOMICS of securitization require that a large percentage of the receivables be refinanced at rates associated with AAA securities. Since the raw unenhanced receivable pool that is being securitized cannot be funded at AAA rates, the bulk of credit risk embedded in the receivable pool must be distilled from the overall receivable pool and allocated to investors willing to finance a multiple of the pool's expected credit losses. Financing more than 90 percent of the receivable pool at yields commensurate with AAA credit ratings is accomplished by concentrating most of the credit risk on a relatively small amount of principal. The resulting classes of securities are leveraged with respect to credit risk and are subordinate interests in the receivable pool. EXHIBIT 5.4 illustrates a typical example of credit-risk leveraging through subordinated class issuance, in this case, of Trust 2000-A.

---- EXHIBIT 5.4 ----

Ford Credit Auto Owner Trust 2000-A

CLASSES OF NOTES AND CERTIFICATES ISSUED BY FORD MOTOR CREDIT 2000-A	PERCENT OF RECEIVABLE POOL FINANCED BY CLASS
Class A1	5%
Class A2	13%
Class A3	35%
Class A4	34%
Class A5	6%
Class B	3%
Class C	2%
Class D	2%

Notes A (A1, A2, A3, A4, A5): fifth level of pool losses (rated AAA)
Note B: fourth level of pool losses (rated AA)
Certificate C: third level of pool losses (rated BBB)
Certificate D: second level of pool losses (rated BB)
Retained Interest: first level of pool losses

A class of interests exists that is structured to absorb delin-quencies and defaults prior to the subordinate certificates. Below the subordinate notes and certificates issued by the trust are the residual interests in the receivable pool that are retained by the seller. Residual interests absorb the first level of credit losses to act as a layer of equity underneath all of the other classes of notes and certificates.

It is common practice for companies that securitize their assets to retain residual interests in the receivable pool. This is an efficient means for extracting profit from the transaction and for tapping the market at the best rates, since the bulk of the credit risk has been absorbed by the transferor. For example, in the Trust 2000-A, inter-ests retained by the seller amounted to about 5 percent of the receiv-able pool, more than the expected losses for the receivable pool over the weighted average life of the class A notes, calculated under the assumption of a 1.5 percent absolute prepayment model. The specif-ics of the transaction are detailed later in this chapter.

A true sale is necessary, but if FMCC were to retain interests in the receivable pool it transferred, the true sale would be jeopardized, as was discussed in the preceding section. If FMCC decided to forgo retention of interest in the receivable pool, to avoid jeopardizing the true sale, it would increase the cost of the transaction by shifting the first loss risk to the marketplace. This is a difficult and costly risk to finance. FMCC has an advantage in managing a portfolio of retained interests in securitized receivables.

The solution to this problem, simultaneously effecting a true sale and allowing FMCC to ensure retention of residual interests in the pool, is the two-step, or two-tier, securitization transaction (see EXHIBIT **5.5** at right).

The Two-Step Securitization Transaction

WHEN FMCC securitizes its receivables, it uses a two-step (two-tier) transaction. In the first step of the transaction, the transferor, FMCC, sells a pool of receivables to a wholly owned special-purpose, bankruptcy-remote subsidiary, Ford Credit Auto Receivables Two LLP. Sales of receivables by FMCC to Ford Credit Auto Receivables Two LLP are structured as true sales at law. This true sale takes the receivables off FMCC's balance sheet and places them beyond the reach of a bankruptcy court should FMCC file for bankruptcy protection.

Not only does the true sale place the receivables beyond the reach of FMCC's creditors; the sale to a special-purpose, bankruptcy-remote subsidiary that is severely limited in the capital structure it may have, in the composition of its directors, in its relationship with FMCC, and in the activities it may pursue, eliminates the possibility that the seller will become involved in bankruptcy proceedings. A bankruptcy-remote special-purpose subsidiary used for securitization transactions cannot have any creditors, nor can it engage in any activities other than buying and selling a well-defined pool or flow of receivables (primary activities) and taking actions (secondary activities) necessary to complete and support the primary activities.

In the second step of the two-step transaction, the seller—Ford Credit Auto Receivables Two LLP—sells the asset pool to a qualifying special-purpose entity (QSPE), in this case Ford Credit Auto Owner

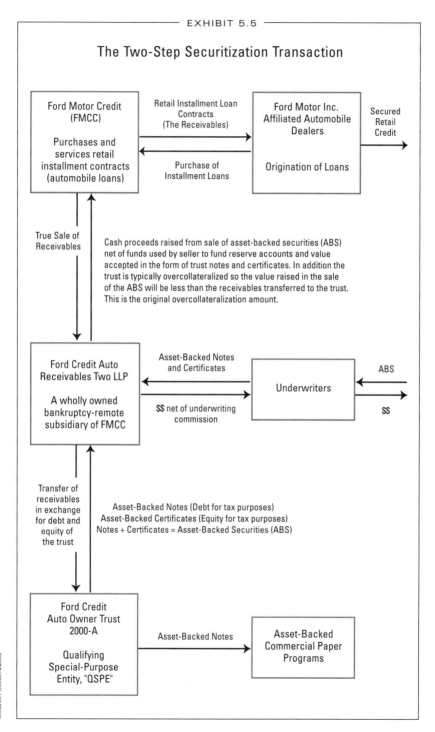

EXHIBIT 5.5

The Two-Step Securitization Transaction

Ford Motor Credit (FMCC)

Purchases and services retail installment contracts (automobile loans)

Retail Installment Loan Contracts (The Receivables)

Purchase of Installment Loans

Ford Motor Inc. Affiliated Automobile Dealers

Origination of Loans

Secured Retail Credit

True Sale of Receivables

Cash proceeds raised from sale of asset-backed securities (ABS) net of funds used by seller to fund reserve accounts and value accepted in the form of trust notes and certificates. In addition the trust is typically overcollateralized so the value raised in the sale of the ABS will be less than the receivables transferred to the trust. This is the original overcollateralization amount.

Ford Credit Auto Receivables Two LLP

A wholly owned bankruptcy-remote subsidiary of FMCC

Asset-Backed Notes and Certificates

$$ net of underwriting commission

Underwriters

ABS

$$

Transfer of receivables in exchange for debt and equity of the trust

Asset-Backed Notes (Debt for tax purposes)
Asset-Backed Certificates (Equity for tax purposes)
Notes + Certificates = Asset-Backed Securities (ABS)

Ford Credit Auto Owner Trust 2000-A

Qualifying Special-Purpose Entity, "QSPE"

Asset-Backed Notes

Asset-Backed Commercial Paper Programs

Source: Stone/Zissu

Trust 2000-A, a Delaware business trust. Due to its QSPE distinction, the assets of the trust are protected from the risks embedded in the transferor and the affiliates of the transferor.

The criteria that must be satisfied to be categorized as a QSPE and treated as such for accounting purposes are set forth in Financial Accounting Standards Board (FASB) 140. While the first SPV in a two-step transaction is a wholly owned subsidiary of the transferor, the second SPV that is set up as a QSPE must be "demonstrably distinct from the transferor."[1] In addition to being demonstrably distinct from the transferor, the activities of the SPV are limited, the assets the SPV may hold are restricted, and its ability to dispose of assets is constrained.

By design and by definition a QSPE is not consolidated with the transferor—in other words, FMCC or affiliates of Ford Credit Auto Receivables Two LLP. Thus, as discussed previously, financial assets owned by a QSPE are insulated from the bankruptcy risk of the transferor.

It is the defined and accepted separation of the seller and the QSPE that allows the seller to enhance the credit quality of the asset-backed securities. The seller enhances them by owning residual interests in the securitized receivable pool. Residual interests expose the seller to the first loss position in the receivable pool. If the losses are below the amount of the residual interest, the excess flows back to the seller either periodically or when the asset-backed securities are retired. In the case of Trust 2000-A, the seller's residual interest takes the form of rights to excess amounts in the reserve fund and overcollateralization account. Other forms of residual interests commonly used are excess spread accounts, where interest payments received that are in excess of amounts necessary to service the obligations of the trust are deposited into an account for the benefit of the seller.

Credit enhancement supplied by the seller makes the securities issued by the trust more marketable. It also offers the transferor a way to extract profit from the transaction.

The transfer of receivables from the seller to the trust may be viewed as secured financing rather than a sale, because the seller finances a significant level of the expected losses of the asset pool by funding the reserve account and holding retained interests and subordinate securities and certificates. In return, the seller receives the value released from the asset pool when it performs better than expected. It is difficult to argue that a transfer should be characterized as a true sale when the seller assumes a multiple of expected losses on the transferred assets and will receive the residual value of the assets.

Normally, characterization of the transfer to the trust as a secured financing would be of concern to investors in the asset-backed notes because a bankruptcy of the seller could tie up the assets of the trust. This is a concern that would translate into a higher required yield. Structuring the seller as a special-purpose, bankruptcy-remote subsidiary of the transferor eliminates the risk that the seller will be declared bankrupt or will declare bankruptcy. Investors are satisfied with the legal assurances offered by the structure. The seller has no creditors and no potential beneficiaries of a bankruptcy filing except the owners of the beneficial interests issued by the trust—the asset-backed certificates and asset-backed notes. The trust owns no assets other than the receivables pool, which is pledged to the indenture trustee for the benefit of owners of the asset-backed notes.

The two-step transaction is the typical approach adopted in asset-backed transactions executed by finance companies that are subject to the U.S. bankruptcy code.

Exhibit 5.6 presents the excerpt from FASB 140 that addresses the issue of two-step securitization transactions. This explanation of the two-step transaction is emphasized because at the core of all securitization transactions is the isolation of the risk associated with the receivables backing the asset-backed securities and the risk embedded in the balance sheet of the transferor. A special-purpose financing structure replaces the general-purpose balance sheet of the originator.

The two-step transaction is tax efficient (no tax on capital gains on sale from transferor to seller) and it allows the transferor, via its ownership of the seller, to efficiently extract profit from the transaction. The seller takes positions in the receivable pool that give it the right to residual cash flows. Residual cash flows are generated when the receivables generate more cash than is necessary to amortize the asset-backed securities issued by the trust. As was noted, residual interests may take the form of a seller's right to excess funds in

EXHIBIT 5.6

FASB 140 on Two-Step Securitization Transations

A. First, the corporation transfers financial assets to a special-purpose corporation that although wholly owned, is so designed that the possibility that the transferor or its creditors could reclaim the assets is remote. The first transfer is designed to be judged to be a true sale at law, in part because the transferor does not provide "excessive" credit or yield protection to the special-purpose corporation, and the Board understands that transferred assets are likely to be judged beyond the reach of the transferor or the transferor's creditors even in bankruptcy.

B. Second, the special-purpose corporation transfers the assets to a trust or other legal vehicle with a sufficient increase in the credit or yield protection on the second transfer (provided by a junior retained beneficial interest or other means) to merit the high credit rating sought by third-party investors who buy senior beneficial interests in the Trust. Because of that aspect of its design, that second transfer might not be judged to be a true sale at law and, thus, the transferred assets could at least in theory be reached by a bankruptcy trustee for the special-purpose corporation.

C. However, the special-purpose corporation is designed to make remote the possibility that it would enter bankruptcy, either by itself or by substantive consolidation into a bankruptcy of its parent should that occur. For example, its charter forbids it from undertaking any other business or incurring any liabilities, so that there can be no creditors to petition to place it in bankruptcy. Furthermore, its dedication to a single purpose is intended to make it extremely unlikely, even if it somehow entered bankruptcy, that a receiver under the U.S. Bankruptcy Code could reclaim the transferred assets because it has no other assets to substitute for the transferred assets.

The Board understands that the "two-step" securitizations described above , taken as a whole, generally would be judged under present U.S. law as having isolated the assets beyond the reach of the transferor and its creditors, even in bankruptcy or other receivership.

EXHIBIT 5.7

Ford Credit Auto Owner Trust 2000-A, Supplement to Prospectus, 9/17/99

"Ford Credit and the seller each intend that each transfer of receivables by Ford Credit to the seller under a purchase agreement constitute a "true sale" of such receivables to the seller. If the transfer constitutes such a "true sale," the receivables and the proceeds thereof would not be part of Ford Credit's bankruptcy estate under Section 541 of the U.S. Bankruptcy Code should Ford Credit become the subject of a bankruptcy case subsequent to the transfer of the receivables to the seller. The seller has received the advice of counsel to the effect that, subject to certain facts, assumptions, and qualifications, in the event Ford Credit were to become the subject of a voluntary or involuntary case under the U.S. Bankruptcy Code subsequent to the transfer of receivables to the seller, the transfer of such receivables by Ford Credit to the seller under the related purchase agreement would be characterized as a "true sale" of such receivables from Ford Credit to the seller, and such receivables and the proceeds thereof would not form part of Ford Credit's bankruptcy estate under Section 541 of the U.S. Bankruptcy Code."

reserve accounts, yield supplement accounts, funds generated from overcollateralization, or excess spread.

An excerpt from the prospectus supplement of Trust 2000-A in EXHIBIT **5.7** is included here to emphasize that the creation of the barrier between the credit risk embedded in the receivable pool and the credit risk embedded in FMCC's balance sheet is considered critical to the successful marketing of the asset-backed securities. The legal hurdles to separate the risk of the receivables issued by the securitization vehicle and the risk of the transferor must be addressed in all securitization transactions by all issuers. Should one of the three pillars be ignored or weakened, whether by choice or circumstance, the cost of refinancing the receivables by means of securitization would increase.

It goes without saying that expert legal and accounting advice is required to work out the issues necessary to achieve a "true sale" to a "bankruptcy-remote special-purpose vehicle." Once the scheme has been designed, reviewed by legal experts and rating agencies, and accepted by investors, subsequent series issued by trusts set up by the seller that adhere to the fundamentals of the structure should require less legal work, rating review time, and marketing expense.

Credit Ratings and On-Balance-Sheet versus Off-Balance-Sheet Cost of Funding

AN ACTIVE ISSUER like FMCC can tap the market at a relatively low cost because rating agencies and investors are familiar with its offerings, the underlying documentation, and, most important, the receivables that are being securitized and the quality of the servicer. In the Trust 2000-A securitization transaction, three of the classes—A1, A2, and the class D certificates—were not offered to the public. Class D was retained by the seller. Classes A2, A3, A4, class B, and class C were underwritten and distributed in the capital markets. Classes A1 and A2, both money market securities rated P-1/A-1, qualified for purchase by FCAR. Although we have no evidence that Trust 2000-A sold these classes to FCAR, it is plausible for this to have occurred, since such a transaction is the purpose of FCAR. It is also possible that the seller privately placed or refinanced these money market classes through a bank-sponsored asset-backed commercial paper conduit.

FCAR has offered FMCC an outlet to the prime commercial paper (CP) market, enabling it to structure its asset-backed securities to take advantage of low money market yields when the opportunity arises. EXHIBIT **5.8** presents the spreads between top-tier dealer-placed CP (A-1/P-1) and second-tier CP (A-2/P-2) at the beginning of December 2002. At that time, FMCC had a short-term rating of A-2/P-2, whereas paper issued by FCAR was rated A-1/P-1. The value of having access to the asset-backed CP market becomes evident from the spreads in exhibit 5.8. However, the spread is not the whole story. The second-tier CP market is not as liquid, so the preferred maturities of an issuer with short-term ratings of A-2/P-2 may not be marketable. Note that the gaps in the maturities for second-tier CP illustrated in exhibit 5.8 indicate that no quotes were available on December 5, 2002, for 21-

EXHIBIT 5.8

Yield Spreads between Top-Tier and
Second-Tier Commercial Paper

HISTORICAL SPREADS

	DEALER CP TOP TOP	DEALER CP 2ND TIER	
	Yield	Yield	Spread
1 DAY	1.20000	1.43000	-0.23000
7 DAY	1.23000	1.51000	-0.28000
15 DAY	1.26000	1.60000	-0.34000
21 DAY	1.29000		
30 DAY	1.30000	1.75000	-0.45000
45 DAY	1.32000	1.74000	-0.42000
60 DAY	1.32000	1.77000	-0.45000
90 DAY	1.32000	1.90000	-0.58000
4 MONTH	1.34000	1.94000	-0.60000
5 MONTH	1.35000	1.95000	-0.60000
6 MONTH	1.36000		
7 MONTH	1.37000		
8 MONTH	1.39000		
9 MONTH	1.44000		
1 YEAR			

day paper and for paper issued with maturities beyond five months.

Top-rated asset-backed CP typically trades at a small discount to top-rated dealer-placed CP. On December 3, 1998, asset-backed CP yielded 18 basis points (bp) more than dealer-placed paper, and on December 3, 2002, the yield difference was 2 bp. EXHIBIT 5.9 shows how short-term yields have declined steadily from 1998 through 2002, while yield spreads have fluctuated.

Successful securitization relies on leveraging credit risk so that most of the receivable pool is financed at rates associated with AAA credit ratings. Unless the credit spreads at the A to BB level widen significantly, deterioration of a firm's credit quality has a more significant effect than a general widening of credit spreads on the efficacy of securitization.

Between January 31, 2000, and January 28, 2003, the average spread between BBB-rated retail installment loan automobile-backed securities with a weighted average life (WAL) of three years to the Treasury strip curve was 177 bp. The high of this spread was 248 bp on December 31, 2002, and the lowest value was 136 bp, on May 31, 2002.

――――――――――― EXHIBIT 5.9 ―――――――――――

Spreads between Tier One and Tier Two Commercial Paper

DATE	ANNUAL YIELD ON TIER 2 A-2/P-2 CP	ANNUAL YIELD ON TIER 1 A-1/P-1 CP	YIELD DIFFFERENCE BETWEEN TIER 1 AND TIER 2
12/3/98	5.39%	4.97%	42 bp
12/3/99	6.46%	5.90%	56 bp
12/5/00	7.40%	6.44%	96 bp
12/5/01	2.36%	1.82%	54 bp
12/5/02	1.95%	1.35%	60 bp

Assume in a securitization transaction originated by a double-A-rated finance company that 12 percent of the pool was financed at rates in line with a triple-B credit rating and three-year WAL. This 12 percent represents the required credit enhancement so that the remainder of the pool can be refinanced at rates corresponding to AAA-rated credits.

If we compare the marginal increase in the cost of this transaction for a change from the low to the high spreads of BBB-rated auto-loan-backed securities over the Treasury curve, the increase is only 13 bp: (248 bp − 136 bp)×0.12. The same difference in spreads would have a larger impact on a lower-quality receivable pool because it would require a larger amount of credit enhancement. For example, if the amount financed at the BBB level was 50 percent of the pool, the increase would be 56 bp.[2]

The key point is that because the significant credit risk embedded in the receivable is leveraged onto a relatively small principal amount, any decline in a firm's credit rating has a larger impact on the economics of a transaction than does the widening of credit spreads. For receivable pools of equal quality, in terms of their risk profiles, lower-rated firms have more to gain from the securitization of receivables.

A downgrade or weakening of a company's credit quality will increase the value of securitization relative to on-balance-sheet financing provided the general level of credit spreads does not widen so much that funding the credit enhancement needed to support the A classes is too costly to justify the deal.

EXHIBIT 5.10

Commercial Paper Spreads over Treasury Strips

SPREADS TO UST STRIPS

Curve	21	23	25	28
Title	US$ Fin/Bank AAA	US$ Fin/Bank AA1/AA2	US$ Finance A1	US$ Finance BBB1
DATE	3/ 1/02	2/28/02	2/28/02	3/ 1/02
3MO	28.00	33.00	70.00	91.00
6MO	21.00	26.00	66.00	94.00
1YR	40.00	63.00	103.00	147.00
2YR	40.00	61.00	101.00	152.00
3YR	51.00	76.00	115.00	172.00
4YR	75.00	94.00	126.00	180.00
5YR	71.00	91.00	127.00	171.00
7YR	86.00	108.00	139.00	159.00
8YR	82.00	106.00	136.00	152.00
9YR	78.00	102.00	129.00	145.00
10YR	70.00	94.00	122.00	138.00
15YR	64.00	88.00	119.00	168.00
20YR	74.00	85.00	117.00	178.00
25YR	86.00	93.00	121.00	197.00
30YR	93.00	102.00	130.00	206.00

Source: Bloomberg

For example, for a finance company that was downgraded from A to BBB (Bloomberg Composite Ratings) at the beginning of March 2002, the cost of five-year debt would have increased by about 44 bp. EXHIBIT 5.10 indicates how much a downgrade would cost a firm in higher debt costs for various maturities.

The benefits gained by securitization will depend on how many credit notches the company is downgraded, from what level it is downgraded, and the quality of the receivable pool. The quality of the receivable pool determines the principal amount of the subordinate securities that the trust must issue to finance a maximum amount at the AAA level.

Yet more important than the incremental funding advantage a BBB-rated finance company derives from securitization over a single-A-rated firm is the absolute advantage securitization offers over on-balance-sheet financing. For example, on May 7, 2003, the spread between yields on three-year A-rated debt issued by finance companies and BBB-rated paper was 24 bp, while the yield difference between AAA and BBB ratings was 121 bp. It follows that the difference between the yields on AAA-rated and single-A-rated debt issued by finance companies was 97 bp. Securitization offers marginally investment-grade companies access to the AAA-rated debt markets.

Ford Credit Auto Owner Trust 2000-A: A Case Study

ON MARCH 23, 2000, FMCC securitized receivables in the amount of $2.891 million. The securitized structure is summarized in EXHIBIT **5.11**.

There were five sequential senior classes, classes A1 to A5, and three subordinated classes, classes B, C, and D. The weighted average life (WAL) for each class in the last two columns of exhibit 5.11 was based on an expected 1.5 percent and 0 percent absolute prepayment model, respectively. The absolute prepayment model assumes

--- EXHIBIT 5.11 ---

FMCC March 23, 2000 Receivables Securitization

Original receivables portfolio: $3,000,003,021.67

Number of contracts: 212,414

Receivable pool at origination

Weighted average life (WAL): 3 years, 11 months

Original weighted average coupon (WAC): 7.61%

Receivable pool at January 2003

Weighted average maturity (WAM): 1 year, 6 months

Weighted average coupon (WAC): 8.34%

CLASSES	PRINCIPAL AMOUNT	COUPON RATE	FINAL SCHEDULED DISTR. DATE	WEIGHTS	WAL 1.5% ABS	WAL 0% ABS
Class A1	$155,000,000	6.035%	7/17/00	0.05361355	0.1	
Class A2	377,000,000	6.217%	12/15/00	0.130402	0.3	
Class A3	$1,000,000,000	6.82%	6/17/02	0.34589389	0.9	
Class A4	$975,000,000	7.09%	11/17/03	0.33724655	2	0.1
Class A5	$171,480,000	7.19%	3/15/04	0.05931388	2.9	0.5
Class B	$99,200,000	7.37%	7/15/04	0.03431267	3	0.9
Class C	$56,690,000	7.75%	9/15/04	0.01960872	3	1.1
Class D	$56,690,000	9.00%	7/15/05	0.01960872	3	1.3

Source: Ford Motor Credit

that all receivables have same initial amount, same maturity, same coupon rate, and therefore same amortization rate.

A 1 percent absolute prepayment model would mean that each month, 1 percent of the initial number of receivables (in our case, 1 percent of 212,414, or 2,124.14 receivables) prepays the total outstanding balance in that month. A 1 percent absolute prepayment model is expected to have a total of 25,489.68 receivables prepaying in one year (1 percent of 212,414 multiplied by 12), and each subsequent year, until maturity.

The WAL of the different classes is quite sensitive to the absolute prepayment model. This can be observed in EXHIBITS **5.12** through **5.15**, in which the principal cash-flow allocation among the different classes is displayed and graphed over time under two absolute prepayment scenarios.

Exhibits 5.12 through 5.15 show the principal cash-flow allocation among classes A through C, over time, under two absolute prepayment model scenarios. Clearly, the higher the absolute prepayment, the faster the classes amortize.

Class D is structured as a bullet note. It is only paid off after all other classes are fully retired. Its WAL is equal to its final maturity, which depends upon when class C is paid off.

The WAL of the pool when no prepayments occur is 2.08 years. EXHIBIT **5.16** shows how the WAL of each class changes as prepayment speed increases from 0.5 percent to 1.5 percent. For this analysis, the notes and certificates were divided into two groups: one group consisting of the class A notes and another of the subordinate classes (the class B notes and the C and D certificates). The capital structure of the trust is such that the WAL of 92.6 percent of the capital is 1.7 years at a 0.5 percent prepayment rate and 1.28 years at a 1.5 percent prepayment rate.

While the subordinate tranches are leveraged with respect to credit risk, class A is exposed to more prepayment risk than the subordinate classes. This can be seen by comparing how the WAL changes when prepayment speed changes. For example, with a change in prepayment speed from 0.5 percent to 1.5 percent, note C's WAL decreases by 18 percent, whereas note A2's WAL declines by 30 percent. The WAL of the receivable pool is above that of the notes and certificates at both high and low prepayment rates, but at higher prepayment

EXHIBIT 5.12

Cash Flows for Publicly Offered Asset-Backed Notes and Certificates of Ford Credit Auto Owner Trust 2000-A at 0.5% Prepayment

ABS.[1] = 0.5%

A1	A2	A3	A4
78926000	0	0	0
74322500	0	0	0
1751500	72233200	0	0
0	73741200	0	0
0	73439600	0	0
0	73138000	0	0
0	72874100	0	0
0	11573900	61000000	0
0	0	72300000	0
0	0	71400000	0
0	0	65600000	0
0	0	65500000	0
0	0	65400000	0
0	0	65200000	0
0	0	65000000	0
0	0	64900000	0
0	0	64700000	0
0	0	64500000	0
0	0	64300000	0
0	0	64200000	0
0	0	64000000	0
0	0	59300000	0
0	0	22700000	36367500
0	0	0	58987500
0	0	0	58792500
0	0	0	58597500
0	0	0	58500000
0	0	0	57037500

1 ABS.: Absolute prepayment model

A5	CLASS B	CLASS C
o	o	o
o	o	o
o	o	o
o	o	o
o	o	o
o	o	o
o	o	o
o	o	o
o	o	o
o	o	o
o	o	o
o	o	o
o	o	o
o	o	o
o	o	o
o	o	o
o	o	o
o	o	o
o	o	o
o	o	o
o	o	o
o	o	o
o	o	o
o	o	o
o	o	o
o	o	o
o	o	o

(continued)

EXHIBIT 5.12 (CONT'D.)

A1	A2	A3	A4
O	O	O	56842500
O	O	O	55087500
O	O	O	54892500
O	O	O	54795000
O	O	O	53917500
O	O	O	53722500
O	O	O	46312500
O	O	O	46312500
O	O	O	46117500
O	O	O	45922500
O	O	O	45825000
O	O	O	45727500
O	O	O	41242500
O	O	O	O
O	O	O	O
O	O	O	O

EXHIBIT 5.13

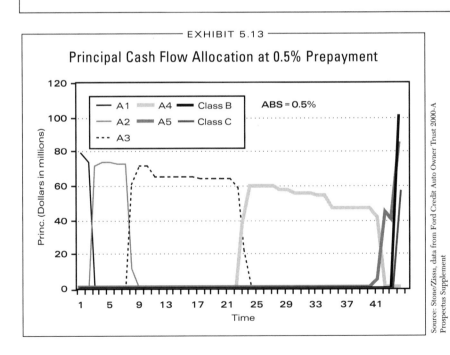

Principal Cash Flow Allocation at 0.5% Prepayment

Source: Stone/Zissu, data from Ford Credit Auto Owner Trust 2000-A Prospectus Supplement

A5	CLASS B	CLASS C
O	O	O
O	O	O
O	O	O
O	O	O
O	O	O
O	O	O
O	O	O
O	O	O
O	O	O
O	O	O
O	O	O
O	O	O
4218408	O	O
43521624	O	O
39646176	O	O
84093792	99200000	56690000

rates the percent difference increases. This ensures that within the normal range of receivable payment rates (including defaults), the notes and certificates will amortize before the asset pool.

In order to create money market securities with a relatively short WAL, it is necessary to extend the WAL of other notes and certificates. The behavior of the underlying pool in combination with market interest rates allows only a certain amount of manipulation. For example, if all cash flows generated from the amortization of receivables were invested in Treasury bills for ten years and then liquidated and distributed to investors, a wedge would be driven between the amortization rate of the pool and the WAL of the notes and certificates. While possible, this scheme would not offer any value. Reinvesting the cash flows from the amortization of the receivables in Treasury bills would ultimately create yields that approach those of Treasury bills without offering their liquidity. Investors can go directly to the Treasury bill market.

EXHIBIT 5.14

Cash Flows for Publicly Offered Asset-Backed Notes and Certificates of Ford Credit Auto Owner Trust 2000-A at 1.8% Prepayment

ABS.[1] = 1.8%

A1	A2	A3	A4
127193000	0	0	0
27807000	92779700	0	0
0	1.18E+08	0	0
0	1.16E+08	0	0
0	50065600	63500000	0
0	0	1.11E+08	0
0	0	1.09E+08	0
0	0	1.07E+08	0
0	0	1.04E+08	0
0	0	97100000	0
0	0	92900000	0
0	0	90700000	0
0	0	88200000	0
0	0	86000000	0
0	0	50600000	33930000
0	0	0	81997500
0	0	0	79560000
0	0	0	77122500
0	0	0	74685000
0	0	0	72150000
0	0	0	69517500
0	0	0	64252500
0	0	0	62010000
0	0	0	59572500
0	0	0	57330000
0	0	0	54892500
0	0	0	52455000
0	0	0	49432500

1 ABS.: Absolute prepayment model

A5	CLASS B	CLASS C
O	O	O
O	O	O
O	O	O
O	O	O
O	O	O
O	O	O
O	O	O
O	O	O
O	O	O
O	O	O
O	O	O
O	O	O
O	O	O
O	O	O
O	O	O
O	O	O
O	O	O
O	O	O
O	O	O
O	O	O
O	O	O
O	O	O
O	O	O
O	O	O
O	O	O
O	O	O
O	O	O
O	O	O
O	O	O

(continued)

EXHIBIT 5.14 (CONT'D.)

A1	A2	A3	A4
0	0	0	46995000
0	0	0	39097500
0	0	0	0
0	0	0	0
0	0	0	0
0	0	0	0
0	0	0	0
0	0	0	0
0	0	0	0
0	0	0	0
0	0	0	0
0	0	0	0
0	0	0	0
0	0	0	0
0	0	0	0
0	0	0	0

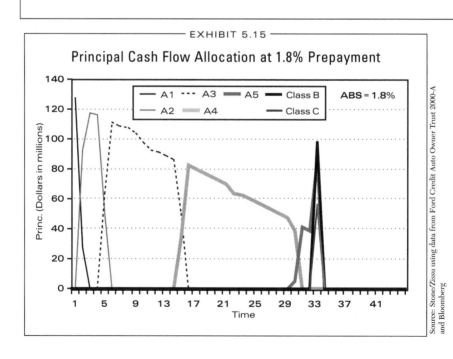

EXHIBIT 5.15

Principal Cash Flow Allocation at 1.8% Prepayment

Legend: A1, A3, A5, Class B; A2, A4, Class C. ABS = 1.8%

Princ. (Dollars in millions) vs. Time

Source: Stone/Zissu using data from Ford Credit Auto Owner Trust 2000-A and Bloomberg

A5	CLASS B	CLASS C
0	0	0
4664256	0	0
41412420	0	0
38977404	0	0
86425920	99200000	56690000
0	0	0
0	0	0
0	0	0
0	0	0
0	0	0
0	0	0
0	0	0
0	0	0
0	0	0
0	0	0
0	0	0

Source: Ford Credit Auto Owner Trust 2000-A and Bloomberg

The point is that while the capital structure of the trust can reallocate the cash flows of the receivable pool, it must do so in a way that creates value for the investors. In the Ford Credit Auto Owner Trust 2000-A transaction, this value was created by offering securities ($2.68 billion in notes and $212.6 million in certificates) at yields that were sufficient to attract investors and offer the seller a profit that was extracted through the retained interests in the pool. The seller's expected profit is reduced or enhanced depending upon the yield actually returned on the notes and certificates, which in turn is tied to the default and delinquency rates of the pool and the prepayment rate.

The sequential structure reallocates the WAL of the asset pool. Cash flows generated from the receivable pool are reallocated to earlier years from later years. This is done by using the cash flowing into the collection accounts from the amortizing receivables to pay down

---
EXHIBIT 5.16

Weighted Average Lives (WAL) of Asset-Backed Securities Issued by Ford Credit Auto Owner Trust 2000-A

	WAL AT 0.5% ABS.[1]	WAL AT 1.5% ABS.[1]
A1	0.10	0.08
A2	0.40	0.28
A3	1.23	0.88
A4	2.61	2.00
A5	3.58	2.93
B	3.64	2.98
C	3.64	2.98
D	3.64	2.98
	Average WAL	Average WAL
A class (A1 + A2 +A3 + A4 + A5)	1.70	1.288
Subordinate classes (B + C + D)	3.64	2.98
A class plus subordinate classes	1.843	1.412
Pool[2]	1.91	1.58

1 ABS: Absolute payment model.
2 Estimates of pool averages are based on information derived from and provided in the prospectus supplement. The numbers are for indicative
purposes only.

Source: Stone/Zissu using data from Ford Motor Credit

a large percent of the note principal and deferring principal payment on other classes.

The design of the sequential structure in this example created two sets of securities: those with a WAL longer than the underlying pool and those with a WAL shorter than the underlying pool. Because of the overcollateralization (discussed previously), the WAL of the pool must be longer than that of the note and certificates.

The FMCC trust is structured to amortize in such a way that the credit enhancement increases over time across various prepayment and default scenarios once the initial money market class is paid off.

The WAL of asset-backed and mortgage-backed securities

depends on the rate at which they are scheduled to be amortized and the flexibility of this schedule in response to change in the rate at which the underlying receivable pool amortizes. In certain collateralized mortgage obligation (CMO) transactions, planned and targeted amortization classes (TACs) are designed to amortize within a very tight band, and this band is insulated by placing securities on both the upside and downside of prepayment rates to absorb fast and slow prepayment rates. When prepayments accelerate, the planned amortization class (PAC) is retired according to schedule, whereas the companion class is retired much sooner than expected. When prepayments decelerate, the PAC still amortizes according to schedule, whereas the companion class life is extended.

In the Trust 2000-A transaction, the classes are scheduled to amortize sequentially, but because auto loan prepayment rates are much less volatile than prepayments on mortgages, and because the WAL of the underlying receivables is much shorter than most mortgages, neither PACs or TACs were employed to reallocate prepayment risk. **Exhibit 5.17** shows that as the WAL changes due to changes in prepayment speeds, the translation into increases or decreases in required yield depends on the shape of the yield curve at that time.

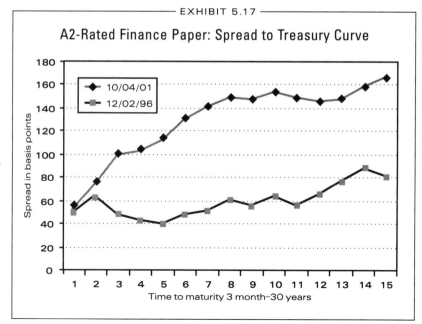

EXHIBIT 5.17

A2-Rated Finance Paper: Spread to Treasury Curve

Spread in basis points

10/04/01
12/02/96

Time to maturity 3 month–30 years

Source: Stone/Zissu using data from Bloomberg

With a steep yield curve, relatively small changes in WAL lead to large changes in required yield. This implies that when the yield curve is relatively steep, prepayment risk is more costly to finance, and spreads for securities with embedded prepayment risk, like those issued by Trust 2000-A, increase. We see that the WAL of class B falls from 3.64 years to 2.98 years when prepayments are calculated at 1.5 percent rather than 0.5 percent. While this is a large difference, it illustrates well the impact on required yields. In September 2001, the difference in spreads between four-year and two-year A-2-rated finance paper was 27 bp. In September 1996, when the yield curve was considerably flatter, the difference was a mere 6 bp (see exhibit 5.17).

Waterfall of Cash Flows

EXHIBIT 5.18 shows the allocation of interest and principal cash flows, according to the different priorities among the different classes. It is typical in a securitization transaction for the originator/transferor of the assets to continue to service the assets that it has sold. As the servicer of the securitized asset pool, the transferor manages the collection of interest and principal from the obligors, the deposit of funds into the collection account, the enforcement of liens attached to the assets, and direction to the indenture trustee to withdraw and distribute funds from the collection account to other accounts held in the name of the trustee. In return for performing the servicing function, the servicer receives a fee from the trust. In the case of Ford Motor Credit, the servicing fee earned by Ford Motor Credit is 1/12 of 1 percent per month of the outstanding principal amount of the receivables held by the Trust 2000-A.

Interest and principal payments that obligors pay to the servicer, FMCC, are distributed to the beneficiaries of Trust 2000-A according to a defined set of rules. For example, class A1 must be retired before any other class receives principal or interest, and class A notes have priority of interest over subordinate notes and certificates. These rules form what is commonly known as the waterfall of cash because of the way it flows down to different accounts and to different beneficial owners of the trust. Cash flows at the top of the waterfall have priority over cash flows at the bottom—that is, they are allocated first.

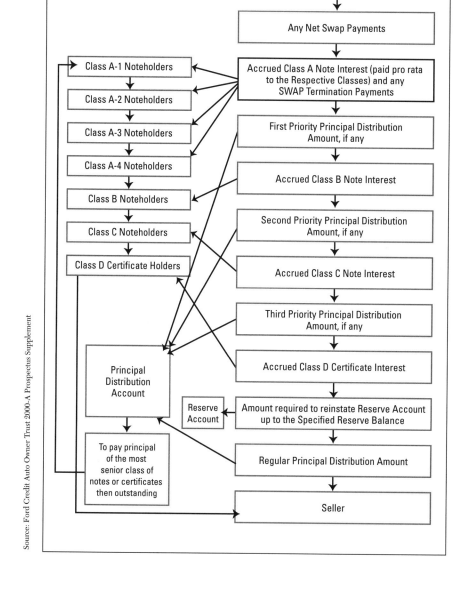

EXHIBIT 5.18

Allocation of Interest and Principal Cash Flows

Source: Ford Credit Auto Owner Trust 2000-A Prospectus Supplement

Exhibit 5.18 diagrams the cash-flow waterfall, or cash-flow allocation, for Trust 2000-A. (The scheme appears in this format in the prospectus supplement of Trust 2000-A.)

Credit Enhancement

THE FIVE senior classes, classes A1 through A5, constitute 92.64 percent of the principal of the asset-backed securities. Classes B, C, and D, subordinated to the A1 through A5 classes, comprise 7.35 percent of the notes and act as credit enhancement. The percentage of credit enhancement for the senior notes increases over time as the senior notes amortize.

EXHIBIT **5.19** shows the number of years a class is outstanding for a given absolute prepayment scenario. For example, class A2 will be fully amortized in six years with a 1 percent prepayment rate.

After A1 is fully retired, the total credit enhancement for the remaining four senior classes, A2 through A5, is 7.77 percent. After A2 is also fully retired, the total credit enhancement for the remaining three senior classes, A3 through A5, is 9 percent. After A3 is fully retired, the total credit enhancement for the remaining two senior classes, A4 and A5, is 15.64 percent. Finally, after the first five senior classes, A1 through A5, are fully retired, the credit enhancement provided by the subordinated notes B, C, and D corresponds to 55.35 percent.

EXHIBIT 5.19

Months Outstanding under Four Prepayment Scenarios of Senior Note Classes

SENIOR NOTE CLASSES	ABSOLUTE PREPAYMENT MODEL			
	.5%	1%	1.5%	1.8%
A1	3	2	2	2
A2	8	6	5	5
A3	23	20	17	15
A4	41	38	34	30
A5	44	41	36	33

Source: Ford Credit Auto Owner Trust 2000-A

When all five A classes are fully retired, the next class to benefit from credit enhancement is class B, enhanced by the remaining classes C and D. At that point, class B benefits from a 53.33 percent credit enhancement constituted by classes C and D. Finally, when all classes senior to C and D are fully retired, class C is credit enhanced by class D, in the amount of 100 percent.

Overcollateralization

BESIDES THE subordination of note and certificate classes, there are other forms of credit enhancement internal to the structure. At time of issue, the trust assets represented 103.76 percent of the principal amount of classes A1 through A5, B, C, and D. The 3.76 percent overcollateralization of the trust constitutes additional credit enhancement.

A trust is overcollateralized when the assets transferred to the trust exceed the face value of the securities issued by the trust. For example, in the case of Ford Credit Auto Owner Trust 2000-A, the receivable pool transferred to the trust—$3,000,003,021.76—exceeding the principal amount of the notes and certificates issued by the trust ($2,891,060,000) by 3.76 percent. The amount by which Trust 2000-A is overcollateralized is not fixed for the life of the transaction.

Depending on the rate at which the receivables amortize (in other words, according to defaults and different scheduled repayments and prepayments), the percent of the overcollateralization will vary. In the Trust 2000-A transaction, the notes and certificates are scheduled to amortize faster than the receivables. When securities amortize faster than the underlying receivable pool, as in this case, the overcollateralization amount will increase as a percentage of the outstanding notes and certificates.

EXHIBIT 5.20 is based on the historical performance of the underlying pool of receivables securitized through Trust 2000-A (interest and principal cash flows) and the interest and principal allocation to each class from issuance through May 20, 2003. The bottom line graphs the historical total interest and principal cash-flows allocation to all classes, and the top line the historical interest plus principal payments from the underlying pool of receivables. The space

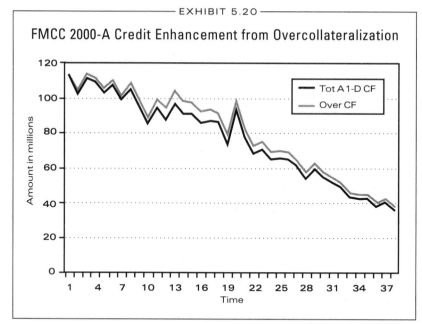

EXHIBIT 5.20

FMCC 2000-A Credit Enhancement from Overcollateralization

Legend:
- Tot A 1-D CF
- Over CF

X-axis: Time (1, 4, 7, 10, 13, 16, 19, 22, 25, 28, 31, 34, 37)

Y-axis: Amount in millions (0, 20, 40, 60, 80, 100, 120)

between the two lines is excess spread. Excess spread enhances the credit quality of the securities issued by the trust, because more cash flow is generated than is needed to amortize the asset-backed notes and certificates. The source of this excess spread is the overcollateralization and the difference between the interest rate charged on the receivables and the interest rate offered on the securities.

As has been noted, overcollateralization creates two forms of credit enhancement: (1) the excess spread generated from the assets in excess of those necessary to amortize the receivables under loss rates below the overcollateralization amount, and (2) the principal in the trust in excess of the principal value of the securities issued. The volume of excess spread varies from period to period, as can be seen from the variability in the distance between the two lines in exhibit 5.20. A large difference between the cash flowing into the trust (from amortizing receivables and interest earned on short-term instruments) and the cash needed to fund the trust's capital structure and fees produces a large excess spread for the period.

The difference between the two lines, or extra cash flow, to the extent that it is not needed to fund the target overcollateralization amount and interest shortfalls, repay servicer advances, and/or maintain reserve accounts, will flow back to the seller. Note that it is typical in a securitization transaction for the servicer of the receivables to advance funds to the SPV to bridge timing differences between cash received by the SPV and required payments of the SPV to investors. Servicer advances are a source of liquidity to the securitization transaction but are not considered as credit enhancement since the servicer has priority with respect to funds it is owed relative to the investors who own the certificates and securities issued by the SPV.

Excess spread is an important source of income for the transferor. **EXHIBIT 5.21** shows the amount of excess spread that would flow to the seller with 0 percent delinquency and loss rates. To calculate the gain from selling assets, the transferor must estimate the present value of its retained interest in the securitized pool. Part of this retained interest is the excess spread. As delinquencies and losses on the underlying asset pool increase, excess spread is diminished. The transferor discounts the amount of excess spread it expects to receive at a discount rate commensurate with the risk of the asset pool.

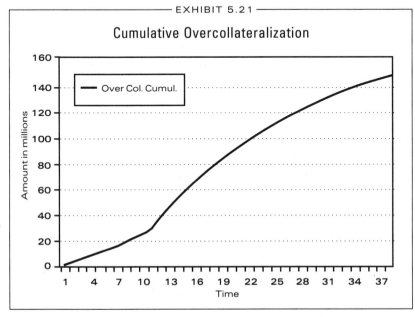

EXHIBIT 5.21

Cumulative Overcollateralization

Source: Stone/Zissu using data from Ford Credit Auto Owner Trust 2000-A

Rating Agency Parameters

Rating agencies require that, even under extreme stresses to the system such as bankruptcy of the transferor or of the servicer of the securitized assets, the securitization structure perform in a manner consistent with the rating of the asset-backed notes and certificates without regard to the credit rating of the transferor. Ratings reflect the likelihood of the timely payment of interest and principal. If bankruptcy of the transferor or of any of the entities in the structure is possible, then bankruptcy is assumed in order to test the integrity of the issuing vehicles' independence and isolation under extreme stress. In the FMCC securitization transactions neither bankruptcy of the seller, Ford Motor Credit Auto Receivables Two LLP, or of the trust, Ford Credit Auto Owner Trust 2000-A, is assumed because the former meets Standard & Poor's special-purpose-vehicle (SPV) criteria and the latter is a qualifying special-purpose entity (QSPE) as defined by FASB 140. In addition, the seller meets Standard & Poor's bankruptcy remoteness criteria. A bankruptcy of FMCC should leave Ford Motor Credit Auto Receivables Two LLP intact as a separate and independent vehicle.

It is critical to the rating decision that even under bankruptcy of the transferor the investors in the asset-backed securities will have unimpeded and timely access to the cash from amortization or liquidation of the receivables. Without comfort in this unimpeded access to the receivables, securitization regresses to secured financing as far as investors are concerned.

"The fundamental tenet of the criteria [the legal criteria of the rating] is to isolate the assets from the credit risk of the seller," according to Standard & Poor's Structured Finance Auto Loan Criteria. Once the rating agencies are comfortable with the strength of isolation of the credit risk of the transferor from the credit risk of the asset-backed notes and certificates, the agencies' focus is on sizing the credit enhancement necessary to support the ratings assigned to each of the classes of notes and certificates issued. The original ratings of the securities issued by Trust 2000-A are given in EXHIBIT **5.22**. Using the criteria of Standard & Poor's, the AAA ratings assigned to the class A notes require a level of credit protection that is equal to between four and five times the cumulative expected losses on the underlying receivables. Standard & Poor's derives this multiple from

---

EXHIBIT 5.22

Ratings Changes for ABS Issued by Ford Credit Auto Owner Trust 2000-A

CLASS	RATING AT ISSUE	LAST RATING
Class A1	A-1+	A-1+ (3/00)
Class A2	A-1+	A-1+ (9/00)
Class A3	AAA	AAA (7/01)
Class A4	AAA	AAA (9/00)
Class A5	AAA	AAA (9/02)
Class B	A	AAA (4/02)
Class C	BBB	AA+ (9/02)
Class D	BB	BBB- (7/02)

---

the loss curve based on the historical performance of FMCC's portfolio of retail installment sales contracts.

As an indication of the expected losses and their impact on the required credit enhancement for each rating, consider the worst year's net losses on FMCC's managed portfolio of retail installment contracts and leases between 1997 and 2001. This was 1.45 percent in 2001. If this worst loss rate is compounded for two years, by about six months more than the WAL of the A classes computed at a 0.5 percent prepayment scenario (1.58 years), the cumulative loss would be 2.1 percent. The A classes of asset-backed securities in the Trust 2000-A then benefit from 12 percent support between five and six times the expected cumulative losses on the underlying receivable pool. The 12 percent is calculated by dividing the sum of the class A note principal amount on the issue date by the sum of the principal amounts on the Class B, C, and D securities, the overcollateralization amount, and the reserve account balance on the issue date. This is a rough calculation because the weighted average life of the securities may be shorter or longer depending upon the prepayment rate of the receivables. As the short-term A1 and A2 classes are retired (WAL of 0.1 and 0.4 years, respectively), the longer-term class A securities will benefit from increased credit support.

Leveraging Credit Risk

Securitization vehicles are capitalized with various classes of securities, certificates, and retained interests that are positioned differently with respect to the credit risk of the underlying pool of receivables. Reallocating all but the most remote credit risk, credit risk associated with AAA-rated securities—from the whole receivable pool to classes that represent a small percentage of the principal amount of the pool—is the process of leveraging credit risk.

Simply selling the receivables to an off-balance-sheet SPV in exchange for a single class of notes that are then placed in the market would be impractical from a financing standpoint. Since the note would bear 100 percent of the credit risk embedded in the receivable pool, the credit enhancement supporting the note would be 0 percent of expected pool credit losses. This scenario would translate into a credit rating of no higher than B to BB. Financing at this rate would not make sense for a finance company that has investment-grade ratings. Another way of making this point is to realize that if Ford issued a single unenhanced class, arbitrageurs would buy the security and securitize it.

In summary, in the Trust 2000-A transaction, five A classes were issued (A1, A2, A3, A4, and A5). Generally, all classes within a single notation (A, B, C, and so on) rank pari passu with respect to credit risk. That is, they share the same position on the credit spectrum, and they share available interest and principal charge-offs on a pro rata basis. In this transaction, there are five different levels of credit enhancement that benefit the A notes. Credit enhancement takes the form of subordination of the class B notes, the class C certificates, the class D certificates, the overcollateralization of the trust, and the reserve fund. In addition to principal amortization of the credit enhancement that is allocated in order of priority to the more senior classes, the excess spread generated in each period also enhances the credit quality of the notes and certificates.

Excess spread is derived from the difference between the periodic interest owed to the note and certificate holders, and the net interest generated by the receivable pool. Excess spread that is not used in one period to support a more senior class or fund the reserve account is not available in subsequent periods; instead it flows to the seller. Since it flows out of the transaction periodically, excess spread does not offer the same credit support to more senior classes of securities as does a reserve account, overcollateralization, or subordinate securities.

One reason for a revision in credit ratings would be a change in the amount of credit enhancement protecting or covering senior classes of securities. Credit losses on the receivable pool erode the credit enhancement protecting each class. If the credit enhancement is sized correctly for each class, the rating of the class should not change. However, if default rates exceed the expected loss rates associated with the rating, then the rating of the securities will be lowered. Credit enhancement may also increase as the receivable pool amortizes, as occurred with the Trust 2000-A transaction presented here.

It is interesting to notice changes in the level of credit enhancement over time and its impact on the ratings of the different classes. We can observe in exhibit 5.22 the changes in ratings for classes B, C, and D. They were all upgraded. This is due to the two forms of credit enhancement that occurred: the first was provided by the subordination of the three classes to the senior classes A1, A2, A3, A4, and A5; the second resulted from overcollateralization.

As explained earlier, as the senior classes amortize and are sequentially retired, the subordinated notes benefit from a decrease in credit risk, leaving less to enhance. The subordinate classes are deleveraged. Overcollateralization as a percent of the trust increases and combines with the decrease in the class A principal relative to subordinate classes B, C, and D to increase the credit quality of the outstanding classes. This is why classes B, C, and D were upgraded.

As testament to the strength of the securitization structure and the separation of the risk of the transferor from the risk of the trust in 2002, it is also interesting to note that FMCC's long-term issuer rating was lowered from BBB+ to BBB by Standard & Poor's, and its short-term rating was lowered from P-1 to P-2, while Standard & Poor's issued twenty-two upgrades of asset-backed securities issued by Ford Credit Owner Trusts and no downgrades. The reason for the upgrades was that credit enhancement increased because the securities amortized faster than the receivables. It is also possible for upgrades to be caused by lower default rates than expected, but this was not the case in 2002.

Chapter Notes

1. A qualifying SPE is demonstrably distinct from the transfer only if it cannot be unilaterally dissolved by any transferor, its affiliates, or its agents, and either (a) at least 10 percent of the fair value of its beneficial interests is held by parties other than any transferor, its affiliates, or its agents, or (b) the transfer is a guaranteed mortgage securitization. An ability to unilaterally dissolve an SPE can take many forms, including but not limited to holding sufficient beneficial interests to demand that the trustee dissolve the SPE, the right to call all the assets transferred to the SPE, and a right to call or a prepayment privilege on the beneficial interests held by other parties. (FASB 140 Paragraph 36)

2. Bear Stearns Asset-Backed Indices on Bloomberg System.

Chapter Six

Asset-Backed Commercial Paper

THE MARKET for asset-backed commercial paper (ABCP) has ballooned in recent years. From $40.7 billion, or 7.5 percent of the total commercial paper (CP) market, in March 1992, it grew to $728.3 billion, or 53.8 percent of that market, by March 2003. Growth in ABCP reflects the fact that this vehicle offers companies access to the prime CP market at better terms than they can attain by issuing CP directly from their own balance sheets. Advantages in using the ABCP market extend beyond lower interest rates and include the opportunity for diversification of funding sources that can act as a cushion against credit downgrades or marginal increase in the cost of on-balance-sheet CP. In addition, ABCP offers investors an alternative access point to a prime money market instrument. (Data are from The Federal Reserve Board Commercial paper Outstanding.)

EXHIBIT 6.1 presents data on the spreads between tier-one and tier-two dealer-placed CP as they were on December 5, 2002. Top tier refers to CP rated A-1/P-1 by Standard & Poor's and Moody's, respectively. Tier two refers to CP rated A-2/P-2 by Standard & Poor's and Moody's, respectively. Dealer placed refers to commercial paper that is distributed for an issuer by a dealer as opposed to directly placed paper that is sold by the issuer to investors without the use of an intermediary. The spreads ranged from 23 basis points (bp) for one day to 60 bp for five months. The spreads between top-tier ABCP and top-tier CP issued from a company's balance sheet are about 1

EXHIBIT 6.1

Tier-One and Tier-Two Commercial Paper Spreads

HISTORICAL SPREADS

DATE   12/ 5/2002

	DEALER CP TOP TOP	DEALER CP 2ND TIER	
	Yield	Yield	Spread
1 DAY	1.20000	1.43000	-0.23000
7 DAY	1.23000	1.51000	-0.28000
15 DAY	1.26000	1.60000	-0.34000
21 DAY	1.29000		
30 DAY	1.30000	1.75000	-0.45000
45 DAY	1.32000	1.74000	-0.42000
60 DAY	1.32000	1.77000	-0.45000
90 DAY	1.32000	1.90000	-0.58000
4 MONTH	1.34000	1.94000	-0.60000
5 MONTH	1.35000	1.95000	-0.60000
6 MONTH	1.36000		
7 MONTH	1.37000		
8 MONTH	1.39000		
9 MONTH	1.44000		
1 YEAR			

Source: Bloomberg

to 2 bp. The spreads on 12/5/02 are indicative of the magnitude of the spreads between the markets for top-tier and second-tier paper in general. As the data indicates, companies pay a relatively high premium for the placement of lower-rated paper, 60 basis points at five months. Below the second tier the market for CP is very thin and becomes uneconomical in most cases. This is where the market for asset-backed CP offers its greatest value to financial and nonfinancial companies. Companies without access to the CP market from their own balance sheets can tap the market via an asset-backed commercial paper conduit. The date December 5th was chosen only as an indication of spreads. Spreads will narrow and widen due to both firm-specific and broad market conditions.

For prime-rated financial, service, and industrial firms—in other words, those rated at the top of the short-term rating spectrum by Fitch (F-1/F-1+), Standard & Poor's (A-1+), or Moody's (P-1)—CP is a primary source of liquidity. However, firms with ratings below the first two prime notches, P-1 and P-2, are priced out of the CP market unless they take the ABCP conduit route. Even firms that possess prime ratings tap into ABCP programs to diversify and expand their sources of liquidity.

Why Companies Use Asset-Backed Commercial Paper Programs

THE MARKET FOR ABCP has grown since its inception in the early 1980s because it offers value to the following three dimensions of the capital market:

➤ Companies gain access to the money markets at lower rates.

➤ Investors gain access to a broader choice of prime-rated CP issuers.

➤ Banks and finance companies that sponsor or administer asset-backed security conduits can offer customers a competitively priced source of liquidity that does not tie up bank capital to the same extent a loan or credit facility would. Sponsors can earn administration fees, and conduits can earn fees for supplying and arranging liquidity and credit enhancement facilities, with little expansion in their capital base.

ABCP programs are designed to give companies access to the top-tier CP market at a premium that reflects the credit and liquidity risks of the receivables or securities they seek to finance. A company that is not rated or is rated below investment grade and is therefore unable to tap the CP market from its own balance sheet can enter the CP market by way of an ABCP program.

Companies that can and do issue CP directly from their own balance sheets may, at the same time, choose to actively securitize receivables through an ABCP program. If the company were to suffer a credit downgrade, it may be closed out of the unsecured CP market. Obviously, in this case the company's reliance on ABCP would increase. Maintaining both on-balance-sheet and off-balance-sheet CP programs offers the company diversity of funding sources and increases the depth of the money markets it can tap at any one time. A company that has saturated the market with its own CP and is facing increasing marginal costs to place additional paper can use the ABCP market as a less expensive alternative.

GE Capital Example

Among companies using ABCP, General Electric Capital Corporation, which has a short-term rating of A-1+ by Standard & Poor's and Prime-1 (P-1) by Moody's, issues CP directly from its own balance sheet as well as securitizing its receivables through third-party ABCP conduits. The rationale for financing working capital in the CP market using both on- and off-balance-sheet instruments is diversification. As the single largest issuer of CP from its own balance sheet, GE Capital is, like all large issuers of CP, exposed both to marginal increases in short-term interest rates and to disruptions in its ability to roll over maturing CP due to either firm-specific reasons or general market conditions. At the beginning of 2003 GE Capital had $66.6 billion dollars in U.S. commercial paper outstanding. If the market were to become saturated with GE Capital CP, the marginal demand for funds could be raised in the ABCP market. If, on the other hand, the asset-backed market becomes relatively costly, then GE can substitute unsecured on-balance-sheet issues of CP for issues of ABCP.

> We believe that alternative sources of liquidity are sufficient to permit an orderly transition from commercial paper in the unlikely event of impaired access to those markets. Funding sources on which we would rely would depend on the nature of such a hypothetical event, but include $54 billion of contractually committed lending agreements with highly rated global banks and investment banks, an increase of $21 billion since December 31, 2001, as well as other sources of liquidity, including medium- and long-term funding, monetization, asset securitization, cash receipts from our lending and leasing activities, short-term secured funding on global assets, and potential asset sales. (General Electric Capital Corporation 10-K, for fiscal year ended 2002)

Just as companies use the ABCP market to diversify funding sources, investment funds use the market to diversify their CP holdings. ABCP conduits that issue CP that satisfies SEC rule 2a-7[1] offer money market funds investments that can broaden their investment choices. It is the obligations of the asset-backed commercial paper conduit that count for diversification purposes, not the companies that are financing their receivables via the conduit. So long as the asset-backed commercial paper conduits satisfy the concentration limits of rule 2a-7, investments in ABCP are driven by the credit quality of the program, not the credit quality of the companies refinancing their assets through the conduit. To satisfy SEC rule 2a-7, no single obligor's receivables that are refinanced through the conduit can represent more than 10 percent of the conduit's assets. If this limit is breached the obligor whose receivables exceeded the 10 percent limit would be treated as the issuer of the commercial paper—as far as a money market mutual fund were concerned.

The quality of an asset-backed commercial paper conduit is monitored by the rating agencies and controlled by the program's administrator. Investors receive periodic reports concerning various dimensions of the program's activities and performance. Funds will typically be constrained by concentration limits with respect to the investments the program makes. Rule 2a-7 sets a regulatory limit but funds may also set their own limits to assure investors of sufficient diversification. Investors consider the program to be the issuer of the CP for purposes of diversification limits, not the underlying obligors of the CP. In other words, only CP issued directly by SONY Corp. and not by an asset-backed commercial paper conduit that funds SONY receivables are counted as investments in SONY obligations. CP issued by an asset-backed commercial paper conduit that finances SONY receivables are counted as investments in the obligations of the asset-backed commercial paper conduit unless, as we have just explained, SONY's assets represented more than 10 percent of the conduit's assets.

Companies use ABCP programs sometimes to complement and other times to replace their bank lines of credit and revolving-loan facilities. Various types of financial assets are funded through such programs. Trade receivables, mortgages, retail automobile loans, credit card receivables, dealer floor plan loans, equipment leases, commercial loans, and asset-backed securities (ABSs) are some of the assets that have been funded in this way.

Ford Motor Credit Example

Ford Motor Credit uses its single-seller ABCP program, FCAR Owner Trust, to refinance ABSs that are created when it securitizes retail installment loans and dealer floor plan loans and leases. (As discussed in Chapter 5, FCAR, a Delaware business trust structured as a bankruptcy-remote special-purpose limited liability company, is administered by Ford Motor Credit; it is primarily used to refinance short-term tranches of ABSs that have been issued to finance the purchase of retail installment contracts.) A single-seller program only purchases interests in receivables pools originated by one company, while a multiseller asset-backed commercial paper program finances receivables originated by multiple companies.

FCAR issues two series of commercial paper. Series I is rated A-1+/P-1 by Standard & Poor's and Moody's, respectively, and Series II is rated A-1/P-1. Each series shares in FCAR's collateral on a pro rata basis. FCAR also issues equity interests in the form of owner trust certificates. The owner trust certificates are subordinate to the CP issued in Series I and Series II. The minimum rating of the ABSs financed by FCAR is AA/Aa2. Liquidity facilities are supplied by a syndicate of A-1+/P-1-rated banks to support Series I and by a syndicate of A-1/P-1-rated banks to support Series II.

Ford Motor Credit also uses bank-sponsored multiseller ABCP programs to finance its receivables and asset-backed securities.

Countrywide Home Loans Example

As was noted above, ABCP conduits are also used by financial institutions to fund the accumulation of loans prior to their refinancing through a term issue of mortgage-backed or asset-backed securities. The conduit makes secured loans to a wholly owned bankruptcy-remote subsidiary of the financial institution that has bought the asset from the originator. The conduit funds itself in the CP markets. When the credits are finally pooled and securitized, the financial institution uses the proceeds from the securitization to repay its secured loan from the conduit. The agreement with the conduit serves as a line of credit to the financial institution that can be drawn upon up to a limit.

Countrywide Home Loans, for example, which is a subsidiary of Countrywide Financial Corporation, uses ABCP to finance the accumulation of conventional mortgages prior to their securitization in the agency or private-label market. Countrywide also uses ABCP conduits as a source of liquidity to fund delinquent Federal Housing Administration and Veterans Affairs mortgage loans that have been securitized. The conduit provides funds that Countrywide uses to bridge the time between foreclosure and liquidation.

ABCP Characteristics

COMPANIES THAT ENTER into ABCP programs have the option of securitizing current and future receivables from designated accounts. Companies enter into an agreement with an ABCP program for a set period of time. A company typically may have a two-year commitment from the ABCP program with an option to renew. Whether the conduit is willing to renew the firm's participation in the program will depend upon the financial condition of the company and the performance of its receivables and servicing over the previous two years.

Relationship of Conduit, Originator, and Seller

Companies that enter into agreements with CP conduits to finance their assets, whether they are trade receivables, loans, or ABSs, have the possibility of renegotiating the receivables purchase agreement that establishes the relationship of the conduit with the originator or servicer and the seller. The seller, which is usually a wholly owned subsidiary of the company that originates the receivables, buys the receivables from the originator and sells interests in the receivables to the conduit, which is called the *purchaser* of the receivables. The seller can also use interests in the pool of receivables to secure loans from the conduit. The purchaser funds itself in the CP market.

Frequently, the value of receivables that the company can securitize in a given period will be increased as the expected performance of the receivables is monitored and confirmed by the administrator of the ABCP program. The premium required by the conduit from the company securitizing its assets may also be changed as the receivable pool either outperforms or underperforms expectations of the program administrator. Access to the program will also be tied to the financial condition of the originator, such as measures of profitability, liquidity, and leverage.

As has been discussed, ABCP programs are conduits from the originator or seller of receivables to the CP market. The program administrator arranges for enhancement of the credit and liquidity of the receivable pool so that the commercial paper it issues will be rated P-1/F-1/A-1. The conduit is structured as a bankruptcy-remote special-purpose company. Thus, it is bankruptcy remote from the sponsor or administrator, but it is not structured as a qualifying special-purpose entity (QSPE). The sponsor/administrator is typically a bank or a finance company such as GE or Citicorp. It is the latitude of the conduit's activities on both the asset and liability side that precludes it from being a QSPE.

Securitization Structure and Cash Flow

The administrator has broad discretion in selecting sellers, sizing credit enhancement, and setting the terms of asset purchases. Securitization of receivables via ABCP paper programs is often structured as two-tier transactions. In the first step, receivables are sold to a special-purpose, wholly owned, bankruptcy-remote subsidiary of the originator. This subsidiary, referred to as the seller in the transaction, then sells interests in its pool of receivables to the conduit, which is referred to as the purchaser.

The sale from the originator to the seller is a true sale for accounting purposes. As has been discussed in earlier chapters, selling the receivables to a special-purpose, wholly owned, bankruptcy-remote subsidiary isolates the assets from the originator. Should the originator enter into bankruptcy, the seller's assets will not be consolidated with the assets of its bankrupt parent. A bankruptcy of the originator would end its participation in the ABCP program.

As the pool of receivables owned by the seller (the bankrupt originator's wholly owned subsidiary) liquidates, the cash is used by the conduit to retire maturing CP and repay liquidity draws, rather than to purchase new receivables from the company. The seller often retains or finances a first-loss position in the receivables that takes the form of a retained subordinate interest, overcollateralization, a letter of credit, or a commitment by a financial institution to buy defaulted receivables from the seller. The seller may also be required to provide a liquidity facility, such as a letter of credit from a bank with a sufficient credit rating to support the receivable pool. The transfer from the seller to the purchaser (the conduit) may be structured as a sale or secured loan.

Credit Enhancement and Liquidity Support

As has been noted, ABCP conduits may be either multiseller or single seller. Multiseller programs buy interests in receivable pools from multiple companies, whereas single-seller programs buy interests in receivable pools from a single company and its subsidiaries. Furthermore, these programs may be either fully supported or partially supported. Support refers to the amount of credit and liquidity enhancement that is available relative to the program's outstanding CP. The gap between the credit quality of a pool of trade receivables and the prime rating of the CP issued by the conduit must be filled with credit enhancement.

Fully Supported versus Partially Supported

A fully supported ABCP program is one in which credit support equal to 100 percent of the program's outstanding CP is in place, while partially supported means that only a fraction of the outstanding CP is covered by a credit enhancement facility. Even in a partially supported ABCP program, the liquidity support arrangements will generally support 100 percent of the program's outstanding CP. At the pool level, overcollateralization, a subordinate retained seller's interest, or a letter of credit will be used to bring each receivable pool purchased by the conduit up to at least an investment-grade level, and often higher. Credit enhancement is arranged to cover a multiple of expected default rates so that a receivable pool can be financed at A-1/P-1 rates. Transaction- or pool-specific credit enhancement is subordinate to program-wide credit enhancement. Program-wide credit support may take the form of letters of credit, asset purchase agreements, or surety bonds supplied by a single bank or syndicate of financial institutions.

Credit enhancement is used to essentially buy out defaulted receivables so that sufficient liquid assets are available to support the outstanding CP. For a fully supported program, the credit rating agencies look directly to the credit quality of the suppliers of liquidity and credit enhancement. In a partially supported program, it is also necessary to analyze the strength of each receivable pool, each originator, and the portfolio effects of funding additional pools by new sellers, as well as the pool- and program-wide liquidity and credit support.

Credit enhancement and liquidity support are sized to cover sufficient losses and delinquencies consistent with a prime rating. Rating agencies also evaluate the strength of the servicer, which is usually the company that originates the assets. A weak or deteriorating servicer can lead to liquidity constraints and, ultimately, strains on the credit quality of the receivable pool.

Liquidity Facilities

Liquidity facilities are put in place to bridge any time gap between the liquidation of receivables and the maturity of CP. Liquidity risk increases as the maturity of the assets funded increases relative to the maturity of the CP issued to finance the asset pool. The liquidity of the securitized assets—that is, the ability to liquidate the assets at their fair value to cover maturing CP—will moderate the amount of liquidity support required. A pool of securities backed by credit card receivables is more liquid than a pool of trade receivables, for example, and the required pool-specific liquidity enhancement will reflect this difference.

In a well-functioning ABCP program, investors roll over maturing CP on the credit and liquidity quality of the program, not on the availability of cash flowing out of specific receivable pools and into the conduit. The liquidation of the receivables in fact is disconnected from the maturity of the CP. Proceeds from liquidating assets are used to buy additional assets, and proceeds from new sales of CP are used to pay off maturing CP. If an asset pool deteriorates in the liquidity or credit dimension, then the pool will not be filled with new receivables, and proceeds generated by the asset pool will be used to pay off maturing CP and the supplier of liquidity enhancement. Investors generally do not rely on information about the content of individual receivable pools or their performance. They rely on the integrity of the liquidity and credit facilities as well as the ongoing monitoring of the receivable pool by ratings agencies and the program administrator.

Liquidity facilities are committed to extend credit to the ABCP conduits up to a preset limit (often 100 percent of each receivable pool) but are not committed to fund defaulted receivables. If a liquidity problem becomes a credit problem, the liquidity facility will stop lending and the credit enhancement arrangement will kick in.

Cost of Funding

A company's cost of funding through an ABCP conduit will be a premium above current commercial paper rates. This component of the cost will vary as market rates across the short end of the yield curve fluctuate. The size of the premium is tied to the expected performance of the receivable pool, past performance of the receivable pool, the credit profile of the company originating the receivables, and the operational efficiency of the company—specifically, its competence in servicing receivables. The premium paid by the seller above the CP or Libor rate refer to spreads above the yields on CP issued by the A-1/P-1–rated asset-backed commercial paper conduit. The premiums can be adjusted either upward or downward by the program administrator over the life of the company's agreement with the CP program.

Credit enhancement costs will be passed back to the company either in the form of a higher discount rate or yield or in the size of the first-loss position the seller is required to assume.

After we explain the mechanics of a partially supported multiseller asset-backed commercial paper program with the use of a hypothetical example, we summarize how and why three different companies (D&K Healthcare Resources, General Electric Capital, and Labor Ready Inc.) use the asset-backed commercial paper market. GE Capital rated A-1/P-1 both administers asset-backed commercial paper programs and finances its own receivables through asset-backed commercial paper conduits. D&K Healthcare and Labor Ready, both unrated companies with no access to the CP market via their own balance sheets, have joined asset-backed commercial paper programs to refinance their trade receivables. D&K eventually substituted its access to the asset-backed commercial paper market with a bank line of credit. Often companies use both bank loans and commitments from asset-backed commercial paper conduits.

Financier Conduit Hypothetical Example

EXHIBIT 6.2 lays out the general scheme of Financier Conduit, a partially supported ABCP conduit that is a bankruptcy-remote special-purpose vehicle of Delaware Corporation. Financier Conduit buys interests in receivable pools or makes loans secured by these interests and funds itself on the CP market. Maturity of the paper can range from 1 to 270 days. Each of the three companies that have entered into a receivables purchase agreement with Financier Conduit has established a wholly owned special-purpose subsidiary that is structured as a special-purpose vehicle (SPV). This SPV is the "seller."

Each seller buys receivables originated by its parent company or a

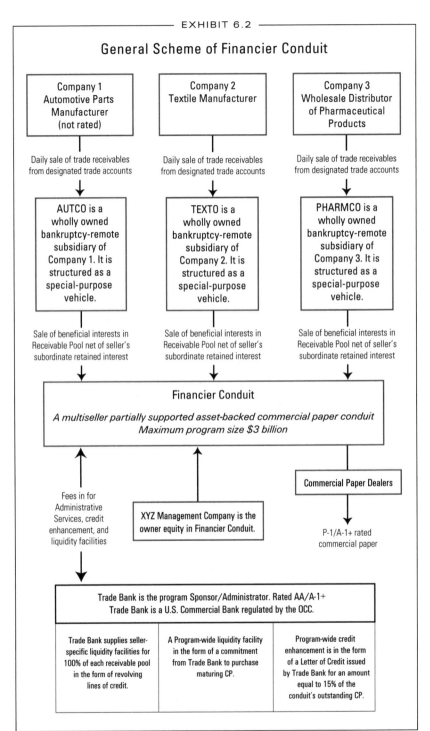

EXHIBIT 6.2

General Scheme of Financier Conduit

Company 1
Automotive Parts
Manufacturer
(not rated)

Company 2
Textile Manufacturer

Company 3
Wholesale Distributor
of Pharmaceutical
Products

Daily sale of trade receivables
from designated trade accounts

Daily sale of trade receivables
from designated trade accounts

Daily sale of trade receivables
from designated trade accounts

AUTCO is a
wholly owned
bankruptcy-remote
subsidiary of
Company 1. It is
structured as a
special-purpose
vehicle.

TEXTO is a
wholly owned
bankruptcy-remote
subsidiary of
Company 2. It is
structured as a
special-purpose
vehicle.

PHARMCO is a
wholly owned
bankruptcy-remote
subsidiary of
Company 3. It is
structured as a
special-purpose
vehicle.

Sale of beneficial interests in
Receivable Pool net of seller's
subordinate retained interest

Sale of beneficial interests in
Receivable Pool net of seller's
subordinate retained interest

Sale of beneficial interests in
Receivable Pool net of seller's
subordinate retained interest

Financier Conduit

A multiseller partially supported asset-backed commercial paper conduit
Maximum program size $3 billion

Commercial Paper Dealers

Fees in for
Administrative
Services, credit
enhancement, and
liquidity facilities

**XYZ Management Company is the
owner equity in Financier Conduit.**

P-1/A-1+ rated
commercial paper

Trade Bank is the program Sponsor/Administrator. Rated AA/A-1+
Trade Bank is a U.S. Commercial Bank regulated by the OCC.

| Trade Bank supplies seller-specific liquidity facilities for 100% of each receivable pool in the form of revolving lines of credit. | A Program-wide liquidity facility in the form of a commitment from Trade Bank to purchase maturing CP. | Program-wide credit enhancement is in the form of a Letter of Credit issued by Trade Bank for an amount equal to 15% of the conduit's outstanding CP. |

Source: Stone/Zissu

subsidiary thereof. These transactions are structured as true sales for accounting purposes. The seller issues undivided beneficial interests in the receivable pool to Financier Conduit and is compensated by Financier Conduit either at the face value of the receivables net of the seller's retained interest or at a discount from face value. When the interests are sold at face value, the seller must pay an explicit rate of interest to the conduit. If the interests are sold at a discount, the yield is earned by the conduit as the receivables liquidate at face value.

Program-wide liquidity facilities in this case are supplied by Trade Bank, which is the sponsor and administrator of a program to buy maturing CP should Financial Conduit be unable to roll over maturing paper. Pool-specific liquidity enhancement takes the form of revolving lines of credit from various banks. These banks make commitments to advance funds to the seller to cover receivable delinquencies in each pool. Each pool is covered by a line of credit up to 100 percent of the conduit's purchase commitments to the seller.

Financier Conduit benefits from credit enhancement at the pool-specific level and the program-wide level. Pool-specific credit enhancement takes the form of a subordinate retained seller's interest in each pool to bring the rating of the beneficial interest issued by the pool to a P-2 rating. At the program-wide level, the credit enhancement is a letter of credit issued by Trade Bank for 20 percent of the conduit's outstanding CP. Financier Conduit is minimally capitalized. The equity of Financier Conduit is owned by a charitable organization.

D&K Example

D&K Healthcare Resources, Inc., is a full-service regional wholesale drug distributor of both branded and generic products that are sold over-the-counter in pharmacies and also to the hospital market. To enhance its liquidity and finance certain trade receivables, D&K entered into an agreement with a bank-sponsored multiseller ABCP conduit in the first quarter of 1999. The original maturity of the agreement with the conduit was three years for an amount of $45 million. To join the ABCP program, D&K had to pay a fee of $225,000 and an additional fee of $75,000 when the program limit was increased.

Originally, the securitization agreement allowed D&K to sell up to $45 million in receivables at any one time. This limit was increased to

$60 million in the second quarter of 1999, then to $75 million in the fourth quarter of 2000, $150 million in June 2002, and finally $200 million in August 2002. After its renewal, the securitization agreement was set to expire in August 2005. However, D&K replaced its access to the ABCP conduit financing with a bank loan in March 2003. Companies are always willing to substitute one form of funding for another to secure better terms, lower rates, less rate risk, and more capacity.

During 1999, the Company and its wholly owned, bankruptcy-remote subsidiary ("Seller") established an accounts receivable securitization program. Under the program, undivided interests in a pool of eligible trade receivables, which had been sold on a nonrecourse basis by the Company to the Seller, were then sold to a multiseller, asset-backed commercial paper conduit ("Conduit"). Purchases by the Conduit were financed with the sale of highly rated commercial paper. The Company utilized proceeds from the sale of its accounts receivable to repay long-term debt, effectively reducing its overall borrowing costs. Funding costs under this program were 4.85 percent on the first $50 million, with the rate on the excess amounts equal to the commercial paper rate. Certain program fees totaled an additional 0.75 percent.

Under the provisions of SFAS No. 125, "Accounting for Transfers and Servicing of Financial Assets and Extinguishments of Liabilities" (as amended by SFAS No. 140, "Accounting for Transfers and Servicing of Financial Assets and Extinguishments of Liabilities"), the securitization transactions had been recorded as sales, with those accounts receivable sold to the Conduit removed from the consolidated balance sheet. The amount of undivided interests in accounts receivable sold to the Conduit were $120 million at June 30, 2002.

The Seller was a separate legal entity from the Company. The Seller's assets were available first and foremost to satisfy the claims of its creditors. Eligible receivables, as defined in the securitization agreement, consisted of trade receivables from our subsidiaries, excluding nonpharmaceutical receivables, reduced for certain items, including past due balances and concentration limits. Of the eligible pool of receivables contributed to the Seller, undivided interests in only a portion of the pool were sold to the Conduit. The Seller's interest in these receivables was subordinate to the Conduit's interest in the event of default under the securitization agreement. The portion of eligible receivables not sold to the Conduit remained an asset of the Seller ($31.7 million as of June 30, 2002). (10-K, 2003)

EXHIBIT 6.3 sketches the basic structure of D&K's relationship to the ABCP program it used and the relationship of the suppliers of program-wide credit enhancement and liquidity facilities to the conduit. D&K extends trade credit to its customers. D&K sells these receivables to a wholly owned bankruptcy-remote subsidiary, D&KRC, which in turn sells undivided interests in its pool of receivables to the asset-backed commercial paper program. The seller D&KRC was overcollateralized, meaning that only a portion of its receivables were refinanced through the conduit while the remaining amount is funded by the originator who holds a residual interest in the receivable pool. This overcollateralization of D&KRC is the source of the seller-supplied credit enhancement.

GE Capital Example

In addition to funding its own financial assets (equipment leases, tranches of asset- and mortgage-backed securities, trade receivables, equipment leases, and commercial loans) through ABCP conduits sponsored by banks and finance companies, GE Capital is itself a sponsor and administrator of ABCP programs. These include Edison Asset Securitization, LLC, the largest ABCP program in terms of outstanding CP as of the second quarter of 2003, with $28.6 billion in outstanding ABCP, according to Standard & Poor's U.S. ABCP Market Statistics. GE Capital is also the sponsor of Fleet Funding Corp., Cooper River Funding Inc., and Redwood Receivables Corp. As of mid-2003, Redwood had $2.1 billion of outstanding CP, rated Prime-1 by Moody's and A-1+ by Standard & Poor's.

Redwood Receivables Corp. is capitalized with equity owned by outside investors unaffiliated with General Electric. Redwood purchases beneficial interests or makes loans and issues letters of credit secured by beneficial interests in receivable pools issued by bankruptcy-remote SPVs that have been established by companies as wholly owned subsidiaries. These wholly owned bankruptcy-remote entities are the sellers in the scheme of ABCP programs.

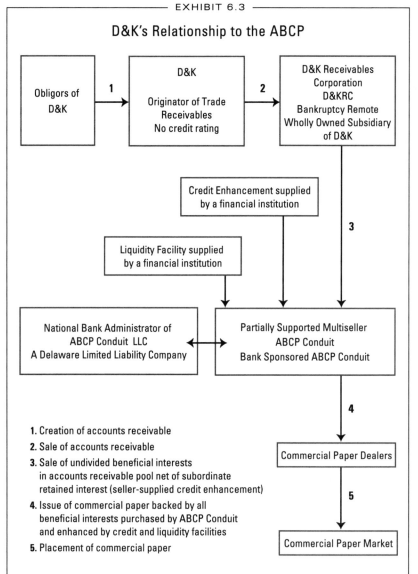

EXHIBIT 6.3

D&K's Relationship to the ABCP

1. Creation of accounts receivable
2. Sale of accounts receivable
3. Sale of undivided beneficial interests
   in accounts receivable pool net of subordinate
   retained interest (seller-supplied credit enhancement)
4. Issue of commercial paper backed by all
   beneficial interests purchased by ABCP Conduit
   and enhanced by credit and liquidity facilities
5. Placement of commercial paper

Source: Stone/Zissu

When investors buy ABCP issued by a multiseller CP program, they are not aware of which company's receivables back the CP issued by the conduit. The CP market is rating driven. Investors look to the rating of the CP issued by the program and the rating agencies' commitment to monitor the conduit's structure and activities. Each time a new seller enters an ABCP program or the purchase limit for an existing seller is increased, the rating agencies will review this decision and the program's rating. As an example, the following press release from Standard & Poor's describes its affirmation of the ratings of Redwood Receivables Corp.:

> Standard & Poor's affirmed its A-1-plus rating on the commercial paper notes of Redwood Receivables Corp. (Redwood). The rating action follows Redwood's purchase of up to $100 million of trade receivables from a special-purpose subsidiary of a temporary staffing company.
>
> The rating on Redwood's commercial paper program is based on liquidity support from liquidity providers with short-term ratings commensurate with Redwood's A-1-plus rating and sufficient pool-specific credit enhancement.
>
> Redwood is a multiseller, partially enhanced asset-backed commercial paper conduit administered by General Electric Capital Corp. (AAA/Stable/A-1-plus), Standard & Poor's said. (Standard & Poor's Ratings Services)

Labor Ready, Inc., Example

Labor Ready, Inc., a supplier of temporary labor for manual jobs, does not have its capital market or money market debt rated. Labor Ready raises funds in the CP market via an ABCP program. The excerpt below from SEC filings by Labor Ready indicates that Labor Ready securitizes its receivables through Redwood Capital Corporation.[2] Labor Ready sells receivables to its bankruptcy-remote, wholly owned subsidiary, Labor Ready Funding Corporation. Labor Ready Funding Corporation secures funding from Redwood based on the value of its receivables. The funds raised by Labor Ready Funding Corporation are then used to secure letters of credit from General Electric or other acceptable lenders.

> In March 2001, we entered into a letter of credit facility and an accounts receivable securitization facility (collectively the "Accounts Receivable Facility") with certain unaffiliated financial institutions that expires in February of 2006. The Accounts Receivable Facility provides loan advances and letters of credit through the sale of substantially all of our eligible domestic accounts receivable to a wholly owned

and consolidated subsidiary, Labor Ready Funding Corporation. The Accounts Receivable Facility includes a corporate guarantee by us and requires that we meet certain financial covenants. Among other things, these covenants require us to maintain certain liquidity, net income, and net worth levels and a certain ratio of net income to fixed expenses. Subject to certain availability requirements, the Accounts Receivable Facility allows us to borrow a maximum of $80 million, all of which may be used to obtain letters of credit. The amounts we may borrow (our borrowing capacity) under this agreement are largely a function of the levels of our accounts receivable from time to time, supplemented by pledged and restricted cash. We currently use this facility to issue letters of credit but if we were to take a loan against this borrowing capacity, interest would be charged at 1.1 percent above the Commercial Paper rate. We are currently in compliance with all covenants related to the Accounts Receivable Facility. (Board of Governors of the Federal Reserve System, Statistical Release, Commercial Paper Outstanding, July 29, 2004)

Accounting Treatment

UNTIL JANUARY 2003, the assets and liabilities of ABCP conduits structured as bankruptcy-remote special-purpose vehicles were not required to be consolidated onto the balance sheets of their sponsors. Thus, financial institutions supplying credit and liquidity enhancements to securitization structures were required to allocate the requisite amount of capital to support these commitments but not to include the assets and liabilities of the program on their own balance sheets. Sponsors did not own the equity of the conduit and therefore did not control the entity, according to Accounting Research Bulletin 51 (ARB 51), *Consolidated Financial Statements* (Fin 46). Financial institutions supplying credit and liquidity enhancements to securitization structures were only required to allocate the requisite amount of capital to support these commitments, but were not required to include the assets and liabilities of the program on their own balance sheets. However, Fin 46 has changed the rules for consolidation of a variable-interest entry (VIE), under which definition ABCP conduits are included.

Financial Interpretation 46

Financial Interpretation 46 (Fin 46), released by the Financial Accounting Standards Board (FASB) in January 2003 and revised in December 2003, interprets ARB 51 for its application to the consolidation of variable-interest entities by business enterprises. While ARB 51 requires a business enterprise to consolidate subsidiaries in which it has a controlling interest, Fin 46 requires the primary *beneficiary* of a VIE to consolidate it. In ARB 51, controlling interests are measured in terms of voting rights, while Fin 46 focuses on the rights to receive residual value and the obligation to fund expected losses.

Qualifying special-purpose entities (QSPEs) as defined by FAS 140 are exempt from Fin 46 and need not be consolidated with another entity even though they meet the definition of a VIE. Securitization vehicles that are not QSPEs are, however, constrained by Fin 46.

Sponsors of ABCP conduits are usually suppliers of credit enhancement and liquidity support to the conduits. General Electric Capital Corporation, for example, sponsors several CP conduits and supplies financial support to these conduits. At year-end 2002, GE Capital had approximately $16.9 billion in credit support outstanding to securitization vehicles and $10.3 billion in liquidity support that could be drawn within the year. In addition, financial institutions that do not sponsor ABCP conduits may supply credit and liquidity support to CP conduits.

By placing themselves in the position of being the primary financier of the credit risk embedded in the pool of assets funded by the ABCP program, the sponsor assumes the role of being the primary risk bearer and thus the "primary beneficiary," according to language within Fin 46:

> The primary beneficiary of a variable-interest entity is the party that absorbs a majority of the entity's expected losses, receives a majority of its expected residual returns, or both, as a result of holding variable interests, which are the ownership, contractual, or other pecuniary interests in an entity that change with changes in the fair value of the entity's net assets excluding variable interests. (Fin 46 R)

Primary Beneficiary Status

Fin 46 defines the primary beneficiary of a VIE as the entity that is exposed to the majority of the VIE's expected losses or the majority of expected residual returns.

For example, even if each seller of assets to the program must fund the first 10 percent of credit losses, the dispersion of risk across the individual sellers disqualifies any one seller from being designated as the primary beneficiary, because no one seller funds a majority of the conduit's expected losses or captures a majority of the residual gains on the program's assets.

According to Fin 46, the primary beneficiary of a VIE must consolidate the VIE's assets with its own.

For example, let's assume that twenty sellers finance assets through an ABCP program. Each seller funds $10 million of assets through the program at all times, and each seller is required to finance the first 10 percent of losses on the outstanding asset pool ($1 million in our case; $10 million × 10%). A credit guarantee for 5 percent of the value of the assets financed by the program is issued by the bank that sponsors the ABCP program. While each seller is in the first-loss position, financing a multiple of expected losses on the specific pool of assets it finances through the program, the total risk funded by the sponsor is $10 million (5 percent of $200 million), which is ten times as large as any single seller's exposure. In this example, the ABCP program is a variable-interest entity (VIE) and the $10 million financial guarantee issued by the sponsor to fund losses is a *variable interest.*

Fin 46 defines a financial entity as a variable-interest entity (VIE), meaning a business entity whose equity is insufficient to permit it to finance its activities without additional subordinated financial support from other parties, or that is financed by equity investors who cannot make significant decisions about the entities operations, or do not absorb the expected losses or receive the expected returns of the entity. ABCP conduits generally meet the definition of a VIE. For one thing, they are minimally capitalized. The value of the conduit's equity owned by entities not affiliated with the program sponsor is well below the level of the expected losses on the assets financed by the conduit, and the conduit does not cede the equity investor any decision-making capacity regarding its operation.

The sponsor or administrator of the ABCP conduit makes the

decisions about day-to-day and long-term management of the conduit. Without the credit enhancement and liquidity support that is generally supplied to the conduit by the sponsor or administrator, possibly through a syndicate of financial institutions, the conduit would not be financially viable.

Risk-Based Capital Regulations

THE FEDERAL banking agencies, Office of the Comptroller of the Currency (OCC), Federal Deposit Insurance Corporation (FDIC), Board of Governors of the Federal Reserve System (FRB), and Office of Thrift Supervision (OTS), have amended the risk-based capital rules regarding the risk-based capital that banks must allocate to finance ABCP conduits. They must consolidate onto their balance sheets due to the implementation of Fin 46. The final regulatory rule, "Risk-Based Capital Guidelines; Capital Adequacy Guidelines; Capital Maintenance: Consolidation of Asset-Backed Commercial Paper Programs and Other Related Issues," became effective September 30, 2004. The amended regulation does not exempt banks from counting the consolidated assets in their tier-one leverage ratio.

Tier-One Leverage Ratio

A bank's tier-one leverage ratio is tier-one capital divided by average total consolidated assets. EXHIBIT 6.4 lists the components of tier-one and tier-two capital.

Banks rated in the top tier of the Uniform Financial Institutions Rating System by regulators must maintain a minimum tier-one leverage ratio of 3 percent. Banks that receive a rating below the highest must maintain a leverage ratio of at least 4 percent.

The sum of tier-one and tier-two capital must be at least 8 percent of risk-weighted assets. Risk-weighted assets must be financed with a minimum of 4 percent of tier-one capital. The interim risk-based capital rule requires banks to deduct from tier-one capital any minority interests in ABCP programs that are consolidated in accordance with Fin 46. Minority interests in consolidated subsidiaries are generally included as a component of tier-one capital.

In summary, if the federal banking agencies had not issued the interim risk-based capital rules governing ABCP programs consolidated

EXHIBIT 6.4

Components of Tier-One and Tier-Two Capital

Capital components are distributed between two categories (Tier 1 and Tier 2). Tier 2 capital elements will qualify as part of a bank's total capital base up to a maximum of 100% of that bank's Tier 1 capital. Beginning December 31, 1992, the minimum risk based capital standard will be 8.0%.

Definition of Capital
Tier 1:

> Common stockholders' equity;
>
> Noncumulative perpetual preferred stock and any related surplus; and
>
> Minority interests in the equity accounts of consolidated subsidiaries.

Tier 2:

> Cumulative perpetual, long-term and convertible preferred stock, and any related surplus;[5]
>
> Perpetual debt and other hybrid debt/equity instruments;
>
> Intermediate-term preferred stock and term subordinated debt (to a maximum of 50% of Tier 1 capital); and
>
> Loan loss reserves (to a maximum of 1.25% of risk-weighted assets).

Deductions from Capital
From Tier 1:

> Goodwill and other intangibles, with the exception of identified intangibles that satisfy the criteria included in the guidelines.

From Total Capital:

> Investments in unconsolidated banking and finance subsidiaries;
>
> Reciprocal holdings of capital instruments[.]

Source: OCC 12 C.F.R. part 3 Appendix A

because of the adoption of Fin 46, banks would have been required to count the consolidated assets as risk-weighted assets. In the example presented above, assuming all of the assets funded through the ABCP program have a risk weight of 100 percent, the sponsor would have had to raise $16 million in equity capital to support the addition of $200 million of assets (8% × 100% × $200 million).

If the bank sponsor is required to consolidate the assets of an ABCP program onto its balance sheet, then any credit enhancement and liquidity facilities it issued to support the program must be converted into on-balance-sheet assets, assigned the appropriate risk weight, and then capitalized with regulatory capital. Liquidity facilities issued by banks to support ABCP programs are generally structured to have maturities of less than one year, so that the conversion factor is 0 percent. That is, there is no capital charge on liquidity facilities that have maturities of one year or less.

Conversion Factor for Liquidity Facilities

LIQUIDITY FACILITIES issued by banks to support ABCP programs are generally structured to have maturities of less than one year. The amended risk-based capital rules have changed the prior 0 percent credit conversion factor to a 10 percent conversion factor. Once converted to an on-balance-sheet credit equivalent, a risk weight that corresponds to the assets being covered by liquidity facility is assigned. For a liquidity facility that supports a CP program that funds trade receivables, the risk weight would be 100 percent for the drawn amount of the facility. If the assets funded through the program were AAA-rated classes of ABSs, the risk weight attached to the portion of the liquidity facilities supporting these securities would be 20 percent.

An asset-purchase agreement issued to enhance the credit quality of an ABCP program is an example of a direct credit substitute. The conversion factor of this direct credit substitute is 100 percent. If the assets funded by the conduit have a 100 percent risk weight, then the capital charge for the asset-purchase agreement is 8 percent times 100 percent times 100 percent of the principal amount of the credit enhancement facility.

The following excerpt from Bank One's 10-Q filing is a good summary of the bank's relationship to the asset-backed commercial paper conduits it sponsors and the way FIN 46 has changed the accounting treatment of the conduits sponsored by the bank. Bank One's management and treatment of the asset-backed conduits it manages is indicative of the way most banks deal with the commercial paper programs they sponsor.

Bank One Corporation, 10-Q for period ending September 30, 2003

The Corporation is an active participant in the asset-backed securities business where it helps meet customers' financing needs by providing access to the commercial paper markets through special purpose entities, known as multi-seller conduits. These entities are separate bankruptcy-remote corporations in the business of purchasing interests in, and making loans secured by, receivables pools and other financial assets pursuant to agreements with customers. The multi-seller conduits fund their purchases and loans through the issuance of highly-rated commercial paper. The primary source of repayment of the commercial paper is the cash flow from the pools of assets. Investors in the commercial paper have no recourse to the general assets of the Corporation. Customers benefit from such structured financing transactions as these transactions provide an ongoing source of asset liquidity, access to the capital markets, and a potentially favorable cost of financing.

As of September 30, 2003, the Corporation administered multi-seller conduits with a total program limit of $70 billion and with $34 billion in commercial paper outstanding. The multi-seller conduits were rated at least A-1 by S&P, P-1 by Moody's and F1 by Fitch.

These multi-seller conduits are a type of variable interest entity ("VIE"), as defined by FIN No. 46. These entities historically have met all of the requirements to be accounted for as independent entities, and, prior to the issuance of FIN No. 46, were not required to be consolidated with the Corporation. Each of the multi-seller conduits administered by the Corporation prepares stand-alone financial statements, which are independently audited on an annual basis.

As administrator of the multi-seller conduits, the Corporation provides deal origination services, asset portfolio monitoring, treasury and financial administration services for these entities. The Corporation structures financing transactions for customers such that the receivables and other financial instruments financed through the multi-seller conduits are appropriately diversified and credit enhanced to support the conduits' commercial paper issuances. As of the date hereof, the Corporation does not service these assets and does not transfer receivables originated by the Corporation into the multi-seller conduits it administers. Each conduit has program documents and investment policies, which govern the types of assets and structures permitted by the conduit. Three of the multi-seller conduits principally purchase interests in, or make loans secured by, trade receivables, auto loans and leases and credit card receivables. One conduit makes loans secured by portfolios of publicly rated marketable investment securities.

The commercial paper issued by the conduits is supported by deal-specific credit enhancement, which is structured to cover more than the expected losses on the pool of assets. The deal-specific credit enhancement is typically in the form of over-collateralization, but may also include any combination of the following: recourse to the seller or originator, cash collateral accounts, letters of credit, excess spread, retention of subordinated interests or third-party guarantees. In a limited number of cases, the Corporation provides the deal-specific credit enhancements as a financial arrangement for the customer. As of September 30, 2003 and December 31, 2002, the Corporation provided such deal-specific enhancements to customers in the form of subordinated interests totaling $154 million and $203 million, respectively. These subordinated interest positions were included in loans on the Corporation's balance sheets as of September 30, 2003 and December 31, 2002.

For three of the multi-seller conduits, the commercial paper investors have access to a second loss credit protection in the form of program-wide credit enhancement. The program-wide credit enhancement consists of a subordinated term loan from the Corporation and a surety bond from an AAA rated monoline insurance company. The subordinated term loans from the Corporation to these conduits totaled $1.0 billion as of both September 30, 2003 and December 31, 2002. One conduit has only deal-specific credit enhancements provided by other financial institutions.

As a means of ensuring timely repayment of the commercial paper, each asset pool financed by the conduits has a minimum of 100% deal-specific liquidity facility associated with it. In the unlikely event of a disruption in the commercial paper market or in the event an asset pool is removed from the conduit, the administrator may draw on the liquidity facility to repay the maturing commercial paper. The liquidity facilities are typically in the form of asset purchase agreements structured such that the bank liquidity is provided by purchasing, or lending against, a pool of non-defaulted, performing assets. Additionally, program-wide liquidity facilities and lines of credit are provided by the Corporation and other financial institutions to the multi-seller conduits to facilitate access to the commercial paper markets.

As discussed on pages 44-46, the Corporation is an active participant in the asset-backed securities business where it helps to meet customers' financing needs by providing access to the commercial paper markets through special purpose entities known as multi-seller conduits. These multi-seller conduits are a type of VIE as defined by FIN No. 46. These entities historically have met the requirements to be treated as independent entities, and, prior to the issuance of FIN No. 46, were not required to be consolidated with the Corporation. The Corporation had previously announced its intent to consolidate certain VIEs related to its asset-backed conduit business in conjunction with the implementation of FIN No. 46. As a result of the Financial Accounting Standards Board's ("FASB") deferral, the Corporation expects to consolidate or restructure these entities in accordance with FIN No. 46 in the fourth quarter. During the third quarter, banking regulators issued interim regulations that provide risk-based capital relief for certain assets that would be consolidated under FIN No. 46.

Restructuring Possibilities

VARIOUS RESTRUCTURING possibilities exist that will enable the sponsor to avoid having to consolidate the ABCP program. One possibility is to compartmentalize a conduit that is a VIE into separate silos that are in turn considered VIEs. Each silo would purchase assets from a seller just as a traditional ABCP conduit does. Financings for each silo have to be structured so that essentially the only source of repayment of the silo's liabilities are the assets owned by the silo and any credit enhancement supplied by the seller. By supplying the credit enhancement, the seller becomes the primary beneficiary of the silo, because it funds the expected losses of the silo and captures the residual value of the silo. As the primary beneficiary of the silo VIE, the seller must consolidate it.

Other restructuring possibilities are structuring the ABCP conduit as a QSPE; selling a majority of the credit risk of the VIE to a third-party investor, or dispersing the risk or residual benefits of the VIE so that no single entity becomes the primary beneficiary.[3]

Citicorp, like many banks that sponsor ABCP programs, has reacted to Fin 46 by either restructuring the conduits it sponsors, winding down current programs, or evaluating the economics of sponsoring ABCP programs when it must consolidate the conduit's assets and liabilities.

Chapter Notes

1. Rule 2a-7 of the Investment Company Act of 1940 limits the credit risk that money market mutual funds may bear by restricting their investments to "eligible" securities. An eligible security must carry one of the two highest ratings ("1" or "2") for short-term obligations from at least two of the nationally recognized statistical ratings agencies. A tier-1 security is an eligible security rated "1" by at least two of the rating agencies; a tier-2 security is an eligible security that is not a tier-1 security. The sum of tier-1 and tier-2 securities will not add up to the total due to ineligible securities. Money funds may hold no more than 5 percent of their assets in the tier-1 securities of any individual issuer and no more than 1 percent of their assets in the tier-2 securities of any individual issuer; moreover, a money fund's holdings of tier-2 securities may constitute no more than 5 percent of the fund's assets. (Board of Governors of the Federal Reserve System, Statistical Release, Commercial Paper Outstanding, July 29, 2004)

2. Receivables Funding Agreement between Labor Ready Funding Corporation, Redwood Receivables Corporation, Labor Ready, Inc., and General Electric Capital Corporation dated March 1, 2001.

3. "Fin 46: New Rule Could Surprise Investors," June 24, 2003, Equity Research. (Credit Suisse First Boston)

PART THREE

Securitization of Revolving Credit

Chapter Seven

Dealer Floor Plan Loans

THE NEXT TWO CHAPTERS discuss how revolving lines of credit are securitized. The receivables that fall into this category comprise a large segment of the asset-backed markets and include dealer floor plan loans, also referred to as wholesale motor vehicle loans, and credit card receivables (the subject of Chapter 8), as well as home equity lines of credit and trade receivables.

Trends in Wholesale Automobile Credit Securitization

TO UNDERSTAND the trend of securitization in the sphere of wholesale automobile credit, consider that the ratio of owned wholesale receivables to managed wholesale receivables had been 4.36 back in August 1990. (Note that "owned" receivables are those that are balance-sheet assets, while "managed" assets are those that have been financed through a securitization vehicle.) Ten years later, that ratio had begun to shift. In August 1990 finance companies had securitized $650 million of wholesale automobile credit, as against $2.81 billion of wholesale automobile credit that they owned. By September 2003 finance companies owned wholesale automobile receivables in the amount of $3.05 billion, and wholesale automobile credit managed (securitized) by finance companies stood at $4.28 billion. The ratio of owned to managed receivables had thus fallen to 0.71. Ever since October 1997 managed wholesale credit to automobile dealers originated by finance companies has exceeded owned wholesale credit.[1]

DaimlerChrysler, like Ford, GMAC, and the other captive finance companies of the automobile manufacturers (in other words, subsidiaries formed to finance customer purchases from the parent corporation), uses securitization to enhance its liquidity and diversify its funding sources. Forgoing the option to securitize in today's financial markets would be the equivalent of forgoing medium-term debt or commercial paper financing tools. The extent to which companies rely on securitization depends on the relative cost of on-balance-sheet funding. Costs depend on the credit rating of the firm, the credit spreads in the market, constraints such as covenants in existing credit agreements, risk-based capital regulations, and accounting rules. A firm's ability to securitize its assets makes its balance sheet more liquid. All things being equal, a liquid balance sheet is more valuable than an illiquid balance sheet. The following excerpt from a recent DaimlerChrysler annual report aptly attests to the role securitization plays in the automobile industry today:

> The Group sells significant amounts of finance receivables as asset-backed securities through securitization to accelerate the receipt of cash related to those receivables. In a securitization, the Group sells a portfolio of receivables to a nonconsolidated, special-purpose entity and remains as servicer, and is paid a servicing fee. In a subordinated capacity, the Group retains residual cash flows, a beneficial interest in principal balances of sold receivables, and certain cash deposits provided as credit enhancements for investors. The recoverability of DaimlerChrysler's retained interests in the sold receivables is heavily dependent upon the credit losses, prepayment speed, and average interest rate within the sold portfolio. (DaimlerChrysler AG, Form 20-F/A, Amendment No. 1, for the fiscal year ended December 31, 2001)

The fundamental difference between dealer floor plan loans and retail installment loans in terms of securitizing each asset class is that the former are relatively short-term floating-rate credits generated from revolving lines of credit while the latter are fixed-rate amortizing loans with fixed maturity. Securitizing retail installment loans involves a single sale of a loan pool to a qualifying special-purpose vehicle (SPV) such as Ford Motor Credit 2000-A (as discussed in Chapter 5).

Securitization of dealer floor plan loans, on the other hand, entails the securitization of the flow of receivables from a designated set of accounts. Receivables are transferred to the trust (CARCO Auto Loan Master Trust in the example discussed below) on a daily basis, as they are generated.

DaimlerChrysler securitizes both its portfolio of retail installment sales contracts and its dealer floor plan loans. While the securitization of dealer floor plan loans and retail automobile installment loans have much in common, there are some important differences. These differences are due primarily to the constraints imposed, on one side, by the revolving nature of the dealer floor plan credits and the uncertain payment patterns of the receivables, coupled with the desire of the originator of the receivables to secure medium-term financing, and on the other side, by investor demand for floating-rate debt with a certain maturity on which their principal is repaid, in full, in one payment.

To shed some light on the dealer floor plan business before we discuss the securitization of dealer floor plan loans, included below are two excerpts, the first from the 2002 10-K filing of United Auto Group, the second-largest publicly traded automotive retailer in the United States as measured by revenues, and the second from the CARCO 2000-B prospectus supplement. CARCO Auto Loan Master Trust (CARCO) is the master trust that DaimlerChrysler uses to securitize its dealer floor plan receivables. Chrysler Auto Receivables Company was the seller in dealer floor plan securitization transactions sponsored by Chrysler Financial Corporation (CFC) until December 2001, when it was replaced by DaimlerChrysler Wholesale Receivables LLC. Ten percent of United Auto Group's 2002 revenues were generated from DaimlerChrysler franchised dealerships.

> We finance the majority of our new and a portion of our used vehicle inventory under revolving floor plan financing arrangements between our subsidiaries and various lenders. In the United States, we make monthly interest payments on the amount financed but are generally not required to make loan principal repayments prior to the sale of the new and used vehicles we have financed.... The weighted average interest rate paid by the Company on floor plan indebtedness during 2002 was 5.13 percent. (United Auto Group 10-K for 2002)

United Auto Group is one among many participants on the demand side of the market for dealer floor plan loans. The finance companies (such as CFC, referred to in the excerpt below) and banks that supply the credit to dealers represent the other side of the dealer floor plan business.

> CFC finances 100 percent of the wholesale invoice price of new vehicles, including destination charges. DaimlerChrysler originates receivables in respect of DaimlerChrysler-manufactured or -distributed vehicles concurrently with the shipment of the vehicles to the financed dealer. (CARCO Auto Loan Master Trust Form 10-K for fiscal year ending December 31, 2002)

Dealer floor plan lines of credit are secured by new and used automobiles and spare parts. The credit must be repaid when the inventory backing the receivable is sold. The dealer can then draw down additional credit. The interest rate on dealer floor plan loans extended by CFC is tied to the prime rate (prime plus a margin). The dealer can make draws up to a predetermined limit that may be negotiated up or pulled back if the dealer performs badly.

Accounts for the securitization transaction are chosen by CFC, which continues to service and own the accounts. These are the designated accounts of the transaction, and it is the future flow of receivables generated by these accounts that is being refinanced by CFC through the CARCO master trust. CFC sells the receivables on an ongoing basis to the seller (DCWR). Sales for cash are characterized as "true sales" for bankruptcy purposes as defined in Financial Accounting Standards Board's No. 140, "Revolving-Period Securitizations," paragraph 79, while exchanges for beneficial interests in the trust are not.

Basics of the Securitization Scheme

CARCO Auto Loan Master Trust issues securities backed by a revolving pool of dealer floor plan receivables. Since December 1991 CARCO has issued $21.5 billion of capital and money market securities in thirty-one different series.

Exhibit 7.1 outlines the basic scheme that Chrysler Financial Corporation (CFC) uses to securitize its dealer floor plan loans. Like

EXHIBIT 7.1

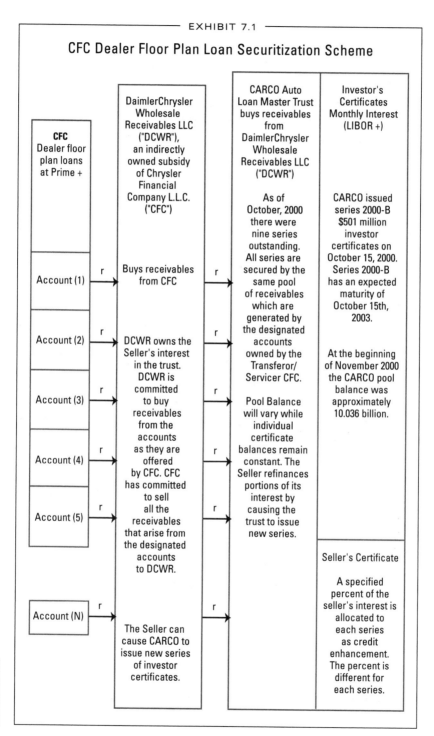

CFC Dealer Floor Plan Loan Securitization Scheme

		CARCO Auto Loan Master Trust buys receivables from DaimlerChrysler Wholesale Receivables LLC ("DCWR")	Investor's Certificates Monthly Interest (LIBOR +)
CFC Dealer floor plan loans at Prime +	DaimlerChrysler Wholesale Receivables LLC ("DCWR"), an indirectly owned subsidy of Chrysler Financial Company L.L.C. ("CFC")		CARCO issued series 2000-B $501 million investor certificates on October 15, 2000. Series 2000-B has an expected maturity of October 15th, 2003.
Account (1)	Buys receivables from CFC	As of October, 2000 there were nine series outstanding. All series are secured by the same pool of receivables which are generated by the designated accounts owned by the Transferor/ Servicer CFC.	
Account (2)	DCWR owns the Seller's interest in the trust. DCWR is committed to buy receivables from the accounts as they are offered by CFC. CFC has committed to sell all the receivables that arise from the designated accounts to DCWR.		At the beginning of November 2000 the CARCO pool balance was approximately 10.036 billion.
Account (3)			
Account (4)		Pool Balance will vary while individual certificate balances remain constant. The Seller refinances portions of its interest by causing the trust to issue new series.	
Account (5)			
Account (N)	The Seller can cause CARCO to issue new series of investor certificates.		Seller's Certificate

A specified percent of the seller's interest is allocated to each series as credit enhancement. The percent is different for each series. |

Source: Stone/Zissu

the Ford Motor Credit transaction discussed in Chapter 5, it is a two-tier transaction. CFC opens the credit lines with DaimlerChrysler's franchised and nonfranchised auto dealers and then sells the receivables generated by designated accounts to "the Seller," DCWR, which is a wholly owned subsidiary of CFC. DCWR is a limited-purpose company designed to be bankruptcy-remote from CFC. Its activities are constrained to eliminate the possibility of DCWR's becoming involved in bankruptcy proceedings.

Each dealer financed by CFC represents an account. (Note that CFC does not designate all of its dealer floor plan accounts for securitization.) The seller transfers the receivables that arise in the designated accounts to CARCO, a master trust established by the seller, in exchange for beneficial interests in the trust. CARCO has the accounting status of a qualified special-purpose entity (QSPE). The beneficial interests received by the seller are then retained or offered as certificates to the public via an underwritten public offer or private placement. CFC continues to service the receivables that are securitized for a servicing fee of 1 percent per year (one-twelfth of 1 percent per month on a 30/360-day basis).

Exhibit 7.1 shows that as receivables (r) are generated by the designated accounts (1 through N), they are sold to the seller and then sold to CARCO either for cash or for an increase in the seller's certificate. Since the seller is a wholly owned subsidiary of the transferor, CFC, the seller's interest is consolidated on the balance sheet of the transferor.

CARCO issues two types of beneficial interests to fund the purchase of the receivables: (1) investor certificates and (2) the seller's certificate. The seller's certificate represents the interests in the trust not funded by investor certificates. It fluctuates as the principal value of the assets owned by CARCO fluctuates. In contrast, each series of investor certificates issued by CARCO finances a fixed principal amount for a fixed term. A portion of the seller's certificate is subordinate to each series of investor certificates issued. For example, the original amount of the seller's interest subordinated to CARCO series 2000-B was $55,666,666.67. In addition to the subordination of part of the seller's interest, a reserve account is funded by the seller for the benefit of each series of investor certificates issued by CARCO. For series 2000-B the reserve account was seeded with $1,753,500, which the seller raised from the sale of the receivables to the trust. The initial subordination amount for series 2000-B was approximately 11.1 percent of the invested amount.

Credit Enhancement

Credit enhancement can be viewed as the equity that protects the certificates from a certain magnitude of credit losses experienced by the receivable pool. The level of credit enhancement is primarily dictated by the rating agencies and, to a lesser extent, by the market. The size of the subordination and the reserve account are imposed by the rating agencies and reflect the agencies' expectations about the loss rate on the receivables generated by the designated accounts and, in this case, the ability of CFC to generate sufficient receivables and service the receivables efficiently. The level of the reserve account and the fraction of the seller interest subordinated to the investor interest are calculated so as to justify the AAA rating on the senior class of certificates.

CARCO series 2000-B benefits from a yield supplement account. The purpose of this account is to moderate the basis risk that exists due to differences in the indices to which the interest rate charged on the receivables and the asset-backed securities (the investor certificates) are tied. There is a possibility that the yield on the receivables will be insufficient to cover the yield on the securities. Up to a limit, the yield supplement account can be drawn down to make up for differences in the asset receivable rate and the certificate rate.

CARCO issues multiple series at different times by filing prospectus supplements according to its pooling and servicing agreement with Chrysler Credit Corporation (CCC) as servicer and Manufacturers and Traders Trust Company, a New York banking corporation, as trustee. Between 1996 and March 2003, fourteen series of investor certificates had been issued by CARCO.

Payment Phases

EXHIBIT 7.2 illustrates the four phases that are typical of a securitization of revolving credit lines. First is the *revolving phase,* during which the trustee maintains the principal of the series by using the series' share of the principal flowing into the trust to buy new receivables from the seller.

─────── EXHIBIT 7.2 ───────

Phases of a Series Issued by a Master Trust

Early Amortization Period

Repayments of principal are used to paydown the series. Early amortization can be triggered when receivable generation of the accounts falls below a designated level or a bankruptcy of CFC among other events. *Can be triggered at any time and can in certain cases be resolved so that the period interrupted is resumed.*

	One to five months	**One bullet payment in the case of CARCO 2000-B October 15th, 2003, expected maturity. Legal final is October 17th, 2005.**
Revolving Period	**Accumulation Period**	**Amortization Period**
Principal use to buy additional receivables from the seller or used to fund principal accumulation of other classes	Repayments are invested in the Principal funding account and are accumulated so that the series can be retired on the expected maturity date.	Funds in the principal funding account and if necessary principal from other series in the revolving or accumulation phase are used either to begin the amortization of the series or finance the full repayment of the series on expected maturity date.

Series 1999-3 is redeemed (expected) 7/15/2002

Source: Stone/Zissu

In the second phase, the series goes through *accumulation*. The accumulation phase in the case of CARCO 2000-B ranges from one to five months. The start of the accumulation period is determined by the service, CFC, according to a formula set up to take into account the invested amounts of all series in accumulation or amortization on the decision date, April 3, 2003, relative to the invested amounts of all other series and the rate at which the receivables are being paid off.

Faster payment rates reduce the accumulation period because more principal flows through the trust in a given period. Slower payment rates increase the accumulation period because less principal flows through the trust in a given period. A relatively large invested amount in accumulation or amortization will increase the accumulation period chosen, and a relatively small invested amount will decrease the accumulation period chosen. When the invested amount in amortization or accumulation is large relative to the total invested amount, less principal will be available for sharing among series. This leaves each series in amortization and accumulation more exposed to the rate at which receivables are being generated and paid, or the revolving rate.

Shorter specified accumulation periods pose more risk to investors because declines in the rate of receivables generation during the accumulation period are more likely to leave the principal funding account short of funds. This is why the architecture of the transaction links the length of the accumulation period to the receivables payment rate and the ratio of invested amounts in accumulation and amortization relative to the total of invested amounts. Larger master trusts with more and larger series outstanding generally have more series in the revolving phase relative to the total than do smaller, less active trusts. If the calculations of the servicer are correct, which they are very likely to be, especially when the servicer is as experienced as CFC and the trust is as active as CARCO, then sufficient principal is accumulated over the calculated period so that on the expected maturity date the series is retired.

The third phase is the *retirement* of the series or, alternatively, the *amortization* of the series. CARCO series 2000-B was designed to be paid off on a single date, October 15, 2003. The prospectus allows for other series issued by CARCO to be issued as soft bullets, meaning that principal is scheduled to be distributed over several periods rather than in a single lump sum.

Also possible is the early amortization of the series. Although early amortization is sometimes called the fourth phase, it does not occur after the third phase. Rather it occurs as an interruption of either the revolving phase or the accumulation phase. Early amortization is triggered when one or more of the following events or trends commences:

> The integrity of the securitization structure is undermined by bankruptcy of the transferor (the source of receivables) or the seller, or by a tax ruling that creates tax liability for the seller.
> The quality of the assets begins to deteriorate.
> The quantity of the assets generated by the accounts declines below a specific level.

If an early amortization event occurred while series 2000-B was in its revolving phase, rather than accumulate principal to maintain the series' principal value, the trustee would distribute principal to the series as receivables are paid off. Since the trigger would likely be due to inadequate receivables generation by the accounts designated in the securitization, the retirement of the series might not occur until after the scheduled date due to the slow accumulation of principal.

Uncertain Maturity Date and Fluctuating Account Balance Considerations

How can a financial institution refinance a pool of revolving loans that have an uncertain maturity date with securities that have a finite principal value and a certain maturity date? In a securitization of a static pool of loans, the pool has a weighted average life (WAL) that is matched by the capital structure of the securitization vehicle, as in Ford Credit Auto Owner Trust 2000-A. From a static pool a series can be tranched into securities that assume different dimensions of the pool's amortization. As the pool amortizes, the securities are retired sequentially. The chain of securities may leverage prepayment risk on one section and deleverage another section. For example, a planned amortization class in a collateralized mortgage obligation (CMO) is deleveraged with respect to the support class.

By contrast, when the pool of receivables that is being securitized revolves, it is not only the current pool of receivables that is being securitized but the future receivable flow from the accounts as well. The volume of this future flow is uncertain. If the trust is going to finance the receivables with fixed-term notes, then a finite cash flow must be carved out of the repayment of the receivables that the accounts produce.

If securities issued by the securitization vehicle have a fixed face value but there is uncertainty about whether the value of the receivables held in the trust at any point in time will cover this amount, there is a risk that must be managed.

Securing Liquidity

BECAUSE OF fluctuating account balances, a method of financing the deviation in the account balances from the security balance must be put in place. In other words, a method of securing the necessary liquidity to retire the securities must be established. This is accomplished by maintaining the trust assets at a level that covers its liabilities. Proceeds from the liquidating receivables are invested in new receivables until the principal is needed to fund the liquidation of the asset-backed securities. Minimizing the accumulation period serves to minimize the time during which principal must be invested in low-yielding money market securities but also increases the risk that insufficient principal will be accumulated.

Fluctuations in the face value of the assets owned by the trust are absorbed by the seller. As seen above, CARCO is capitalized with a seller's certificate and investor certificates. The seller's certificate claim on the trust's assets is not fixed. Declines and increases in the trust's assets are absorbed by the seller's certificate.

By designing the seller's interest to act as a sponge, a fixed principal value can be carved out of a fluctuating trust. The sponge analogy is particularly apt, because the seller interest can absorb receivables and squeeze out receivables to the investor interest. Using this structure makes it possible to finance a fixed principal value with securities that have longer maturities than the underlying receivables and mature on a specific date. As the seller transfers additional receivables to the trust, its interest in the trust increases. This becomes an exchange of receivables for beneficial interests in the trust. DCWR, for example, can refinance portions of its interest by causing the trust to issue additional series of investor notes. A refinancing of the seller's interest shifts the capital structure of CARCO from the seller to investors.

If the accounts do not generate sufficient new receivables to maintain the trust balance, then liquidity can be drawn from the seller as the seller's claim against the pool declines while the investor's claim remains fixed. Should the seller's interest decline to a specified level, an early amortization of the investor series would commence. The magnitude of such a decline in the seller's interest is a warning signal that inadequate receivables are being generated to sustain the securities issued by the trust. Once an early amortization event is triggered, principal allocated to a series, such as series 2000-B, is distributed to retire the series as it flows into CARCO, rather than being invested in new receivables.

Shifts in Seller's Interest and Investor Interest

EXHIBIT 7.3 illustrates how the capital structure of the master trust shifts between the seller's interest and investor interest. It is important to keep in mind that this diagram illustrates the relative size of the seller's interest and the investor interest. Together, the seller's interest and investor interest finance 100 percent of the trust's assets. This diagram also shows how principal is shared across series. The mechanics outlined in the diagram are generally true for all master trust structures. Receivables are sold to the trust daily. The seller funds the increase in trust assets above the amount funded by outstanding investor interests until the seller's corporate treasury officers decide to issue a new series of investor certificates. The new issue refinances part of the seller's interest in the trust. This causes the percentage of the trust funded by the seller to decline and the percentage funded by investors to increase.

The timing of repayments and draws on the auto dealers' credit line determines how much principal per period will flow into the securitization trust. Principal flow determines how long it will take to accumulate sufficient principal to retire a series.

Receivables are transferred to the trust daily, as they are created. When the collection of principal is less than the investment in new receivables, it indicates an increase in the seller's interest. The seller is compensated for the difference between collections of principal and investment in new receivables by an addition to its beneficial interest in the trust. When the investment in new receivables is less than the collections of principal, the trust balance either declines, if principal collections are used to retire a portion of the seller's interest, or remains the same, if collections are used to fund the principal accounts of series that are in the accumulation phase.

EXHIBIT 7.3

Shifting of Master Trust's Capital Structure between Seller's Interest and Investor Interests

Finance Company X

Owner and Servicer of the Dealer Floor Plan Accounts
Sale of new receivables daily

Dealer Floor Plan Credit (The Receivables)

The Seller

A wholly owned subsidiary of Finance Company X

Dealer Floor Plan Credit (The Receivables)

This exhibit illustrates the change in the Seller's interest relative to the Investor's interest. The vertical distance between A and B is 100% of AUSCO's assets.

Gray area represents the percent of receivable pool financed by the Seller's interest. The white area represents the percent of the pool financed by the Investor's interest.

AUSCO MASTER TRUST
The Issuer

A B

Retirement of Series-1 brings receivables back into the seller's interest

Issue of Series-2 refinances a portion of seller's interest

Seller's interest will increase when account draws exceed repayments

Issue of Series-3 refinances a portion of seller's interest causing the decline

← – – – Series 3 and 4 share principal with series (1999-1 and 1999-2) – – – →

Series 1
End of revolving
period is retired
or amortized

Series 2
End of accumulation
period

Series1999-3
Middle of revolving
period

Series1999-4
Beginning of revolving
period

This diagram is a snapshot of AUSCO, a hypothetical Master Trust on June 1st, 2003. The series in this exhibit were issued in 1999.

Source: Stone/Zissu

Seller's Claim on Receivable Pool

THE LEVEL of receivables generated by the accounts determines the size of the receivables pool. Since the size of the pool may vary, whereas investors have financed only a fixed amount of principal, there must be a mechanism to raise capital to fund the addition of receivables to the pool. This mechanism is the seller's certificate. As has been discussed, the seller's certificate is designed to absorb fluctuations in the size of the receivables pool. It does so by financing additions of receivables to the pool above the amount that is financed by the investor certificates, and by decreasing the share of the pool it finances as the principal amount of receivables in the pool declines.

It bears repeating that the seller's claim on the receivable pool varies, while the investor's interest is disconnected from variations in the pool balance. For example, if investors have a claim of $6 billion on the trust's total assets of $9 billion, and the pool balance increases to $11 billion, due to either the addition of dealer floor plan accounts by the transferor or the increased net generation of receivables by existing accounts, the seller's beneficial interest in the trust would jump by $2 billion to $5 billion, while the investor's beneficial interest would remain at $6 billion. On the other hand, a net decline in the pool balance from, say, $9 billion to $7 billion would be borne by the seller's interest.

Should the seller want to refinance part of its interest in the pool, it can cause the trust to issue a new series of investor certificates, providing that the new issue released by the master trust (such as that of CARCO in the example illustrated here) does not threaten the credit quality of the outstanding series. Maintaining the quality of the outstanding series is accomplished by prohibiting dilution of the outstanding series of investor certificates. Even after the new issue, all the series must be collateralized with sufficient receivables and credit enhancement to preserve their credit ratings and to satisfy the conditions of the trust indenture. Credit enhancement takes the form of a portion of the seller's interest and reserve accounts for each series.

In a revolving structure, the ability of the seller to replace receivables as they are repaid is critical if the trust is going to issue securities with fixed terms. If the designated accounts do not generate sufficient receivables, the securities issued by the trust will lack support and, according to the terms of the pooling and servicing agreement, will be amortized as principal flows into the trust, unless the originator (such as CFC, in this case) can designate additional accounts to the transaction and sell the receivables of these accounts to the seller, who in turn would sell them, in this case, to CARCO. When receivables are purchased by the seller either in the initial transfer or in subsequent transfers, the actual sale of receivables does not take place until the seller receives compensation other than beneficial interests in the trust.

When the designated accounts generate more receivables than are necessary to capitalize the investor's interest in the trust, the seller's interest increases in principal value. Since the seller's balance sheet is consolidated with the originator's (in this case, CFC's), the seller must be able to finance the increased size of the seller's interest. The seller may choose to finance the increase in seller's interest as it grows, or it may choose to refinance portions of its interest in the pool by having the trust issue additional investor certificates. As was noted, issuing a series to refinance a portion of the seller interest shifts trust assets from the seller to the investor interest.

EXHIBIT **7.4** on the following page shows the seller's interest as a percentage of CARCO's assets over time, with the dates corresponding to issues of new series highlighted. The seller does not maintain its investment in the master trust at a constant percentage. The timing of new issues depends on conditions in the asset-backed market and the cost of balance sheet liquidity.

Factors in Credit Line Variability

SINCE THE BALANCE of a credit line, by its very nature, varies as draws are made and repaid, the timing of principal payments and the amount of interest earned on the line is uncertain. There are two components of the variability in a credit line: the firm-specific factor and the market factor. For example, a general decline in auto sales will decrease the rate at which the inventory is sold and replaced. This is a general factor and will decrease the rate at which new receivables are generated and extend the time it takes for outstanding credit to be repaid. Inventory turnover is important, because without sufficient receivable generation, the principal of the trust cannot be maintained

---

EXHIBIT 7.4

Seller's Interest in Receivable Pool, November 2000 through May 2003

TIME	SELLER'S INTEREST IN POOL (%)	TIME	SELLER'S INTEREST IN POOL (%)
November 2000	28.27	March 2002	28.06
December	21.75	April	35.57
January 2001	25.30	May	41.82
February	19.91	June	22.21
March	19.94	July	34.81
April	21.06	August	25.38
May	21.08	September	27.65
June	30.09	October	28.16
July	30.64	November	36.71
August	21.88	December	30.69
September	19.16	January 2003	31.98
October	22.77	February	29.33
November	16.39	March	37.32
December	15.79	April	27.25
January 2002	19.52	May	23.91
February	17.36		

Source: Stone/Zissu, CARCO Auto Loan Master Trust

---

to keep outstanding series afloat, and this slows the accumulation of principal needed to retire the securities issued by the trust.

It may also be that one brand—for example, Toyota—is declining relative to another brand—for example, Ford. Such a decline is also market-wide and not dealer specific and would cause Ford dealer accounts to increase financing volume relative to Toyota dealers.

A dealer that is being badly managed will have a relatively low inventory turnover, which will reduce the generation of new receivables from the dealer's account. A dealer that is in financial difficulty may, either by choice or because of bankruptcy constraints, be delinquent on its floor plan credit. A small number of badly managed dealers would not threaten the integrity of a securitization transaction or cause investors to suffer losses; however, an overall deterioration in the quality of the dealer accounts would disrupt the flow of receivables and trigger an early amortization of the securities issued by the trust, because the flow of new receivables would be insufficient to replace repayments. It is important to recognize that two dealers in similar markets may have very different payment patterns; at the same time, dealers under the same type of ownership structure typically tend to have similar payment patterns through various phases of the economic cycle.

Pool Size Matters

As was noted, timing of the draws and repayments of revolving credit lines is uncertain, but with large enough pools of accounts, transactions can be built on the expected behavior of the pool. Pooling receivables generated from a large number of accounts diversifies the dealer-specific risk and allows financial architects to build a securitization structure around the expected behavior of the accounts that generate the receivables.

The following excerpt from the CARCO 2000-B prospectus supplement illustrates how securitization transactions depend on large numbers of receivables so that reliable projections about the cash flows generated from the accounts or from the receivables, in the case of static pools, can be made. The construction of asset-backed securities that perform in a reliable manner depends on backing them with large pools of assets. The law of large numbers helps to ensure that idiosyncratic behavior of the receivables will be eliminated, because this behavior across the individual receivables is uncorrelated. Even though the behavior of the asset pool is variable, the variability can be forecasted. While it is not possible to accurately predict the prepayment behavior of a single mortgagor or auto dealer, it is possible to forecast the behavior of a large pool of obligors. In other words, pooling thousands of receivables allows us to become more certain about the nature of uncertainty.

As of September 30, 2000, with respect to the Accounts in the trust:

➤ there were approximately 2,960 Accounts and the principal receivables balance was approximately $10 billion;

➤ the average credit lines per dealer for new and used vehicles (which include Auction Vehicles) were approximately $3.73 million and $0.51 million, respectively; and the

➤ average balance of principal receivables per dealer was approximately $3.39 million; and

> ➤ the aggregate total receivables balance as a percentage of the aggregate total credit line was approximately 79.9 percent. (CARCO 2000-B prospectus)

IN SUMMARY, it is worth noting that the main difference between credit card receivables, home equity lines of credit, and dealer floor plan loans is credit risk. Dealer floor plan loans are significantly more certain than home equity lines and credit card receivables (discussed in Chapter 8). Dealer floor plan loans are secured by new automobiles and a dealer's inventory of parts, while credit card loans are unsecured and home equity lines of credit have a subordinate lien on the owner's equity in the mortgaged property. The franchises that establish dealer floor plan credit lines with bank and finance companies are monitored carefully by the automobile manufacturers whose brands they deal in, and assistance is also forthcoming to the dealer from the manufacturers. Additional risk embedded in home equity lines and credit card receivables is reflected in the higher levels of credit enhancement that must be built into securitizations of those asset classes. Financing for the additional credit enhancement is available from the relatively high yields on these riskier receivables.

The similarities between dealer floor plan loans, credit card receivables, and home equity lines of credit are that the receivables are generated by accounts that offer revolving lines of credit to the obligors. Each time a borrower repays all or part of an obligation under the line of credit, the account balance declines, and each time the borrower draws on the line of credit, the account balance increases. In a securitization of revolving lines of credit, it is the activity of the accounts designated for the transaction that are securitized, not the accounts themselves. The accounts remain with the originator—in our example, CFC. Repayment of dealer floor plan credit is directly linked to the sale of the automobile that secures the credit.

Chapter Notes

1. Federal Reserve, Release G.20, Historical Data on Finance Companies, Owned and Managed Receivables.

C h a p t e r 8 *E i g h t*

Credit Card Receivables

A FTER MORTGAGES, the asset class comprised of credit card receivables constitutes the largest segment of the asset-backed security (ABS) market. Securities backed by credit cards were valued at $401.8 billion at the end of the second quarter of 2003, making up 24.8 percent of the overall asset-backed market. This compares with values outstanding of $315.5 billion for securities backed by home equity loans (19.4 percent of the market) and $228.6 billion for securities backed by automobile loans (14.1 percent of the market). In 1985 there were $153.1 billion of credit-card-backed securities outstanding, representing 48.4 percent of the ABS market. The volume of ABSs backed by credit card receivables grew at a compound rate of about 12.8 percent over this eighteen-year period. The decline in the percent of the market comprised of credit card ABSs is due to the growth in the collateralized loan obligation (CLO) and collateralized bond obligation (CBO) and, to a lesser extent, home equity segments of this market.

In 1998 revolving consumer credit amounting to $586.2 billion was held by commercial banks, finance companies, credit unions, savings institutions, nonfinancial businesses, and pools of securitized assets. Pools of securitized assets, as has been discussed, are finance receivables that have been securitized and are now held by securitization vehicles such as asset-backed commercial paper (ASCP) conduits, master trusts, and other special-purpose vehicles (SPVs). As of

June 2003 revolving consumer credit owned by these institutions and entities had grown by 23 percent, to $721.1 billion. According to the Federal Reserve, as a percent of revolving credit, securitized pools increased from 46 percent in 1998 to 58 percent by June 2003.[1]

EXHIBIT **8.1** graphs the distribution of revolving consumer credit across the major owners of this type of credit. The outstanding point here is how an increasing share of revolving consumer credit has moved from the balance sheets of financial institutions to securitization vehicles. While ABS issuers hold the largest share of revolving consumer finance, the issuers do not originate the credits. Most revolving consumer credit is originated by financial institutions, commercial banks, savings institutions, finance companies, and credit unions. Securitization has enabled the separation of origination and servicing of the loans from its financing. This phenomenon of disintermediation—the movement of funds from financial intermediary to financial institutions in order to invest in instruments yielding a higher return—is occurring not only in revolving consumer credit but also in the mortgage market, consumer automobile loans, and certain types of business credit, such as dealer floor plan loans (discussed in Chapter 7).

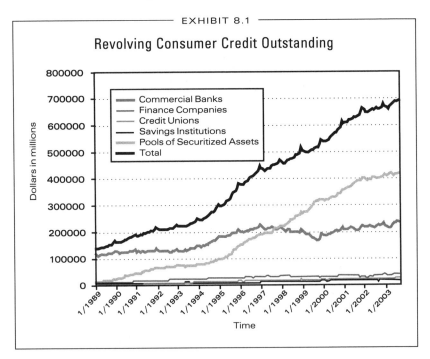

EXHIBIT 8.1

Revolving Consumer Credit Outstanding

Source: Federal Reserve Statistical Release G19, Consumer Credit, 9/8/03

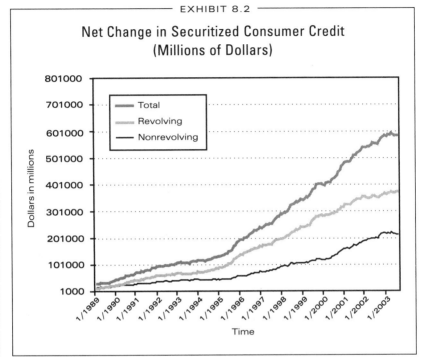

EXHIBIT 8.2

Net Change in Securitized Consumer Credit
(Millions of Dollars)

Source: U.S. Federal Reserve Flow of Funds, Table F.222

EXHIBIT **8.2** graphs the value of revolving and nonrevolving credit that has been securitized. Revolving consumer credit is securitized via master trusts and asset-backed commercial paper programs.

EXHIBIT **8.3**, from the Federal Reserve's Flow of Funds data, gives the sources of consumer credit. Note that a negative entry for ABS issuers and positive numbers for the banking segment appear in the second quarter of 2002. This indicates that receivables financed via securitization trusts such as credit card master trusts were amortizing faster than new series were being issued. The receivables were coming back onto the balance sheets of financial institutions faster than they were being refinanced via securitization.

When ABS issuers have a positive flow of consumer credit and financial institutions a negative flow, it does not mean that ABS issuers are originating consumer credit; rather, it indicates that financial institutions are securitizing more consumer credit than they are originating. Receivables that are held on the balance sheet are flowing into special-purpose vehicles (SPVs) sponsored by the originators or by third-party financial institutions, as in the case of ABCP con-

EXHIBIT 8.3

Sources of Consumer Credit*

		1995	1996
1	**Net change in liabilities (Households)**	**147.0**	**103.6**
2	**Net change in assets**	**147.0**	**103.6**
3	Nonfinancial corporate business	−1.6	−7.3
4	Nonfarm noncorporate business	0.0	0.0
5	Federal government	3.2	7.7
6	Commercial banking	43.2	24.8
7	Savings institutions	1.6	4.6
8	Credit unions	12.3	12.2
9	Government-sponsored enterprises	4.0	−0.6
10	ABS issuers	66.6	59.5
11	Finance companies	17.7	2.8

* Billions of dollars; quarterly figures are seasonally adjusted annual rates

EXHIBIT 8.4

Pools of Securitized Assets as a Percent of Total Revolving Consumer Credit

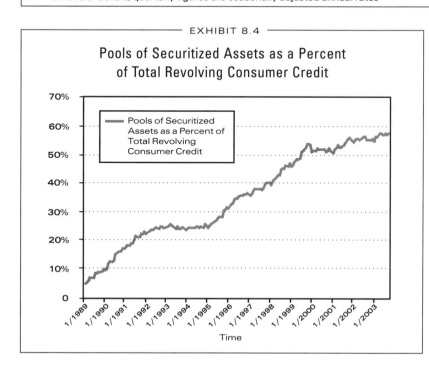

Source: Federal Reserve Board, Federal Reserve Statistical Release G.19, Consumer Credit Historical Data

1997	1998	1999	2000	2001	2002	2003	
62.1	96.8	112.1	165.2	137.7	81.4	101.6	1
62.1	96.8	112.1	165.2	137.7	81.4	101.6	2
1.2	-2.7	2.5	4.0	-0.4	-0.1	-7.5	3
0.0	0.0	0.0	0.0	0.0	0.0	0.0	4
10.8	9.0	13.6	16.1	13.1	12.7	1.3	5
-14.2	-3.6	-9.2	41.7	17.0	28.7	49.3	6
2.5	4.4	9.9	3.0	4.5	-0.6	9.2	7
8.2	3.0	12.5	16.5	5.1	6.2	14.0	8
-4.2	-1.2	5.4	-3.9	2.4	-2.6	-7.1	9
45.3	72.0	59.0	68.9	78.4	37.4	-10.3	10
12.6	15.8	18.3	18.9	17.6	-0.3	52.8	11

Source: U.S. Federal Reserve Flow of Funds

duits. ABS issuers do not originate consumer credit; they refinance consumer credit that was originated by financial institutions.

EXHIBIT 8.4 shows how securitized asset pools have progressed from being a marginal means of funding of revolving consumer credit in 1989 to being the dominant source of revolving consumer credit by 2003.

Consumer loans, of course, encompass more than just credit card receivables. Student loans are counted as consumer loans, as are term loans originated to finance the purchase of consumer durables. This chapter focuses on credit card receivables, the debt created when consumers and businesses use their credit cards to make purchases and borrow funds, because as noted previously, from the standpoint of investors in ABSs, this constitutes the lion's share and most significant component of consumer credit.

Elements of a Master Trust
Pooling and Servicing Agreement

MASTER TRUSTS formed by pooling and servicing agreements between the seller that sponsors the transaction and the trustee are at the core of the securitization of both credit card receivables and dealer floor plan loans (discussed in Chapter 7). The pooling and servicing agreement is not unique to master trusts; it is central to all securitization transactions. The pooling and servicing agreement includes the trust indenture. This agreement spells out the way the securitization transaction functions, from the sale of receivables to the issuance of securities, as well as the legal obligations and responsibilities of all parties involved, including third-party suppliers of credit enhancement.

The pooling and servicing agreement contains specific directions concerning the following:

1   conveyance of receivables
2   administration of receivables
3   rights of certificate holders
4   allocation and application of collections
5   distribution and reports to certificate holders
6   legal form and registration requirements of the certificates

The securities issued by MBNA Master Credit Card Trust II, the focus of the case study that follows, are registered under the 1933 Securities Act pursuant to rule 415, which is commonly referred to as a shelf registration. A prospectus is filed with the Securities and Exchange Commission (SEC) as part of the shelf registration. The prospectus lays out the general static and dynamic components of the transaction, such as the allocation of cash flows and defaults, characteristics of the receivables, servicing responsibilities, capital structure of the trust, tax treatment of the trust and securities, Employment Retirement Income Security Act (ERISA) rules applicable to the securities issued by the trust, legal and accounting status of the receivable transfers, and legal relationships between the parties involved in the transfers.

Before the master trust can issue a series of publicly offered certificates, it must file a prospectus supplement. The prospectus supplement makes specific the general terms of the prospectus. In the prospectus supplement, all of the parameters of the notes and certificates that compose the series to be issued are enumerated, such as interest rates, amortization schedules, and credit enhancement levels. Included below is an excerpt from a 1997 SEC registration statement for the MBNA Master Credit Card Trust II.

> The Prospectus Supplement relating to a Series to be offered thereby and hereby will, among other things, set forth with respect to such Series: (a) the initial aggregate principal amount of each Class of such Series; (b) the certificate interest rate (or method for determining it) of each Class of such Series; (c) certain information concerning the Receivables allocated to such Series; (d) the expected date or dates on which the principal amount of the Certificates will be paid to holders of each Class of Certificates (the "Certificate holders"); (e) the extent to which any Class within a Series is subordinated to any other Class of such Series or any other Series; (f) the identity of each Class of floating-rate Certificates and fixed-rate Certificates included in such Series, if any, or such other type of Class of Certificates; (g) the Distribution Dates for the respective Classes; (h) relevant financial information with respect to the Receivables; (i) additional information with respect to any Enhancement relating to such Series; and (j) the plan of distribution of such Series. (February 4, 1997, SEC, Amendment No. 2 to Form S-3, Registration Statement under the Securities Act of 1933, MBNA America Bank, National Association, the originator of MBNA Master Credit Card Trust II)

Basics of the Securitization Scheme

THE SCHEME financial institutions use to securitize credit card receivables is similar to the one used to securitize dealer floor plan loans, as discussed in the previous chapter. This is because the dynamics of the two asset classes are similar. Both are generated by revolving lines of credit. In both cases, it is important to consider that the accounts that generate the receivables remain the property of the originator; it is the *receivables* generated by the accounts that are securitized. Should a seller choose or be forced to wind up a credit card securitization transaction, then the originator/seller must have the resources to finance the receivables that will come back onto its balance sheet. Winding up or terminating a securitization transaction may be the decision of the seller, or it may be a result of the poor performance of the securitized pool of assets. In the former case, the seller decides to finance all new receivables not needed to support the outstanding classes of the master trust's ABSs that are generated by the designated accounts via its own balance sheet or a new securitization structure. In the latter case, amortizing receivables are used to pay down outstanding classes as quickly as possible, and no new series are issued by the trust.

If the value of the receivables backing the series is not refinanced with another series, the originator must raise the capital necessary to finance the receivables on its own balance sheet. Thus, the liquidity of the originator is an important element in its ability to securitize the future flow of receivables. Without adequate liquidity the future solvency of the seller is potentially diminished, which in turn increases the chances that the seller will not be able to generate a future flow of receivables to support a trust's outstanding series of ABSs. If the liquidity problem were to become severe, it might trigger early amortization of the master trust's outstanding ABSs. Such a trigger mechanism is set to protect investors.

Assets of master trusts like the one discussed in Chapter 7 that DaimlerChrysler uses to securitize its dealer floor plan receivables, DaimlerChrysler Master Owner Trust, and the one highlighted in this chapter that MBNA[2] uses to securitize its credit card receivables, MBNA Master Credit Card Trust II, are allocated between the investor interest and the seller's interest. The seller's interest absorbs fluctuations in the receivables balance of the master trust so that series of certificates that finance the investor interest can remain constant until they are retired. Exhibit 8.4 sets forth the general capital structure of a credit card master trust and the basics of how cash flowing into the trust is allocated among the different interests in the trust. The zigzag shape of the seller's interest illustrates how the principal amount funded by the seller's interest varies according to fluctuations in the investor interest receivables, that is, the principal amount funded by investors, which varies as new series are issued and outstanding series mature.

Cash Flow Allocation

EXHIBIT **8.5** shows the dynamics of the capital structure of a credit card master trust over time. The share of the trust funded by the seller declines at T1 as a new series is issued. The share of the trust funded by the seller increases between T1 and T2 as the creation of new receivables exceeds the payment rate on outstanding receivables. Between T2 and T3 the portion funded by the seller declines as the payment rate exceeds the rate at which new receivables are created. From T3 to T4 the percent of the pool funded by the seller increases as the new receivables growth rate exceeds the payment rate on outstanding receivables. At T4 the seller again refinances part of its interest by having the trust issue a new series, series 2000-B. While the seller's interest grows from T5 to T6 the seller funds the increase. At T6 the trust issues series 2000-C. From T7 to T8 the seller's interest increases gradually, and then at T8, when series 1997-C matures and the principal financed by this series comes back onto the seller's balance sheet, the seller's interest jumps.

EXHIBIT **8.6** shows the basic nexus of contracts connecting MBNA, the securitized portfolio of credit card receivables, and the asset-backed notes issued by the MBNA Credit Card Master Note Trust. MBNA owns credit card accounts, which it designates for the securitization transaction via Master Trust II. Receivables generated from these designated accounts are sold to Master Trust II. Sales of receivables are governed by the pooling and serving agreement between the master trust and MBNA as originator and servicer of the receivables.

The collateral certificate is issued like other series of asset-backed certificates, and its terms are specified in a series supplement. Rather than being distributed to investors like other series of certificates, the collateral certificate is purchased by the Master Note Trust. It serves as collateral for the asset-backed notes issued by the MBNA Credit Card Master Note Trust. The general rights of the note holders to the liquidation proceeds of the receivables secured by the collateral certificate and the responsibilities of the indenture trustee for the allocation and distribution of the cash flows are detailed in the note indenture. Specifics of note holder rights for each class of notes and the indenture trustees' responsibilities to each class appear in the indenture supplement.

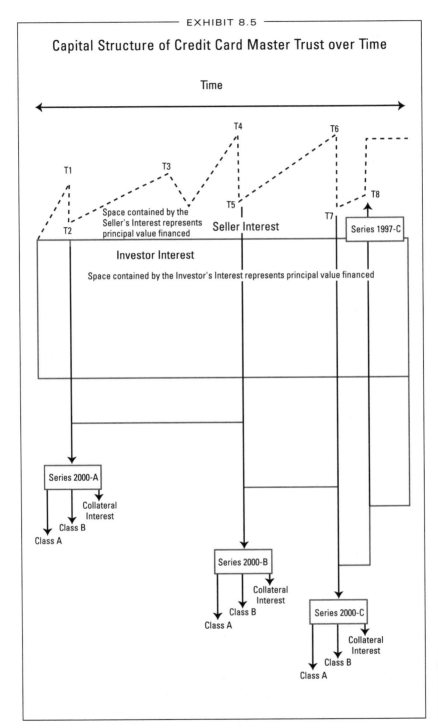

EXHIBIT 8.5

Capital Structure of Credit Card Master Trust over Time

Time

T4

T6

T1

T3

Space contained by the
Seller's Interest represents
principal value financed

T5

Seller Interest

T8

Series 1997-C

T2

T7

Investor Interest

Space contained by the Investor's Interest represents principal value financed

Series 2000-A

Collateral
Interest

Class B

Class A

Series 2000-B

Collateral
Interest

Class B

Class A

Series 2000-C

Collateral
Interest

Class B

Class A

Source: Stone/Zissu

EXHIBIT 8.6

Key Operating Documents

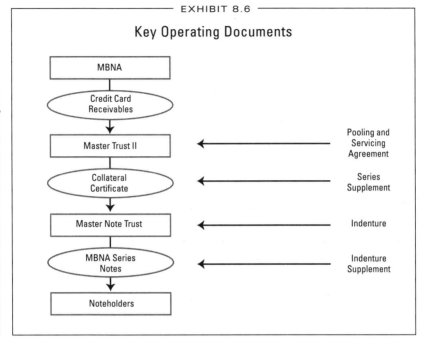

A prospectus and prospectus supplement are published with each issue of a tranche of a class of asset-backed notes. The general terms and conditions of series of ABSs issued by the MBNA Credit Card Master Note Trust as well as the mechanics of the securitization scheme are presented in the prospectus, while the specifics of each offering are spelled out in the prospectus supplement.

Looking at the MBNA Credit Card Master Trust II as a typical example of revolving credit securitization, each series issued passes through three phases: revolving, accumulation, and amortization. Typically, principal is accumulated so that a sufficient amount is available to retire each class of certificates that comprise a series with a single payment on its scheduled maturity date. This is called a *controlled accumulation* period. It is also possible to structure a class so that it amortizes gradually. This is referred to as a *controlled amortization* period. If rapid amortization is triggered, then certificates will be retired in sequence: A, then B, then the collateral interest as principal becomes available. As principal is accumulated for the A and B classes, then the collateral interest can be reduced.

Collateral interests are the most subordinate class of investor interest. In credit card securitizations, it is typical for each series to have a collateral interest as credit enhancement for the A and B classes. Reduction in the required credit enhancement that results from the funding of the principal accumulation accounts releases principal to the collateral interest holder.

Principal Collections and Reallocations

The master trust allocates principal collections and defaults among the series in proportion to their invested amounts. When a series is in the revolving phase, principal collections are used to buy new receivables from the seller. This maintains the asset base of the trust so that outstanding series in their revolving phase remain fully collateralized. Series already in the accumulation phase will be collateralized by their share of the receivables in the trust net of funds that have been accumulated for the series in its principal funding account. Each series issued by the trust has its own principal funding account where principal collections are invested during the accumulation phase.

Principal can also be reallocated from one series to another. Such reallocation of principal collections from one series to another is known as the *sharing of principal*. It may be that a relatively large series is in the accumulation phase while several smaller series are in the revolving phase. The extra principal collections from the series that are in the revolving phase can be used to accumulate principal for the larger series if needed.

Principal is released to the seller after all series have been either funded to the appropriate level for their stage of accumulation or the trust has sufficient receivables to support all outstanding classes of all series.

Principal that flows into the trust is allocated across series in relation to the principal value of the series relative to the trust. EXHIBIT 8.7 outlines how principal is allocated in a typical credit card master trust. The broken boxes on the left side of the two thick vertical two-way arrows indicate how principal is allocated across the series. Larger rectangles correspond to larger series and are thus allocated more principal. Principal is then distributed across classes in order of priority. Class A receives principal allocation prior to class B, and class B prior to the collateral interest.

EXHIBIT 8.7

Series Issued and Outstanding from Hypothetical Credit Card Master Trust

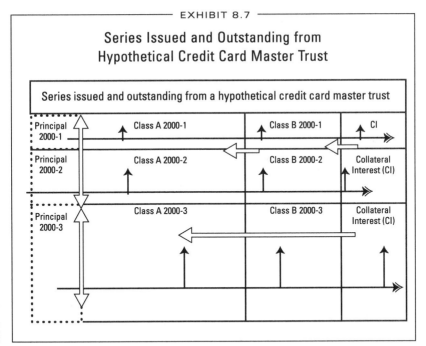

The three thin horizontal arrows going from left to right, with thin vertical arrows rising into each series' respective rectangle, illustrate that each class is allocating its share of principal collections for that series. The thicker right-to-left horizontal arrows that cross between classes of a series (for example, from CI to class A in series 2000-3 and from CI to class B and from class B to class A in series 2000-2) indicate that principal will be redirected from subordinate classes to senior classes to make senior classes whole and to cover any fee or interest shortfalls that may have resulted from insufficient collections of finance charges. The two thick two-way vertical arrows on the left are shown crossing between series to indicate that when principal allocated to a series is not needed for accumulation or liquidation of the series, it is then shared with other series that may need the cash for accumulation or liquidation purposes. For example, series 2000-3 may be in the accumulation phase while series 2000-2 and 2000-1 are in the revolving stages. If the principal claimed by series 2000-2 and 2000-1 is not needed, the principal flows will be shared with series 2000-3 and allocated among the classes of this series. If the principal is not required by series 2000-3 it would be used to amortize the seller's interest. The seller's interest is also allocated its own share of collections, principal, and interest.

Finance-Charge and Remaining Collections

Finance-charge collections are allocated among the investor interest and the seller's interest on a pro rata basis depending on the size of each interest. Once the allocation between the seller's and investor interest has been made, the share allocated to the investor interest is then allocated among the different series that comprise the investor interest. Depending on the design of the master trust, allocation of finance-charge collections among series is based on the relative size of the series or the relative cost of the series. In MBNA Master Credit Card Trust II, finance-charge collections are allocated based on the relative size of the series. The finance-charge collections allocated to a series (see EXHIBIT 8.8) then trickle down to each class in the order laid out in the prospectus supplement for the series.

After the distribution of interest to the class A and class B certificates and the servicing fees allocated to each class, A, B, the collateral interest, and the class A default amount, the remaining collections are categorized as excess spread. The value of defaulted receivables is allocated to each class within a series according in the same proportion as principal collections. Excess spread is then allocated to first make class A whole with respect to interest payments, default amounts, and amounts that may have been written down in previous periods. Next, the excess spread is used to complete the allocation of interest, servicing obligations, default amounts, and previous principal write-down of class B. Exhibit 8.7 shows how a typical so-called nonsocialist trust (discussed further below) allocates finance-charge collections.[3] Finance-charge collections allocated to a given series cascade from box to box, filling each category before being allocated to the next section.

Each class is responsible for its share of the servicing fee. Funds allocated to the series but not distributed are used to fund deposits to required reserve accounts and then may be shared among other series of the master trust. This sharing of excess finance-charge collections is indicated in exhibit 8.8 by the dark arrow labeled "Excess spread" coming out of the box "CI default amount."

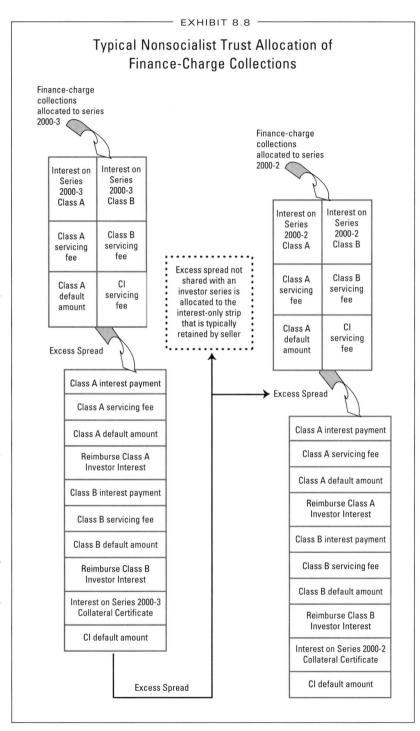

EXHIBIT 8.8

Typical Nonsocialist Trust Allocation of Finance-Charge Collections

Excess finance-charge collections are distributed in one of three ways. Depending on the design of the master trust, excess finance-charge collections may not be shared among series; rather, any excess flows directly to the seller. In other trusts, known as socialist trusts, finance-charge collections are distributed on a pro rata basis according to the expense of the series relative to the combined expense of all series. Such expenses include certificate interest, servicing fees, and default amounts. More costly series thus have a claim on a greater share of the finance-charge collections. Allocation of finance-charge collections are based on the need of the series. Excess collections of finance charges are allocated among series based on the relative shortfall for each series, which is equivalent to distributing the funds based on the relative cost of each series.

Finally, as illustrated in exhibit 8.8, a nonsocialist trust allocates finance-charge collections based on the relative size of the series. Unlike in the socialist trust, a large low-coupon series will receive more finance collections than a small high-coupon series even if the latter is more costly and has a larger shortfall of interest income. If there are any excess finance-charge collections after each series has received its full allocation, then the excess is distributed pro rata among other trust series within the group based on the size of the finance-charge shortfall for each series.

As the following excerpt from its prospectus indicates, the MBNA Credit Card Master Note Trust is designed as a socialist trust.

> MBNA series Available Funds for any month remaining after making the seventh application described under "Application of MBNA Series Available Funds" will be available for allocation to other series of notes in Group A. Such excess including excesses, if any, from other series of notes in Group A, called shared excess available funds, will be allocated to cover certain shortfalls in Available Funds for the series in Group A, if any, which have not been covered out of Available Funds allocable to such series. If these shortfalls exceed shared excess available funds for any month, shared excess available funds will be allocated pro rata among the applicable series in Group A based on the relative amounts of those shortfalls in Available Funds. To the extent that shared excess available funds exceed those shortfalls, the balance will be paid to the issuer. (MBNA Credit Card Master Note Trust)

Case Study: MBNA Master Credit Card Trust II

THE CASE STUDY that follows focuses on how MBNA, a credit card bank that specializes in issuing affinity cards, securitizes its credit card receivables. Affinity cards are credit cards that are endorsed by groups and marketed to members of the group. The members have a common interest by being affiliated with the same organization. Affinity groups include alumni organizations; professional groups; students, alumni, faculty and administrators of a university; and customers of a retail group. MBNA issues both Visa and MasterCard credit cards.

MBNA is the leading issuer of affinity credit cards in the world. Groups endorsing MBNA credit card products receive valuable benefits such as relatively low rates and high usage points. The benefits can be greater for holders of affinity cards than for holders of unaffiliated cards. Affinity programs offer the issuer marketing economies and are also a filter against weaker credit (while not perfect, the filter is better than taking applications from the general public). MBNA also uses a strict and efficient underwriting methodology; its underwriting standards are the same for accounts designated for securitization and those that are not.

MBNA's portfolio of credit card accounts lies on the high end of the credit spectrum. Members of affinity groups to whom MBNA markets its products are self-selected. For example, the American College of Surgeons and the London School of Economics both endorse MBNA credit card products. Membership in such professional organizations offers a certain level of security to MBNA, not as a guaranty but as a tie representing financial responsibility.

This chapter's discussion of how MBNA uses securitization and structures its securitization transactions can be generalized to other credit card banks and financial institutions with large credit card operations. In 1996 $28.5 billion of receivables from the credit card accounts of MBNA were financed by securitization vehicles; by September 2002 this value had grown to $74.7 billion. The primary vehicle through which MBNA securitizes its U.S. portfolio of credit card receivables is the MBNA Master Credit Card Trust II. MBNA completed more securitizations in the public markets in 2002 than any of its competitors.

MBNA's issuance of Visa and MasterCard credit cards in the United States is second only to Citibank's. MBNA had outstanding credit card receivables of $75.8 billion in 2002. Citibank had $98.5 billion of U.S. credit card receivables outstanding at that time. In 2002 MBNA was the most active securitizer of credit card receivables in terms of number of public transactions and principal financed.[4] MBNA Master Credit Card Trust II was formed on August 4, 1994, under a master agreement between MBNA America Bank National Association, as seller and servicer of the receivables, and The Bank of New York, as trustee. The trust is a master trust under which one or more series are issued through a series supplement to the master agreement. MBNA has estimated that in 2004, $11.1 billion of credit card receivables it has funded by securitization trusts will have matured, and in 2005, $12.7 billion will have matured. Credit card receivables are created as card holders use their Visa and MasterCard credit cards. The receivables are composed of principal and finance-charge balances owed to MBNA by the card holder.

The Seller's Interest and Investor Interest

ASSETS OF MBNA Master Credit Card Trust II are allocated between the investor and the seller's interests. As a series matures, the seller's interest increases and the investor interest declines. The seller is committed by the pooling and servicing agreement (the master agreement) to maintain the seller's interest at a level that does not drop below 4 percent of the average principal receivables of the trust for the interest period, or, with approval of the credit rating agencies that are monitoring the trust, below 2 percent of the average principal receivables. If the seller's interest declines below this minimum, an early amortization of the trust's outstanding series will occur.

The seller has committed to sell all receivables generated from the pool of designated accounts to the master trust. It is up to the seller to decide when to issue a new series of ABSs. When account balances grow above the amount funded by the outstanding series of investor certificates, the seller's interest increases. When the account balances decline, the seller's interest declines as existing receivables amortize faster than they are replaced. While a series is in its revolving phase, principal allocations to the series are reinvested in new receivables. Even when the seller's interest is declining, due to a combination of high payment rate and low rate of borrowing, the investor interest remains constant because receivables are bought with principal that belongs to the investor interest.

If the seller's interest declines to a trigger level set in the prospectus supplement, an early amortization of the series commences. A large or rapid decline of the investor interest indicates that new receivables are not being generated at a rate that is sufficient to support the outstanding series of the trust.

EXHIBIT **8.9** plots the percent of the MBNA Master Credit Card Trust II financed by the seller's interest and that financed by the investor interest between February 1996 and June 2001. While the total is always 100 percent, the weights shift back and forth between the two interests. The trend since the MBNA Master Credit Card Trust II was formed is clearly toward a smaller percent financed by the seller. The jagged line between the seller's interest and the investor interest are caused by the issuing of additional series of ABSs and

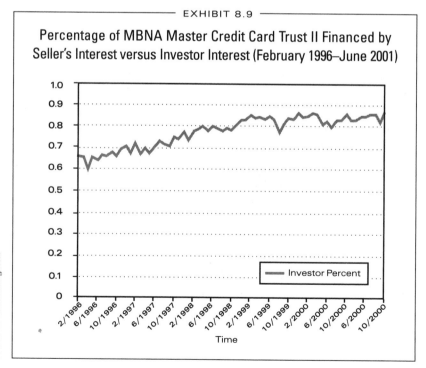

EXHIBIT 8.9

Percentage of MBNA Master Credit Card Trust II Financed by Seller's Interest versus Investor Interest (February 1996–June 2001)

Source: www.FitchRatings.com

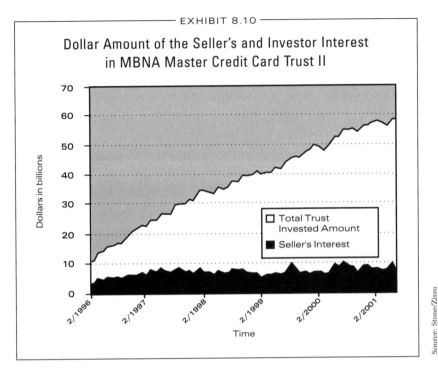

EXHIBIT 8.10

Dollar Amount of the Seller's and Investor Interest in MBNA Master Credit Card Trust II

by the amortization of outstanding series. When a series amortizes, the future value of receivables funded by the series must now be funded by the seller.

Exhibit 8.10 plots the dollar amount of the seller's interest and the investor interest. Growth in the trust can be financed by either the seller's interest or the investor interest. Increases in the investor interest are a result of new series being issued to finance a growth in the receivable pool rather than a refinancing of a maturing series. The first series out of MBNA Master Credit Card Trust II was in 1994. By May 2001, there were seventy-one series outstanding. As of January 19, 2001, 92 percent of MBNA's credit card portfolio was securitized. The earliest scheduled amortization of a series was in 2003. This indicates that the new series being issued by MBNA Master Credit Card Trust II between 1994 and 2003 were to finance the receivables associated with the addition of new designated accounts to the existing pool and increased levels of credit extended under the accounts.

Retained Interest

PART OF the investor interest may be owned by the seller. For example, if the seller retains an interest in the trust that takes the form of a subordinate collateral interest or a subordinate class of securities issued by the trust, the seller would own a beneficial interest in the receivable pool that is allocated to investors. In other words, the seller can be, and usually is, also an investor in the trust.

A retained interest may also take the form of a spread account or interest-only (IO) strip. In this case, the investment in the trust is a right to excess periodic collections: collections not allocated to the seller's interest or the investor interest or to pay fees owed to the trustee, the servicer, or the supplier of credit enhancement. An IO strip does not represent an undivided ownership stake in the assets of the trust. This retained, or residual, interest is a right to excess cash flows generated by the receivable pool owned by the trust. The source of these cash flows is excess spread. The IO strip absorbs the excess cash flow that is periodically released from the trust. Excess spread includes projections of interest income, late fees, and charged-off loan recoveries, less gross credit losses, contractual servicing fees, and the interest rate paid to investors.

Accounting Treatment

The IO strip is accounted for as a receivable, and it is marked to market or revalued quarterly, with changes in valuation credited to the securitization or other income of the seller—in our case, MBNA. When the original pool of credit card receivables is sold to the master trust, and when subsequent sales of receivables are made, the gain on the sale is calculated in the following way. The carrying value of the sold receivables is allocated between the share sold for proceeds other than retained interests in the trust (cash) and the share exchanged for retained interests.

Retained interests may be securities backed by transferred assets, cash reserve accounts, and IO strips. The gain on sale is the difference between the net proceeds of the receivables sold and the carrying value of the retained portion of the loans. The retained interest is recorded at the carrying value of its share of the receivables pool prior to its securitization. The Financial Accounting Standards Board

(FASB) offers the following rationale for the accounting treatment of the retained interest in a securitized pool of receivables.

> The Board decided that all other interests in the transferred financial assets held after a securitization or other transfer of financial assets should be measured at their previous carrying amount, allocated between the assets sold, if any, and the retained interests, if any, based on their relative fair values at the date of the transfer. Retained interests in the transferred assets continue to be assets of the transferor, albeit assets of a different kind, because they never left the possession of the transferor and, thus, a surrender of control cannot have occurred. Therefore, the retained interests should continue to be carried at their allocated previous carrying amount, with no gain or loss recognized. Defining this category as the residual set of interests in transferred instruments held after the transfer (those interests that are neither derivatives nor liabilities of the transferor) establishes a clearer distinction between assets and liabilities that are part of the proceeds of the transfer and retained interests. (Measuring Retained Interests in Assets Sold at Allocated Previous Carrying Amount, FASB 140 paragraph 273)

Sources of and Changes in Securitization Income

Securitization of credit card receivables enables originators, owners, and servicers of credit card accounts to reallocate valuable capital from the banking process by stripping out a high-yield residual interest from a pool of credit card receivables. The stripped-out interest has a high expected yield due to its risk profile. Default amounts and interest shortfalls that would otherwise reduce the balances or lower the yield of the investors' interest in the asset pool are first absorbed by the retained interest. The retained interest assumes the first-loss position in the receivable pool. Residual cash flows are first used to make up interest shortfalls and keep whole the more senior interests in the pool.

Changes in the value of the IO strip accrue to changes in securitization income. For example, all things being equal, an increase in default rates on the pool of receivables held by a master trust would lower the excess spread as finance charges were allocated to the investor interest to compensate for the increased loss rate. Lower excess spread would lower the securitization income of the seller. It is important to distinguish between cash flows received from the retained interest and income changes. Income from a securitization will change as the assumptions regarding future performance of the securitized receivables change. For example, income would increase due to a decrease in the default rate assumption for a pool of securitized receivables. This lower default rate assumption increases securitized income in the current period as the retained interest is revalued. The additional cash will flow to the seller over time.

Securitization income is a function of the level of securitized interest-earning assets, the net interest margin on securitized assets, fee income, and net charge-offs. In addition, as noted previously, changes in the present value of the IO strip are accounted for as changes in securitization income.

Since market values of residual interests in securitization trusts are not available, the seller must estimate their value. Retained interests are important sources of income for financial institutions that securitize their receivables. Accurate estimates of the value of retained interests are necessary data for managers, owners, and creditors interested in estimating the value of the company. Furthermore, IO strips are a leveraged position in the receivable pool. Adverse changes in variables such as loan payment rate, gross credit losses, excess spread, and the discount rate will lead to a change in the value of the retained interest in the credit card master trust that exceeds the percentage loss in value of the assets owned by the trust. Credit card banks include a table in their 10-K reports that calculates the change in value of the retained IO strip for adverse changes in these variables. For example, in 2002 MBNA estimated that a 20 percent decline in excess spread would lead to a 20 percent decline in the value of the IO strip, and a 20 percent increase in gross defaults would lead to a 22.4 percent decline in the bank's residual interest in its securitization trusts.

Credit Risk and Credit Enhancement

WHILE DEALER floor plan loans (see Chapter 7) are secured by new and used automobile inventory extended to automobile dealers, credit card receivables are typically unsecured loans extended to individuals. These differences become manifest in the underlying credit risks of the two portfolios (see EXHIBIT **8.11**).

Receivable balances vary with the payment rate. Credit card contracts require a minimum monthly payment of principal. For example, as indicated in a recent 10-K report, MBNA requires a minimum payment of 2 percent of the outstanding balance or 2.25 percent for accounts that are ninety or more days delinquent or drawn over their credit limit. By contrast, dealer floor plan loans must be repaid as vehicles are sold.

The interest rate charged on credit card balances reflects the higher expected default rates on this class of receivables. It is interesting to see that starting with two very different pools of assets in terms of credit risk, the outcome of the securitization process in terms of the yield on AAA-rated credit card–backed securities and dealer floor plan receivables is quite similar. In other words, yields on ABSs may reflect differences in liquidity and prepayment expectations, yet credit risk can be brought to equivalent levels for disparate groups of receivables originated by institutions with different credit ratings. This is accomplished by building in the appropriate levels and forms of credit enhancement.

EXHIBIT 8.11

Dealer Floor Plan Credit versus Credit Card Receivables

MBNA Credit Card Master Note Trust

	2002	2001	2000	1999	1998
Total charge-offs as a percent of average principal receivables outstanding	5.5%	5.24%	5.1%	4.93%	4.99%

U.S. Wholesale Portfolio of DaimlerChrysler

	2002	2001	2000	1999	1998
Net losses as a percent of average principal receivables balance	0.11%	0.02%	0.01%	0.00%	0.12%

Source: MBNA and DaimlerChrysler

Levels of credit enhancement needed to bring a credit card ABS up to an AAA rating exceed the amount of credit enhancement necessary to bring a dealer floor plan loan ABS up to AAA. To illustrate this point, exhibit 8.11 is a comparison of a tranche of class A notes issued by the MBNA Credit Card Master Note Trust alongside a series issued by DaimlerChrysler Master Owner Trust. The MBNA Credit Card Master Note Trust is a successor vehicle to MBNA Credit Card Master Trust II that MBNA has subsequently used as the issuing vehicle in its securitization transactions.

Tranches of class A notes issued by the MBNA Credit Card Master Note Trust have been indexed to the one- and three-month London interbank offer rates (Libor). Of the class A note tranches indexed to one-month Libor, the margin has ranged between 5 and 25 basis points. The second tranche of the class A notes—Class A (2003-2), issued on March 26, 2003—had a coupon of Libor plus 5 basis points. It had an original principal amount of $1 billion and an expected maturity date of March 2006. The 2003-2 tranche of class A is supported by about 16 percent of subordination consisting of class B and class C notes of the MBNA series. This does not mean that the outstanding amount of the B and C notes issued by the trust is 16 percent of class A (2003-2), because the class B and class C notes support all of the outstanding tranches of class A notes in the MBNA series. In other words, the 16 percent subordination is the portion of the class B and class C notes allocated to support the (2003-2) tranche of the class A note.

DaimlerChrysler Master Owner Trust series 2003-A was issued on February 25, 2003, in the amount of $1.5 billion. The series was composed of a single class A note that had a coupon of Libor plus 5 basis points and an expected maturity of February 15, 2006. Credit enhancement supporting class A is in the form of overcollateralization of the trust by approximately 10 percent.

Exhibit 8.12 lays out the general scheme of the MBNA Credit Card Master Note Trust.

The MBNA Credit Card Master Note Trust is the vehicle that MBNA designed to take the place of the MBNA Master Credit Card Trust II as the issuing vehicle in its securitization transactions. In 2001, MBNA Credit Card Master Note Trust issued series 2001-D to MBNA Master Credit Card Trust II. The notes issued by the Master

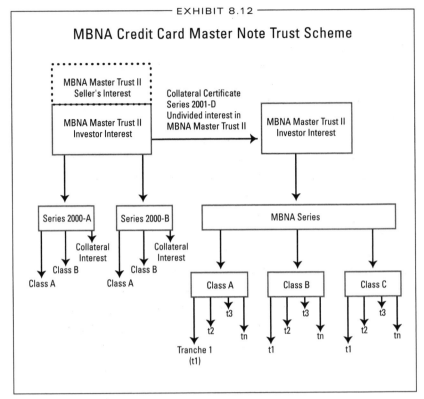

EXHIBIT 8.12

MBNA Credit Card Master Note Trust Scheme

Source: Stone/Zissu

Note Trust are collateralized by series 2001-D issued by MBNA Master Credit Card Trust II.

Series 2001-D is a collateral certificate that, like the other investor series issued by the trust, has a claim on an undivided interest of the trust's assets. Whereas series 2001-D represents a beneficial interest in MBNA Master Credit Card Trust II, the notes issued by MBNA Credit Card Master Note Trust do not give the investors a beneficial interest in the assets of MBNA Master Credit Card Trust II. The notes do not represent beneficial interests in a pool of securitized credit card receivables. This is important for ERISA purposes. A pool of finance receivables generated by a large number of accounts poses the risk that a conflict exists between a pension plan and the investment in the ABSs. This is due to the possibility of obligors of the securitized receivables also being beneficiaries of the retirement plan. The constraints posed by ERISA on asset-backed securitization transactions are discussed in more detail below.

Series 2001-D was issued in May 2001. At this time, there were seventy-one other investor series outstanding from the MBNA Master Credit Card Trust II that funded approximately $47.86 billion of credit card receivables. The seller interest at this time funded the remainder of the trust, approximately $10.31 billion. As of September 2003, the collateral certificate (series 2001-D) funded $29.294 billion of credit card receivables owned by the MBNA Master Credit Card Trust II, up from $1.5 billion in July 2001, according to Fitch Ratings. By September 2003 the investor interest net of Series 2001-D was $33.74 billion. Series 2001-D by this time had grown to $29.294 billion.

MBNA Master Credit Card Trust II has not issued additional series since the collateral certificate 2001-D. The implications of this are that the collateral certificate's undivided interest has grown relative to the other investor certificates issued by MBNA Master Credit Card Trust II. The seller exchanges interests in the seller certificate for the proceeds of notes issued by the MBNA Credit Card Master Note Trust. The collateral certificate functions like a variable funding certificate. Rather than issue new series out of the MBNA Master Credit Card Trust II, series 2001-D absorbs the shift in principal from the seller to the investor interest. The increase in series 2001-D is funded by notes issued by the MBNA Credit Card Master Note Trust. For example, the Master Note Trust might choose to issue another tranche of class C notes or a tranche of class A notes if sufficient credit enhancement were available to support it.

MBNA estimates that from 2003 through 2007, $76.96 billion of securitized principal will mature that will have to be either refinanced via securitization or financed through its own balance sheet. While the investors in ABSs are insulated from the credit quality of the seller because the receivables are sold to a QSPE (qualified special-purpose entity), the general creditors of the seller, that is, the investors who supply equity and credit directly to the seller, are exposed to the risks that the outstanding credit card receivables will eventually come back onto the seller's balance sheet, against its will, if the asset-backed market becomes inaccessible at the seller or industry level. It bears repeating that the seller's liquidity position is of concern to the owners and creditors of the seller and to the investors in the ABSs issued by seller-sponsored trusts. Insufficient liquidity on the part of the seller can trigger early amortization of trust certificates if the liquidity problem affects the ability of the seller to service its receivables or originate sufficient new receivables.

MBNA America Bank National Association, the seller of the credit card receivables to MBNA Master Credit Card Trust II, is a national banking organization regulated by the Office of the Comptroller of the Currency (OCC). The OCC is authorized to appoint the Federal Deposit Insurance Corporation (FDIC) as the conservator or receiver of MBNA if the financial condition or operating procedures of the bank warrant that action. Banks subject to receivership by the FDIC are not subject to the U.S. Bankruptcy Code. This is why MBNA and most banks that securitize their receivables do not structure their transactions as two-tier securitizations. MBNA sells its credit card receivables directly to the MBNA Master Credit Card Trust II rather than first to a wholly owned bankruptcy-remote special-purpose entity (SPE).

When the seller is not subject to the U.S. Bankruptcy Code, the logic of the two-tier transaction does not apply. As was explained in Chapter 5, the two-tier transaction is used to isolate the receivables from the transferor. Once the receivables are isolated from the transferor by structuring the transfer as a true sale to a wholly owned bankruptcy-remote SPE, a bankruptcy of the transferor should not give a bankruptcy court or the transferor access to the sold receivables or their associated cash flows.

Before the passage of the Financial Institutions Reform, Recovery, and Enforcement Act of 1989, which amended the Federal Deposit Insurance Act, the FDIC would have had access to the transferred receivables. The FDIC could have recharacterized a sale of receivables to a bankruptcy-remote SPE as a secured loan. Once this took place, the receivables could have been used to satisfy compensatory damages. This would deprive the investors who own the ABSs issued by the qualifying SPE (QSPE) from the cash flows necessary to service their obligations. The FDIC has placed itself beyond the reach of assets sold in securitization transactions provided that certain conditions of the transaction are met.[5]

Case Study: MBNA Credit Card Master Note Trust

AS WAS NOTED, the MBNA Credit Card Master Note Trust has essentially taken the place of the MBNA Master Credit Card Trust II as the issuing vehicle used by MBNA to securitize its credit card receivables. This is because the Master Note Trust offers the seller the ability to reach a deeper pool of capital and coordinate issues more precisely with market conditions.

The first Credit Card Master Note Trust was implemented by Citibank in 2000 in a program called Citibank Credit Card Issuance Trust, which has become the model for the programs developed by other banks. The master note structure introduced by Citibank in fact is becoming the preferred securitization structure for credit card banks and other significant issuers of credit cards.[6] An innovation of the master note trust is its ability to tranche the classes of notes and then issue the tranches in separate transactions. This allows the seller to gauge the timing and size of issues more accurately than is possible for the traditional master trust structure. For example, the MBNA Master Credit Card Trust II issues series of certificates composed of multiple classes of certificates, but all of the classes are tied together and must be issued simultaneously.

Tranches for A, B, and C Classes

THE MBNA Credit Card Master Note Trust issues three classes of asset-backed notes: A, B, and C. Class C enhances the credit quality of classes B and A, and class B is in turn subordinate to class A. Classes are in turn tranched. Each tranche of a class may have different interest rates and payment terms, but all tranches of a class rank equally with one another in terms of principal repayment. The tranches of notes can be issued separately. That is, a tranche of class C notes may be issued at a different time than a tranche of class A or class B notes. As noted, this is different from the traditional master trusts, such as MBNA Master Credit Card Trust II, which issues all certificates that comprise a series simultaneously.

However, the MBNA Credit Card Master Note Trust cannot issue tranches of class A notes unless there is sufficient credit enhancement in the form of class B and class C notes outstanding to support the

──────── EXHIBIT 8.13 ────────

MBNA Credit Card Master Note Trust Tranches 1 and 2 of Classes A, B, and C Notes

CLASS	ISSUANCE DATE	NOMINAL LIQUIDATION AMOUNT	NOTE INTEREST RATE	EXPECTED PRINCIPAL PAYMENT DATE	LEGAL MATURITY DATE
Class A (2001-1)	5/31/01	$1 billion	5.75%	May 2006	October 2008
Class A (2001-2)	7/26/01	$500 million	One-month Libor + 0.25%	July 2011	December 2013
Class B (2001-1)	5/24/01	$250 million	One-month Libor + 0.375%	May 2006	October 2008
Class B (2001-2)	9/6/01	$250 million	One-month Libor + 0.36%	August 2006	January 2009
Class C (2001-1)	5/24/01	$250 million	One-month Libor + 1.05%	May 2006	October 2008
Class C (2001-2)	7/12/01	$100 million	Not to exceed one-month Libor + 1.15%	July 2008	December 2010

Source: Prospectus Supplement to MBNA Credit Card Master Note Trust, dated March 11, 2003

new issue. The required credit enhancement for a tranche of class A notes is specified in the prospectus supplement for the issue.

EXHIBIT **8.13**, showing the first two tranches of A, B, and C notes issued as part of the MBNA series, illustrates how tranches of notes are issued at different times and with different terms. This flexibility allows sellers such as MBNA or Citibank to time and market the issues effectively. As of October 28, 2003, the MBNA series consisted of twenty-nine tranches of class A notes, twelve tranches of class B notes, and nineteen tranches of class C notes. The principal value of the MBNA Credit Card Master Note Trust series as of September 2003 was approximately $29.3 billion.

The MBNA Credit Card Master Note Trust issued its first notes in May 2001. The first issue of notes as part of the MBNA series out of the MBNA Credit Card Master Note Trust was a $250 million tranche of class C notes. EXHIBIT **8.14** plots the principal amount of credit card receivables funded by the MBNA Credit Card Master

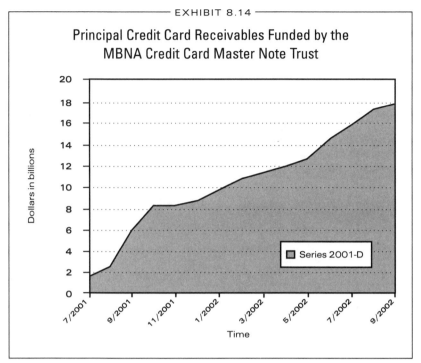

EXHIBIT 8.14

Principal Credit Card Receivables Funded by the MBNA Credit Card Master Note Trust

Note Trust since its inception. EXHIBIT 8.15 on the following page graphs the investor interest of MBNA Master Credit Card Trust II net of series 2001-D, the collateral certificate for the MBNA Credit Card Master Note Trust. The increase in the principal value of series 2001-D (exhibit 8.14) and the decline in the investor interest in the MBNA Master Credit Card Trust II net of series 2001-D (exhibit 8.15) illustrates that the MBNA Credit Card Master Note Trust is funding an increasing proportion of the credit card receivables securitized by MBNA.

ERISA Restrictions

A KEY INNOVATION of the Master Note Trust is that all of the notes issued by the credit card master note trusts are eligible investments for benefit plans governed by ERISA rules. All classes of notes are debt of the master note trust, the beneficiary of which is MBNA in our case example. Only the senior (A) class of certificates issued by traditional credit card master trusts like MBNA Master Credit Card

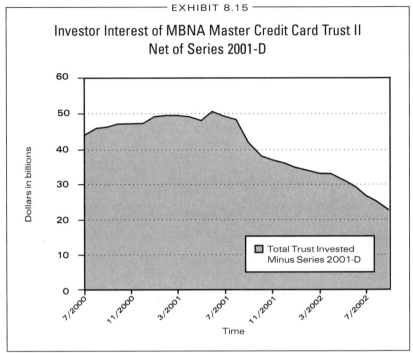

EXHIBIT 8.15

Investor Interest of MBNA Master Credit Card Trust II
Net of Series 2001-D

Source: Stone/Zissu using data from MBNA Master Credit Card Trust and Fitch Ratings

Trust II are eligible investments for benefit plans, however, and then only if the certificates meet the criteria of ERISA's plan asset regulation (see EXHIBIT **8.16**). Those criteria are:

➤ the securities must be publicly offered, or

➤ equity participation in the entity by benefit plan investors must not be significant.

For example, the First USA Master Credit Card Trust relies on publicly offering the A class of its certificates. When the certificates meet the ERISA criteria of being publicly offered, they are eligible investments for benefit plans, whereas they would otherwise be prohibited investments according to ERISA rules.

Benefit plans for retirees—such as pension plans, profit sharing plans, individual retirement accounts, annuities, employee annuity plans, and Keogh plans—are prohibited from engaging in certain types of transactions. The source of the prohibitions is section 406 of the Employee Retirement Income Security Act of 1974 (ERISA). Prohibited transactions can be divided into two general categories:

EXHIBIT 8.16

Administrative Exemption Granted to MBNA

The Department of Labor has issued an individual exemption, Prohibited Transaction Exemption 98-13 (Exemption Application No. D-10304), 63 Fed. Reg. 17,020 (April 7, 1998), to MBNA relating to (1) the initial purchase, the holding and the subsequent resale by plans of senior certificates representing an undivided interest in a credit card trust with respect to which MBNA is the sponsor; and (2) the servicing, operation and management of such trust, provided that the general conditions and certain other conditions set forth in the exemption are satisfied. The exemption will apply to the acquisition, holding and resale of the Class A certificates by, on behalf of, or with "plan assets" of a plan, provided that certain conditions, including the conditions described in "ERISA Considerations" in the accompanying prospectus, are met.

The seller believes that the MBNA exemption will apply to the acquisition and holding of the Class A certificates by plans and that all conditions of the exemption, other than those within the control of the investors, will be met. (MBNA Prospectus Supplement, Series 2001-A)

first, the benefit plan and its fiduciaries cannot engage in transactions with a party that has an economic interest in or relationship with the benefit plan. For example, if the notes issued by the Master Note Trust were deemed to be debt of MBNA and MBNA contributed to the benefit plan, investment in the notes by the benefit plan would be a prohibited transaction.[7] If the fiduciary of the benefit plan were also the trustee for the note issuer, under ERISA rules an investment by the benefit plan in the notes would be a prohibited transaction. These are only two examples of potential prohibited transactions. It is the responsibility of the fiduciary of the benefit plan to realize the source of potential conflicts and detect these conflicts if they exist.

EXHIBIT 8.17

Plan Asset Regulations of ERISA

Under certain circumstances, the Plan Asset Regulation treats the assets of an entity in which a Benefit Plan holds an equity interest as "plan assets" of such Benefit Plan. Because the Class A Certificates will represent beneficial interests in the Trust, and despite the agreement of the Transferor and the Certificate Owners to treat the Class A Certificates as debt instruments, the Class A Certificates are likely to be considered equity interests in the Trust for purposes of the Plan Asset Regulation, with the result that the assets of the Trust are likely to be treated as "plan assets" of the investing Benefit Plans for purposes of ERISA and Section 4975 of the Code, unless the exception for "publicly offered securities" is applicable as described in the attached prospectus. No restrictions will be imposed on the transfer of the Class A Certificates.

The underwriters expect that the Class A Certificates will be held by at least 100 or more investors who are independent of the issuer and of one another ("Independent Investors") at the conclusion of the initial public offering although no assurance can be given, and no monitoring or other measures will be taken to ensure, that such condition is met. The Bank expects that the other requirements will be met so the Class A Certificates will be "publicly offered securities" as described in the attached prospectus. The Class A Certificates will be sold as part of an offering pursuant to an effective registration statement under the Securities Act and then will be timely registered under the Exchange Act. (Prospectus Supplement to Prospectus dated May 3, 2001, First USA Master Credit Card Trust, Class A and Class B Series 2001-4)

The second category of prohibited transactions is potentially more limiting. According to the plan asset regulation of ERISA (29 CFR Sec. 2510-3.101),[8] certain equity investments made by benefit plans would cause the assets underlying the investment to become plan assets. This would result in the managers of the assets becoming fiduciaries of the plan (see EXHIBIT **8.17**). If this were to happen, the actions of the trustee, servicer, and seller that are parties to the securitization transaction would be potential sources of prohibited transactions for the benefit plan. The benefit plan would be constrained not only by the potential for prohibited transactions executed by its fiduciary but also by transactions regarding the assets owned by the securitization trust made by the trustee, servicer, and seller.

The constraints posed by the plan asset regulation clearly dampen the interest of benefit plans in credit card ABSs in particular and ABSs generally. According to 29 CFR 2510.3-101 (definition of "plan assets"—plan investments) of the ERISA rules, a purchase of a beneficial interest in a trust is an equity investment. Since the class A certificates convey to the owner a beneficial interest in the trust's assets, a benefit plan that invests in the class A certificates becomes the owner not only of the class certificate but also of the underlying assets themselves. The way around this problem is either to receive an exemption from ERISA or to satisfy the criteria for being a publicly offered security. ABSs issued out of a trust that have equity features or do not qualify as debt would, according to the plan asset regulation, convey ownership of the trust's assets to any benefit plan that invests in the certificates issued by the trust. In this case, any transaction by the trust would be considered a transaction involving benefit plan assets and thus would be a potential prohibited transaction. When the trust buys receivables from the seller, it's as if the benefit plan assets are being invested in the receivables. If, by chance, obligors of the credit cards were also beneficiaries of the benefit plan, this would be a prohibited transaction. It is a prohibited transaction because plan assets are financing parties with an economic interest in the benefit plan. Just the cost of detecting whether a conflict exists is time-consuming and somewhat futile, because the accounts feeding the receivable pool change over time.

Fiduciaries of benefit plans find a way around these constraints either by investing in notes issued by the trust that qualify as publicly offered securities[9] or by investing in notes that are covered by an ERISA exemption. ERISA grants three types of exemptions: statutory, regulatory, and administrative. The excerpt in exhibit 8.17 comes from the administrative exemption that MBNA was granted by the Department of Labor in 1998. The administrative exemption MBNA received is referred to as an underwriter exemption. Many conditions are placed on the operation, capital structure, and management of the securitization structure for the senior class of certificates issued by the MBNA Master Credit Card Trust II to be covered by the exemption. All of the conditions are designed to ensure that the risks of the class A certificates (the exempt securities) are transparent and manageable and not subject to management discretion.

Chapter Notes

1. Federal Reserve Statistical Release, Flow of Funds Accounts of the United States, Flows and Outstandings, second quarter, 2003.

2. MBNA America Bank, National Association, a national banking association located in Wilmington, Delaware.

3. A detailed discussion of this topic can be found in Standard & Poor's Structured Finance Credit Card Criteria, at www.standardandpoors.com/ratings.

4. Bank Credit Card ABS Sector Overview and Issuer Profiles, Global Structured Finance Review, J. P. Morgan Securities, Inc., September 25, 2002.

5. The FDIC shall not, by exercise of its authority to disaffirm or repudiate contracts under 12 U.S.C. 1821(e), reclaim, recover, or recharacterize as property of the institution or the receivership any financial assets transferred by an insured depository institution in connection with a securitization or participation, provided that such transfer meets all conditions for sale accounting treatment under generally accepted accounting principles, other than the "legal isolation" condition as it applies to institutions for which the FDIC may be appointed as conservator or receiver which is addressed by this section. (FDIC Rules and Regulations, Part 360-Resolution and Receivership Rules, § 360.6 Treatment by the Federal Deposit Insurance Corporation as conservator or receiver of financial assets transferred in connection with a securitization or participation)

6. Fitch maintains an informative Web page at www.FitchRatings.com dedicated to following these so-called credit card issuance trusts. As of 2004 Fitch provided data and analysis on three credit card issuance trusts: Capital One Multi-Asset Execution Trust, Citibank Credit Card Issuance Trust, and MBNA Credit Card Master Note Trust.

7. "A violation of the prohibited transaction rules could occur if any series of certificates were to be purchased with "plan assets" of any plan if the seller, the trustee, any underwriters of such series, or any of their affiliates were a party in interest with respect to such plan, unless a statutory, regulatory, or administrative exemption is available or an exception applies under a plan asset regulation issued by the Department of Labor. The seller, the trustee, any underwriters of a series, and their affiliates are likely to be parties in interest with respect to many plans. Before purchasing certificates, a plan fiduciary or other plan investor should consider whether a prohibited transaction might arise by reason of the relationship between the plan and the seller, the trustee, any underwriters of such series, or any of their affiliates and consult their counsel regarding the purchase in light of the considerations described below." (Prospectus Supplement to Prospectus Dated January 29, 2001, MBNA Master Credit Card Trust II, series 2001-A)

8. "Generally, when a plan invests in another entity, the plan's assets include its investment, but do not, solely by reason of such investment, include any of the underlying assets of the entity. However, in the case of a plan's investment in an equity interest of an entity that is neither a publicly offered security nor a security issued by an investment company registered under the Investment Company Act of 1940, its assets include both the equity interest and an undivided interest in each of the underlying assets of the entity, unless it is established that—

(i) The entity is an operating company, or

(ii) Equity participation in the entity by benefit plan investors is not significant.

Therefore, any person who exercises authority or control respecting the management or disposition of such underlying assets, and any person who provides investment advice with respect to such assets for a fee (direct or indirect), is a fiduciary of the investing plan." (Code of Federal Regulations, 29 CFR 2510.3-101, Definition of "plan assets"—plan investments)

9. "A publicly offered security is a security that is:

(a.) freely transferable;

(b.) part of a class of securities that is owned, immediately subsequent to the initial offering, by 100 or more investors who were independent of the issuer and of one another; and

(c.) either is:

(i.) part of a class of securities registered under Section 12(b) or 12(g) of the Securities Exchange Act of 1934, as amended; or

(ii.) sold to the plan as part of an offering of securities to the public pursuant to an effective registration statement under the Securities Act of 1933, as amended, and the class of securities of which such security is a part is registered under the Securities Exchange Act of 1934, as amended, within 120 days (or such later time as may be allowed by the SEC) after the end of the fiscal year of the issuer during which the offering of such securities to the public occurred."

(Prospectus Supplement to Prospectus Dated May 3, 2001, First USA Credit Card Master Trust Class A Floating Rate Asset Backed Certificates, Series 2001-4, Class B Floating Rate Asset Backed Certificates, Series 2001-4)

PART FOUR

Searching for Value in the Mortgage- and Asset-Backed Markets

Chapter Nine

Investment, Speculation, and Hedging

PREVIOUS CHAPTERS have discussed the process of reallocating different risks among different groups of investors via the securitization of assets. For example, an asset such as a mortgage carries credit risk, prepayment risk, and interest-rate risk. A bank holding mortgages on its balance sheet absorbs the three risks. When these assets are securitized, risks can be redistributed among different groups of investors by "slicing and dicing" the cash flows, as well as slicing and dicing the credit risk from the underlying assets. This chapter highlights some of the investors' concerns and provides some simple examples of strategies developed to minimize or redistribute credit risk, interest-rate risk, and prepayment risk.

Target Investment

WHERE HAVE ALL the mortgage- and asset-backed securities gone, all $6.44 trillion of them? They have gone to state and local employee retirement funds and private pension funds; fixed-income mutual funds, including private retirement accounts and variable-annuity accounts; money market funds; hedge funds; commercial banks, both domestic and foreign; savings banks; real estate investment trusts (REITs); private investment partnerships and companies; insurance companies; corporate treasuries; and individual investors.

For example, the TIAA-CREF Bond Plus Fund had $328,606,230 in net assets as of June 30, 2002, according to the TIAA-CREF Mutual Funds 2002 semiannual report. Of this amount, 4.32 percent was invested in asset-backed securities (ABSs) and 36.91 percent in mortgage-backed securities (MBSs). The asset-backed holdings of the fund were created from the securitization of a diverse set of assets. All of the ABSs of the fund were rated AAA. In addition, the fund's short-term investments included asset-backed commercial paper.

The investment objective of the Bond Plus Fund is "favorable long-term rate of return, primarily through high current income consistent with preserving capital." The benchmark index for the fund is the Lehman Brothers Aggregate Bond Index. In their description of the fund's performance, management points out that one of the main strengths of mortgage- and asset-backed securities is that they are insulated from management.

> Yield spreads on corporate bonds—the difference between their yields and those of Treasuries—became extremely volatile as investors shied away from firms with accounting or corporate malfeasance issues. As a result, sectors less prone to credit concerns, including mortgage-backed, asset-backed, and government-agency bonds, performed well, while corporates lagged similar-duration Treasuries. (Semiannual Report, TIAA-CREF Bond Plus Fund, six months ended June 30, 2002)

The purpose of this chapter is not to account for every penny of the MBS and ABS market. If it were, a good place to start would be the Flow of Funds Accounts of the United States, published by the Board of Governors of the Federal Reserve Board. The intent instead is to provide some insight into how mortgage- and asset-backed securities fit into various investment strategies. For example, asset/liability managers at banks use the mortgage-backed market to adjust the durations of their balance sheets. Certain fund managers build investment strategies around the mortgage- and asset-backed market, and others incorporate mortgage- and asset-backed securities into their fixed-income portfolios to enhance portfolio yield within certain duration, convexity, and risk constraints.

Agency pass-through securities are an important source of liquidity for financial institutions. Agency MBSs are used as collateral for dollar rolls (repurchase agreements), and they have lower risk weights than whole loans—20 percent for Federal National Mortgage Association (FNMA) and Federal Home Loan Mortgage Corporation (FHLMC) MBSs and 0 percent for Government National Mortgage Association (GNMA) MBSs. The lower risk weights afforded to MBSs relative to whole loans mean that a bank that exchanges its whole loans for MBSs will be more liquid than an institution that continues to hold whole mortgage loans. Its balance sheet will be more liquid because the institution will need less capital to fund its portfolio of MBSs.

Data from the Board of Governors of the Federal Reserve Statistical Release H.8, Assets and Liabilities of Commercial Banks in the United States indicates that the share of bank assets invested in mortgage- and asset-backed securities as a percent of total assets grew from 3.99 percent in July 2000 to 4.25 percent as of June 2003. MBSs as a percent of commercial bank assets over the same period grew from 8.77 percent to 11.91 percent.

Bankers use the secondary market as both buyers and sellers. They liquidate the bank's fixed-rate and adjustable-rate mortgage loans, and they buy segments of mortgage portfolios in the form of liquid securities that meet their risk-management and asset-allocation objectives. Mortgage originators can swap their mortgages for pass-through securities issued by FNMA and FHLMC. If approved by GNMA, mortgage originators can pool mortgages and issue GNMA-guaranteed securities backed by mortgage pools that are composed of qualifying mortgages.

MBSs received in exchange for mortgage pools or, in the case of GNMA, issued by the lender can be retained or sold in the secondary market. Proceeds from the sale can be used to buy various classes of agency and private-label MBSs that have risk profiles that meet their asset/liability goals; to extend new loans; or for general corporate purposes. When origination capacity and demand for mortgage credit exceeds an institution's capacity for financing the mortgage assets originated, securitization provides an outlet to the capital and money markets. When the mortgages originated by an institution do not meet the underwriting standards of GNMA, FNMA, or FHMLC, the private-label market provides an alternative source of funds. An example of the private-label market is the GMAC-RFC RFMSI (General Motors Acceptance Corporation–Residential Funding

Corporation Residential Funding Mortgage Securities) mortgage securitization program. The private market also competes for whole loans directly with the FNMA and FHLMC. EXHIBIT 9.1 outlines the general flow of mortgage credit through the U.S. markets. Again, securitization is primarily a source of liquidity.

Mortgage-backed pass-through securities received in exchange for mortgages naturally have a lower yield than the mortgages, because they are more liquid and they have been guaranteed with respect to the timely payment of interest and principal. Credit risk of the whole loan portfolio is assumed by the agency for a fee, and the bank that originated the loans continues to service the portfolio for a fee. Lenders offer consumers thirty-year fixed-rate mortgages, a relatively bulky and illiquid loan, at rates that reflect their ability to liquidate portfolios of these loans in the secondary market. Consumers thus benefit from the bank's access to the securities market. This process of swapping mortgage loans for MBSs is clearly stated by Hibernia Corporation in the following excerpt from its 2002 annual report.

> The Company securitized and retained $305,245,000 of its first residential mortgage loans with recourse provisions through the Federal National Mortgage Association (FNMA) during 2001. The loans were reclassified to investment securities. Investment securities resulting from mortgage loan securitizations had carrying values of $125,830,000 and $255,837,000 in securities available for sale at December 31, 2002, and 2001, respectively, and $140,525,000 and $249,884,000 in securities held to maturity at December 31, 2002, and 2001, respectively.

One example of the exchange of mortgages for guaranteed FNMA pass-through certificates is the sale by Hibernia National Bank of a pool of 417 fixed-rate mortgages to FNMA. These mortgages were then transferred by FNMA to a trust for securitization. The mortgages owned by the trust comprise FNMA pool number 617729. The trust financed the mortgage pool by issuing the FNMA-guaranteed mortgage pass-through certificates, CL-617729, CUSIP 31388XHE7. The pool balance at origination, July 1, 2002, was $46,240,645.33, according to the FNMA Prospectus Supplement. The security description is FNMS 06.0000 CL617729. (The 06.0000 represents the pass-through rate on the certificates.)

EXHIBIT 9.1

Flow of Mortgage Credit Through U.S. Markets

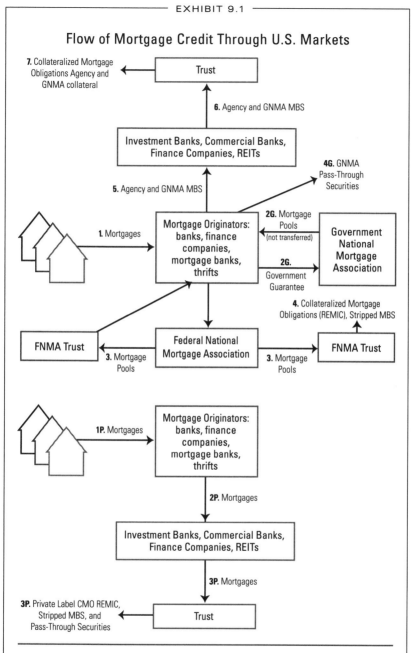

7. Collateralized Mortgage Obligations Agency and GNMA collateral ← Trust

6. Agency and GNMA MBS

Investment Banks, Commercial Banks, Finance Companies, REITs

4G. GNMA Pass-Through Securities

5. Agency and GNMA MBS

1. Mortgages → Mortgage Originators: banks, finance companies, mortgage banks, thrifts

2G. Mortgage Pools (not transferred)

Government National Mortgage Association

2G. Government Guarantee

4. Collateralized Mortgage Obligations (REMIC), Stripped MBS

FNMA Trust ← **3.** Mortgage Pools — Federal National Mortgage Association — **3.** Mortgage Pools → FNMA Trust

1P. Mortgages → Mortgage Originators: banks, finance companies, mortgage banks, thrifts

2P. Mortgages

Investment Banks, Commercial Banks, Finance Companies, REITs

3P. Mortgages

3P. Private Label CMO REMIC, Stripped MBS, and Pass-Through Securities ← Trust

The numbers modified by a "P" in the lower half of the diagram, i.e., "1P" marks the route of mortgages through the Private-label market. P stands for private-label. In the upper half of the diagram the number modified by "G" indicates the route for the creation of GNMA MBS. We only show FNMA but FHLMC operates in a similar and parallel way to FNMA. This is why we use the term Agency. Agency stands for both FHLMC and FNMA.

Source: Stone/Zissu

The average interest rate of the mortgage pool is 6.553 percent. The pass-through securities, or MBSs, issued by the trust represent beneficial interests in FNMA pool 617729. FNMA-guaranteed mortgage pass-through certificates are issued in minimum denominations of $1,000. Hibernia National Bank did not hold all of the beneficial interests in the pool that it received from FNMA in exchange for the mortgages. It sold at least some of the certificates. As of November 30, 2002, the Hyperion Strategic Mortgage Income Fund, Inc., had an investment in $3,418,000 (principal value) of FNMA guaranteed pass-through certificates, FNMS 06.0000 CL 617729 (beneficial interest in FNMA mortgage pool 617729).

In addition to the "single-class" MBSs, FNMA, via its Fannie Majors program, can pool mortgages from multiple mortgage lenders in a single securitization trust. Each lender receives a pro rata share of the beneficial interests issued by the FNMA trust. The beneficial interests are FNMA guaranteed pass-through certificates.

Three of the closed-end Hyperion funds that have exposure to the mortgage- and asset-backed markets are the Hyperion Investment Grade Opportunity Term Trust (see sample prospectus excerpt that follows), the Hyperion Total Return Fund, Inc., and the Hyperion Strategic Mortgage Income Fund. Shares of the funds trade on the New Stock Exchange under the symbols HTO, HTR, and HSM, respectively. Each fund has a different investment objective, and this translates into different MBS and ABS investments.

The Trust [HTO] is a closed-end investment company whose objectives are to provide a high level of current income consistent with investing only in investment-grade securities and to attempt to return $10 per share [the initial public offering price per share] to investors on, or shortly before, November 30, 2005. The Trust pursues these objectives by investing in a portfolio primarily of mortgage-backed securities (MBS), issued or guaranteed by either the U.S. Government or one of its agencies or instrumentalities, or rated "investment grade" by a nationally recognized rating agency (e.g., Standard & Poor's Corporation or Fitch Ratings, Inc.) at the time of the investment. No assurance can be given that the Trust's investment objectives will be achieved....

Though the economic outlook and prospect for corporate credit risk may be very dismal, some of the best places to invest are in high credit quality collateralized securities. Unlike unsecured corporate bonds, where the bondholders are a creditor of the corporation, collateralized securities have their interest secured by "tangible" assets—for example, residential and commercial real estate, consumer receivables, and automobiles.

The general strategy we have been pursuing for the portfolio has been to purchase securities that would exhibit lower sensitivities to prepayment risk. We purchased Agency residential pass-throughs that have, we believe, a tendency for slower prepayment activity. These securities are characterized by low mortgage balances that, due to the high relative fixed costs of refinancing, make them less attractive for borrowers to refinance.

The credit quality of the portfolio remains high—in excess of the requirements of the Trust's "AAf" rating. In fact, over 80 percent of the portfolio is in securities rated AA and higher.

As of June 30, 2002, the Trust was being managed with an average duration of 1.6 years, as measured on a net asset basis [duration measures a bond portfolio's price sensitivity to changes in interest rates]. The duration of total assets as of June 30, 2002, was 2.6 years.

The Trust utilizes leverage to enhance portfolio yield and total return. As of June 30, 2002, leverage represented 32.5 percent of total assets. (Hyperion 2005 Investment Grade Opportunity Term Trust, Semiannual Report, June 30, 2002). (See EXHIBIT **9.2**.)

Investing in credit risk that is based on a quantifiable variable offers an alternative to corporate bonds that are subject to events such as accounting irregularities or dilution. The private-label collateralized mortgage obligation (CMO) market is rich with opportunities, because each issue offers a wide range of possible risk profiles with respect to both prepayment risk and credit risk.

The Treasury market is segmented along the duration, coupon, and premium/discount spectrum; and the agency MBS market is further divided along the premium/discount, prepayment, and duration, coupon, and liquidity spectrum. When we say divided along the coupon spectrum, we are referring to the choice between floating, fixed, inverse-floating, zero, and inflation-indexed coupons. The additional

---

EXHIBIT 9.2

Three Hyperion Fixed Income Funds: Allocation of Assets

Investment in Securities Market value (may be estimated)
Leverage as measured by Reverse Repurchase Agreements divided by investments in Securities
U.S. Government Agency Collateralized Mortgage Obligations
U.S. Government Agency Pass-Through Certificates
U.S. Treasury Obligation
Asset-Backed Securities
Municipal Zero Coupon Securities
Commercial Mortgage-Backed Securities
Non-Agency Senior Collateralized Mortgage-Backed Securities 16.8%
Non-Agency Subordinate Collateralized Mortgage-Backed Securities
Non-Agency Collateralized Mortgage Obligations (REMICS)
Interest-Only Securities
Corporate Obligations/preferred stocks

---

prepayment dimension offers extended opportunities relative to the Treasury markets. Securitizations of mortgages through the private-label market require that credit risk of the mortgage pools be financed. This is typically done by having the trust issue series of securities that include mezzanine and subordinate securities. The credit risk embedded in private–label MBSs offers traders and fund managers a link between the corporate bond market and the MBS market.

Dime Savings Bank liquidates portions of its fixed-rate mortgage portfolio and invests in segments of the MBS market to modify the risks and liquidity of its balance sheet. This is common practice for managers of short-funded mortgage lenders.

HTO	FUNDS HTR	HSM
$257,915,043	$414,306,738	$209,495,788
33.17%	32.66%	32.58%
31.9%	9.8%	
29.3%	39.6%	75.4%
1.9%	1.2%	
7.7%	32.6% (26.5% housing related, 2% franchise receivables)	2.8% (nonhousing related)
6.1%		
19.9%	20.1%	17.4%
16.8%		
29.9%	35.4%	51%
0.3%		
5.6%	7.6%	
	4% / 1.3%	

Source: Semiannual Reports for the period ending June 30, 2002 for the Hyperion Investment Grade Opportunity Term Trust, the Hyperion Total Return Fund, and the Hyperion Strategic Mortgage Income Fund

Mortgage-Backed Securities. Mortgage-backed securities provide the portfolio with investments consisting of desirable repricing, cash flow, and credit quality characteristics. Mortgage-backed securities yield less than the loans that underlie the securities because of the cost of payment guarantees and credit enhancements that reduce credit risk to the investor. Although mortgage-backed securities guaranteed by federally sponsored agencies carry a reduced credit risk compared to whole loans, such securities remain subject to the risk that fluctuating interest rates, along with other factors such as the geographic distribution of the underlying mortgage loans, may alter the prepayment rate of such mortgage loans and thus affect both the prepayment speed and value of such securities. However, mortgage-backed securities are more liquid than individual mortgage loans and may readily be used to collateralize borrowings. In addition to its superior credit quality as a result of the agency guarantees, the mortgage-backed securities portfolio also provides the Holding Company and the Bank with important interest rate risk management features, as the majority of the portfolio is adjustable rate, and the entire portfolio provides monthly cash flows for reinvestment at current market interest rates.

The Company's consolidated investment in mortgage-backed securities totaled $291.5 million, or 10.4 percent of total assets, at June 30, 2002, the majority of which was owned by the Bank. Approximately 55.8 percent of the mortgage-backed securities portfolio was composed of securities guaranteed by GNMA, FHLMC, or FNMA. At June 30, 2002, the Bank had $213.6 million in Collateralized Mortgage Obligations ("CMOs") and Real Estate Mortgage Investment Conduits ("REMICs"), which comprised the largest component of its mortgage-backed securities portfolio. All of these CMOs and REMICs were either U.S. agency obligations or issued by highly reputable financial institutions. In addition, all of the non-agency-backed obligations were rated in the highest ratings category by at least one nationally recognized rating agency at the time of purchase. Further, none of these securities had stripped principal and interest components, and all occupied priority tranches within their respective issues. As of June 30, 2002, the fair value of these securities was approximately $4.1 million above their cost basis.

The remaining mortgage-backed securities portfolio was composed of a $57.5 million investment in ARM MBS pass-through securities with a weighted average term to next rate adjustment of less than one year, a $17.9 million investment in seasoned fixed-rate GNMA, FNMA, and FHLMC pass-through securities with an estimated remaining life of less than three years, and a $2.5 million investment in balloon-mortgage-backed securities, which provide a return of principal and interest on a monthly basis, and have original maturities of between five and seven years, at which point the entire remaining principal balance is repaid (the "Balloon Payment Securities").

The maturities on the Bank's fixed-rate mortgage-backed securities (Balloon Payment Securities, seasoned GNMAs, FNMAs, and FHLMCs) are relatively short compared to the final maturities on its ARM MBS and CMO portfolios. The Bank typically classifies purchased MBS and CMOs as available for sale, in recognition of the greater prepayment uncertainty associated with these securities, and carries these securities at fair market value. (Dime Community Bancshares, Inc., Form 10-K for the fiscal year ended June 30, 2002)

The combined size of the mortgage- and asset-backed market is nearly twice the size of the $3.3 trillion U.S. government debt market. The corporate debt market stands at $4.1 trillion. Of the $7.33 trillion of assets on the balance sheets of U.S. commercial banks as of mid-2003, 5.95 percent was composed of ABSs and 11.91 percent consisted of MBSs, according to the Federal Reserve's Bank Credit File Series and the Bond Market Association. The following Bank of New York 10-K excerpt exemplifies this breadth:

> As of 12/31/02 the $18.028 billion fixed-income portion of Bank of New York portfolio was composed of 56.7 percent mortgage–backed securities and 16 percent asset-backed securities. Banks classify their securities as either held for sale or held to maturity. Loans that a bank intends to securitize would be classified as held for sale. (The Bank of New York Company, Inc., Form 10-K for the period ending December 31, 2002)

The investment-grade segment of the mortgage- and asset-backed market (BBB and above) is more visible than the sub-investment-grade market. It is considerably larger, and the securities in the investment-grade sector are bought by pension funds, mutual funds, and commercial banks, which file detailed reports to the SEC that reveal their holdings. Mutual funds also buy the subordinate classes of MBS and ABS series. Private investment companies do not report detailed information about their holdings, and these often include the riskier tranches—in both credit and prepayment risk—of the MBS and ABS market.

The bulk of the $6.44 trillion MBS and ABS market—$4.66 trillion —consists of AAA MBSs, such as pass-throughs and REMIC CMOs guaranteed by GNMA, FNMA, or FHLMC. Therefore, approximately 72 percent of the MBS and ABS market is an AAA market. If we separate the mortgage-backed from the asset-backed market, 96 percent of the MBS market is AAA rated due to government or agency guarantees.

Subordinate Segment of Private-Label MBSs

SUB-INVESTMENT-GRADE classes of both the asset- and mortgage-backed markets are generally bought by private investment funds or specialized mutual funds or retained by the entity that sells the asset pool to the securitization vehicle. To give an idea of the size of the sub-investment-grade market in MBSs, we looked at a few private-label REMIC pass-through security transactions and found that only about 0.4 percent of pool principal was funded with unrated or below-investment-grade securities (subordinate classes), and about 2.1 percent of the pool was funded with securities rated below AAA but within the investment-grade segment (mezzanine classes).

For example, Residential Funding Mortgage Securities Inc. securitized 978 fixed-rate mortgages that had a principal value of $410,977,069 through the RFMSI Series 2000-3-S10 Trust. Seventeen classes of securities were issued by the trust. Fourteen of the classes were distributed to the public, and three classes, B1, B2, and B3, were privately placed. Class B1 was rated BB, class B2 was rated single B, and class B3 was unrated. The three subordinate classes financed 0.4 percent of the mortgage pool.

The same figures can be calculated from the summary of Banc of America Funding Corporation's mortgage pass-through certificates, series 2003-1 (see EXHIBIT **9.3**). The $1,015,681,968 mortgage pool was funded with a series that was composed of senior, mezzanine, and subordinate classes of securities. The senior classes, rated AAA, funded 97.45 percent of the mortgage pool. The mezzanine securities funded 2.1 percent, and the subordinate (sub-investment-grade) funded just 0.45 percent of the pool.

If we project the numbers found by looking at a few private-label MBS transactions to the entire $186 billion private-label market, then about 97 percent of this market is AAA rated at issue, and about 2.75 percent is below AAA but investment grade, while the 0.45 percent is either not rated or issued below investment grade. These estimates are obviously very rough—for one thing, they do not take into account credit downgrades or, for that matter, upgrades, or the fact that the level of subordination will not be constant across the economic cycle.

The numbers are only meant to indicate the magnitude of the subordinate segment of the private-label MBS market. If applied to the outstanding stock of private-label MBSs, the numbers would suggest a figure of approximately $1 billion. Perhaps the estimate is more applicable to the flow of new securities into the market than to the stock of outstanding securities, since subordination levels fluctuate over time due to expectations about the rate and timing of mortgagor defaults. Applying the 0.45 percent estimate to the $100.7 billion in new private-label residential MBSs issued in 2002 places the value of below-investment-grade and unrated subordinate classes issued at $453.1 million.

Of course, the guarantees that FNMA, FHLMC, and GNMA supply must be financed. It is incorrect to simply say the credit risks of the agency MBS market have been eliminated. These risks are being financed in the agency debt market and the U.S. government Treasury market.

Ford Credit Auto Owner Trust securitizations of retail installment contracts typically issue one sub-investment-grade class that is retained by the seller. This is class D in the Ford Motor Credit transaction discussed in Chapter 5. This subordinate class is designed to absorb a multiple of expected losses and is itself protected by reserve accounts established by the seller and owned by the securitization trust.

While the original subordination in both mortgage- and asset-backed securities is a small percent of the amount financed at AAA credit ratings, there are three important points to keep in mind. First, as the senior classes in the sequence are retired, the subordination increases as a percent of the outstanding pool. Second, subordinated securities amortize more slowly than the senior classes, often not receiving any principal at all during the first years after issue (the lockout period). Third, the level of subordination is generally sufficient to protect the senior classes.

Consider GMAC-RFC, which securitizes its fixed-rate mortgage originations through its RFMSI program. Fitch Ratings analyzes the RFMSI securitization program of GMAC-RFC, and between 1992 and 2002 RFMSI issued 1,025 mortgage-backed securities to finance $113.6 billion of mortgages.[1] The cumulative loss rates on the mortgage pools securitized by RFMSI since 1996, when Fitch began rating the issues of RFMSI, have never exceeded Fitch's loss

EXHIBIT 9.3

Banc of America Funding Corporation, Mortgage Pass-Through Certificates, Series 2003-1

CLASS	INITIAL CLASS BALANCE (1)	PASS-THROUGH RATE	PRINCIPAL TYPES (2)
Offered Certificates			
Class A-1	$993,910,000	6.000%	Senior, Pass-Through
Class A-R	$100	6.000%	Senior, Sequential Pay
Class A-WIO	(4)	(5)	Senior, Notional Amount
Class A-PO	$345,868	(6)	Senior, Ratio Strip
Class B-1	$13,264,000	6.000%	Subordinated
Class B-2	$4,591,000	6.000%	Subordinated
Class B-3	$3,571,000	6.000%	Subordinated
Non-Offered Certificates			
Class B-4	$1,531,000	6.000%	Subordinated
Class B-5	$1,530,000	6.000%	Subordinated
Class B-6	$1,530,828	6.000%	Subordinated

(1) Approximate. The initial class balance of the Offered Certificates may vary by a total of plus or minus 5%.

(2) See "Description of the Certificates—Categories of Classes of Certificates" in the Prospectus for a description of these principal and interest types, and see "Description of the Certificates—Priority of Distributions" and "Allocation of Losses" in this Prospectus Supplement for a description of the effects of subordination.

(3) See "Certificate Ratings" in this Prospectus Supplement. The Depositor has requested ratings of the Class B Certificates only from Standard & Poor's, a division of The McGraw-Hill Companies, Inc.

(4) The Class A-WIO Certificates are Interest-Only Certificates, have no principal balance, and will bear interest on the Class A-WIO Notional Amount (initially

allowance for the single-B rating category. Included in EXHIBIT **9.4** is the summary of the transition matrix for RFMSI securitizations that is presented by Fitch in its June 2002 Residential Mortgage Special Report, "GMCA-RFMSI Securitization Performance."

The CMO market offers a vast investment choice to fund managers. Because of the fine tranching of prepayment risk and the use of support as well as planned and targeted amortization classes, it is pos-

| INTEREST TYPES (2) | INITIAL RATING OF CERTIFICATES (3) | |
	MOODY	S&P
Fixed Rate	Aaa	AAA
Fixed Rate	None	AAA
Variable Rate, Interest Only	Aaa	AAA
Principal Only	Aaa	AAA
Fixed Rate	None	AA
Fixed Rate	None	A
Fixed Rate	None	BBB
Fixed Rate	N/A	N/A
Fixed Rate	N/A	N/A
Fixed Rate	N/A	N/A

approximately $1,013,444,166) as described in this Prospectus Supplement under "Description of the Certificates—Interest."

(5) Interest will accrue on the Class A-WIO Notional Amount as of any Distribution Date at a per annum rate equal to (i) the weighted average of the Net Mortgage Interest Rates of the Premium Mortgage Loans (based on the Stated Principal Balances of the Premium Mortgage Loans on the due date in the month preceding the month of such Distribution Date) minus (ii) 6.000%. For the initial Distribution Date occurring in May 2003, this rate is expected to be approximately 0.54677% per annum.

(6) The Class A-PO Certificates are Principal-Only Certificates and will not be entitled to distributions in respect of interest.

Source: Banc of America Funding Corporation

sible to take well-calculated bets on prepayment speeds and therefore yields. Credit risk is leveraged onto subordinate classes or funded by guarantors like FNMA, FHLMC, or GNMA.

EXHIBIT 9.5 illustrates that two funds managed with different investment objectives (liquidity, duration, yield, and credit risk) will have different positions not only in terms of their total exposure to the mortgage-backed market and to the various segments of the mar-

EXHIBIT 9.4

Residential Funding Mortgage Securities I, Inc.
Fitch Ratings Transitions Summary 1992–2002

RATING	UPGRADED (%)	DOWNGRADED (%)
AAA	Not applicable	0.00
AA	58.09	0.00
A	55.65	0.00
BBB	56.59	0.00
BB	50.81	0.81
B	43.59	0.85

Source: Fitch Ratings June 2002, Residential Mortgage Special Report, GMCA-RFMSI Securitization Performance, www.FitchRatings.com

ket (see exhibit 9.2) but also within a single market sector. The CMO market thrives because the demand for various risk/reward is quite varied and can be satisfied with the various CMO tranches carved out of a pool of mortgages. Exhibit 9.5 presents the exposure of two Hyperion funds to the FHLMC REMIC segment of the MBS market to make this point. Keep in mind that only one subsegment is compared across the two funds. FNMA securities or private-label securities also provide the same types of investment plays as the FHLMC REMIC market.

Inverse floaters are securities that are created when floating-rate MBSs are issued to fund a pool of fixed-rate mortgages. The risk of funding a pool of fixed-rate mortgages with floating-rate liabilities is offset by creating a class of MBSs that floats inversely to interest rates. In this way an increase in the yield on the floating-rate class is offset or hedged by a decrease in the yield on the inverse floater. In hindsight we can certainly see why inverse floaters were the right bet for a fixed-income fund over the period from 2000 to 2004, but the fact that they are support classes complicates the investment decision. While the inverse floater provides a hedge against a fall in interest rates or a bet that interests will fall, they are also sensitive to prepayment rates. Support classes are designed to bear the brunt of the prepayment risk that stems from the rate at which the underlying mortgage collateral is refinanced. A fall in interest rates that increases the yield on inverse floaters that are structured as a support class

Source: The Hyperion Total Return Fund, Inc. and the Hyperion Investment Grade Opportunity Fund, Inc. Annual Reports for the period ending November 30, 2002

—————— EXHIBIT 9.5 ——————

Freddie Mac REMIC Investments as of November 30, 2002

Hyperion Total Return Fund Inc.

ISSUER	SERIES	CLASS	TYPE	STATED MATURITY	WAL AT ISSUE FOR PREPAYMENT RANGE 0%–500% PSA
FHLMC	2050	PG	100%–250% PSA PAC	2/15/23	11–5.3
FHLMC	2369	A	SEQ	7/15/28	18–2.2
FHLMC	2149	TF	100%–250% PSA PAC	5/15/24	19.6–4.5
FHLMC	2187	QA	Pass-through Inverse floater	5/15/29	19.3–2

Hyperion Investment Grade Opportunity Fund Inc.

ISSUER	SERIES	CLASS	TYPE	STATED MATURITY	WAL AT ISSUE FOR PREPAYMENT RANGE 0%–450% PSA
FHLMC	1675	KC	Accretion directed	10/15/10	13.8–11.1 0–500% PSA
FHLMC	1659	SD	Support / Inverse floater	1/15/09	14.7–0.9 0–450% PSA
FHLMC	1565	L	Support/ Inverse floater	8/15/08	14.7–0.8 0–450% PSA
FHLMC	1604	MC	Support/ Inverse floater	11/15/08	14.3–1.1 0–600% PSA
FHLMC	1604	SB	Support/ Inverse floater	11/15/08	14.3–1.1 0–600% PSA
FHLMC	1587	SK	Support/ Inverse floater	10/15/08	14.8–0.7 0–450% PSA
FHLMC	1587	SF	Support/ Inverse floater	5/15/08	13.7–1.6 0–450% PSA

EXHIBIT 9.6

The MBS and ABS Exposure of
Three Different Intermediate Bond Funds

12/31/04	ASSET-BACKED SECURITIES	CORPORATE BONDS INVESTMENT GRADE	SHORT-TERM CORPORATE, AGENCY, AND CDS
The Regions Morgan Keegan Select Intermediate Bond Fund 12/31/02	73% (includes commercial mortgage-backed securities)	16.5%	
SSgA Intermediate Fund 2/28/03	3.9%	31%	
Intermediate Bond Fund of America 2/28/03	16.6% (includes Commercial MBS)	19.2%	15.39%
Intermediate Bond Fund of America 8/31/97	15.16%	6.18%	5.84

within a CMO will also pay down faster if the decline in interest rates accelerates the prepayment rate on the underlying mortgages. If the securities were purchased at a premium, their yield as principal is returned to the investor at a faster rate than would occur in a slower prepayment scenario.

It is also interesting to compare the mortgage- and asset-backed investments of two funds with similar objectives or the same benchmark index, for example, the Lehman Brothers Intermediate

MORTGAGE-BACKED SECURITIES	PREFERRED STOCKS	INTERNATIONAL DEBT	US GOVERNMENT AGENCIES	US GOVERNMENT TREASURIES	EURODOLLAR TIME DEPOSITS
3.2%	0.9%				5.9%
7.1% (includes commercial mortgage-backed securities)		7.5%	19.5%	31.8%	
30.68%			6.5%	17.5%	
46.36%	2.15%	27% $$ denominated foreign government debt	22%		

Source: Regions Morgan Keegan Select Funds, Semiannual Report, December 31, 2001; SSgA Funds, Semiannual Report, February 28, 2003; Intermediate Bond Fund of America, Semiannual Report, February 28, 2003

Aggregate Index.[2] EXHIBIT **9.6** compares the exposures to various segments of the mortgage- and asset-backed markets for three intermediate bond funds. "Intermediate" is a very general term, as can be seen from the objectives of the funds and, more strikingly, from their respective investments. Within the scope of intermediate funds that seek to preserve capital there are a number of parameters that can be changed without violating the intermediate maturity and capital preservation objectives. Not only do their relative exposures to the mortgage- and asset-backed markets and their exposures to the sub-segments of the market (REMIC, IO, pass-through, private label, agency, home equity, auto, subordinate, mezzanine, senior) differ, but within each segment the securities chosen will differ due to the analysis driving the investment decisions.

Not all AAA-rated classes of an asset-backed security are equivalent. Securities depend on the specifics of the underlying collateral and their position relative to the other securities in the series. This is not to say that similar securities cannot be compared. If they couldn't, trading would not be possible. It is clearly easier to compare inverse floaters created as part of FHLMC REMICS that are collateralized by similar pass-through securities than to compare inverse floaters across market segments, such as private-label to agency. More difficult comparisons, while more costly, also offer more opportunities.

The Regions Morgan Keegan Select Intermediate Bond Fund seeks to provide a high level of income by investing in intermediate-maturity, investment-grade bonds. The fund seeks capital growth as a secondary objective when consistent with the fund's primary objective. The fund targets investment-grade debt securities with effective maturities between one and ten years. (Regions Morgan Keegan Select Funds, Semiannual Report, December 31, 2002)

The SSgA Intermediate Fund seeks a high level of current income while preserving principal by investing primarily in a diversified portfolio of debt securities with a dollar-weighted average maturity between three and ten years. (SSgA Funds, Semiannual Report, February 28, 2003)

Intermediate Bond Fund of America seeks to earn current income, consistent with preservation of capital, by investing primarily in fixed-income securities with an average effective maturity of no more than five years and with quality ratings of A or better (as rated by Standard & Poor's Corporation or Moody's Investors Service) or equivalent unrated securities. The fund's investments include U.S. government and federal agency securities; pass-through securities, such as mortgage- and asset-backed securities; and high-quality corporate obligations. (Intermediate Bond Fund of America, Semiannual Report, February 28, 2003)

Source: Intermediate Bond Fund of America, Semiannual Report, August 31, 1997 and February 28, 2003

EXHIBIT 9.7

CMO Investments of the Bond Fund of America at August 31, 1997 and February 28, 2002

	INTERMEDIATE BOND FUND OF AMERICA 2/28/03	INTERMEDIATE BOND FUND OF AMERICA 8/31/97
Federal Agency Pass-Through Certificates	25.84%	28.77%
Federal Agency CMO	3.36%	5.64%
Commercial Mortgage-Backed Security	5.39%	
Private-Label CMO	1.48%	11.45%

Striking about this comparison of intermediate bond funds is the absolute and relative concentration of the Morgan Keegan fund in the asset-backed market. Clearly, the managers have chosen this market over the corporate bond market and the MBS market, while the Intermediate Bond Fund of America has taken a heavier position in the MBS market. This is what makes horse races.

It is also important to keep in mind that managers trade their asset holdings as market conditions change and as their expectations regarding the future change. The same fund compared across time will reveal different investments in securities. Within the MBS and ABS market, positions are revised with respect to prepayment risk exposure, asset class and credit risk, duration, and convexity. For example, compare the holdings of the Bond Fund of America at August 31, 1997, and February 28, 2002 (the last two rows of exhibit 9.6) and the fund's exposure to the CMO market on these same two dates (see **EXHIBIT 9.7**). Again, asset allocations do not reveal as much about the mortgage- and asset-backed market as the classes and structure of securities held do.

Private pension funds and state and local retirement funds have liabilities to the household sector of $8.014 trillion. Of this amount $1.56 trillion was held in the form of credit market securities (this excludes corporate equities and mutual fund shares). Narrowing it down to investments in "agency securities," the amount at the end of 2002 was $430 billion. Agency securities include GNMA, FNMA, and FHLMC pass-through securities and REMICs. This compares to investments in corporate and foreign bonds of $723 billion.

The market value of the investments of the California Public Employees Retirement System (CalPERS) as of April 30, 2003, was $137.8 billion, of which 10.16 percent was invested in MBSs and ABSs. Of the total market value, $39 billion was invested in fixed-income securities. Approximately 35 percent of the fixed-income portfolio was invested in mortgage- and asset-backed securities. CalPERS' fixed-income portfolio is managed to exceed the return of the Salomon Smith Barney Large Pension Fund Index (LPF). CalPERS uses the following risk parameters to constrain the composition of the portfolio: credit, benchmark, interest-rate, yield-curve, convexity, sector, structure, reinvestment, liquidity, and currency risks. Structure risk, described in the following excerpt, is particularly relevant to the mortgage- and asset-backed market.

> Structure Risk arises from the options implicit in bonds (e.g., callable and optional sinking fund bonds) or the rules governing cash flow that differs from expectations. Structure risk shall be managed using option-adjusted and scenario analysis as well as prepayment variability analysis on CMOs. (CalPERS Statement of Investment Policy for Dollar-Denominated Fixed Income Program)

EXHIBIT 9.8 presents the view of CalPERS toward the system's investment in CMOs.

CalPERS has set the sector range for mortgage- and asset-backed securities at 10 percent to 60 percent of the fixed-income portfolio. The Citigroup Large Pension Fund (LPF) index gives this sector a 30 percent weight.

The minimum rating for an MBS or ABS bought by the fund is A. A maximum of 3 percent of the fixed-income portfolio can be composed of leveraged MBSs. A typical example of leveraged MBSs securities is inverse floaters.

CalPERS manages two short-term fixed-income funds that can be tapped as assets by other CalPERS funds that are seeking relatively liquid short-duration portfolios that earn enhanced returns relative to

EXHIBIT 9.8

Collateralized Mortgage Obligations (CMOs)

1. Philosophy

CMOs are considered an important strategic tool for fixed-income management. They segregate mortgage cash flows into instruments with different risk/return characteristics than the underlying mortgage pools. These instruments shall be purchased when valuations indicate a superior return versus other securities in the fixed-income universe. Selected instruments shall generally exhibit positive convexity and superior call protection versus conventional mortgages. They shall only be purchased after performing the appropriate scenario, break-even, option adjusted, implied duration, and cash flow analyses.

2. Purpose

Use of CMOs shall enhance return opportunities and manage risk at appropriate valuation levels while exercising prudence. (CalPERS, 2002)

their benchmarks. The two funds are the High Quality Libor Fund (HQL) and the Short Duration Fund (SDF). Both funds are indexed to the PERS Custom Daily Libor Index.

The HQL fund is managed to "slightly exceed" the returns on the PERS Custom Daily Libor Index, whereas the SDF is managed to "moderately exceed" the same index.

Both funds are managed within a set of constraints that include, but are not limited to, maximum option-adjusted duration of the portfolio, minimum credit rating for investments, maximum sector concentrations, and maximum exposure to counter parties.

The maximum option-adjusted duration of the HQL fund is 90 days, and that of the SDF is 180 days.

The HQL Fund exposure to a single issuer of AAA-rated fixed-rate asset-backed securities that have a maturity of greater than one day cannot compose more than 5 percent of the portfolio, and the fixed-rate asset-backed segment of the portfolio that has maturities greater than one day cannot compose more than 20 percent of the fund's assets.

> It is also expected that floating-rate asset-backed securities will represent a majority of the SDF's assets, but the credit rating will not be limited to AAA. (California Public Employees Retirement System of Investment Policy for Dollar-Denominated Fixed-Income Short-Duration Investment Policy, June 13, 2003)

The minimum credit rating of the MBSs and ABSs held by the HQL fund is AAA.

Prohibited investments within the mortgage- and asset-backed universe are inverse floaters, CMOs, home equity asset-backed securities, manufactured housing home asset-backed securities, and cost of fund index floating-rate securities (or any securities whose interest reset period significantly lags short-term interest rates).

The SDF fund is able to invest in non-AAA-rated mortgage- and asset-backed securities. Within the permitted AAA asset-backed sector there is a 75 percent limit to the SDF's exposure to each of the following asset classes: credit card, auto, and student loans. For other classes of allowable AAA-rated asset-backed securities, the fund's exposure is capped at 20 percent for each asset class. For the non-AAA-rated segment of the asset-backed market that is permitted (credit card, auto, stranded assets, real estate–based, equipment, recreational vehicles, and student loans), each asset class is restricted to 10 percent of the fund's assets. There is an overall 50 percent restriction on non-AAA-rated securities. The minimum credit rating that is permitted on asset-backed securities owned by the SDF fund is Baa2/BBB.

In general the restrictions on the SDF fund are not as tight as those on the HQL fund. The looser restrictions allow the SDF fund to be managed to "moderately exceed" its benchmark rather than "slightly exceed" it, as is the case for the HQL fund. The SDF is permitted broader and deeper exposure to the mortgage- and asset-backed market than the HQL fund. Like the HQL fund, the SDF is not permitted to invest in CMOs.

Life insurance companies are significant investors in mortgage-backed securities. At the end of 2002, life insurance companies held $312.9 billion of agency securities, which include FNMA, FHLMC, and GNMA MBSs and $249.4 billion of mortgages, which include whole loans as well as private-label MBSs. For asset/liability purposes, MBSs are liquid securities with a wide range of duration choices that offer sufficient yields to cover the value of insurance liabilities.

As an example we looked at AIG SunAmerica Life Assurance Company. Mortgage-backed securities accounted for 21.5 percent of the company's $7.19 billion investment portfolio.

> As part of its asset/liability matching discipline, the Company conducts detailed computer simulations that model its fixed-rate assets and liabilities under commonly used stress-test interest-rate scenarios. With the results of these computer simulations, the Company can measure the potential gain or loss in fair value of its interest-rate-sensitive instruments and seek to protect its economic value and achieve a predictable spread between what it earns on its invested assets and what it pays on its liabilities by designing its fixed-rate products and conducting its investment operations to closely match the duration of the fixed-rate assets to that of its fixed-rate liabilities. The Company's fixed-rate assets include: cash and short-term investments, bonds, notes and redeemable preferred stocks, mortgage loans, policy loans, and investments in limited partnerships that invest primarily in fixed-rate securities. At December 31, 2002, these assets had an aggregate fair value of $7.19 billion with a duration of 3.8.... The Company's fixed-rate liabilities include fixed-annuity, universal life, and GIC reserves. At December 31, 2002, these liabilities had an aggregate fair value (determined by discounting future contractual cash flows by related market rates of interest) of $6.47 billion with a duration of 3.8. (AIG SunAmerica Life Assurance Co., Form 10-K, for the fiscal year ended December 31, 2002)

At the end of 1995 real estate investment trusts (REITs) owned $14.1 billion in mortgage assets. By the end of 2002 REITs owned $28.3 billion of mortgage assets that were composed of single-family (17.4 percent), multifamily (0.8 percent), and commercial mortgages (7.5 percent), according to the U.S. Flow of Funds Accounts.

Following is a summary of two REITs, Apex Mortgage Capital Inc., the shares of which trade on the New York Stock Exchange (NYSE) under the symbol AXM, and Anthracite Capital Inc., which trades on the NYSE under the symbol AHR. REITs attempt to create value for their shareholders through a dividend yield that is sufficient to finance and service their capital structure. If the dividend yield is not sufficient, capital will run out of the REIT, and its portfolio will necessarily be liquidated. Using leverage to generate the necessary dividend yield is an economic, not legal, constraint. Apex has a target leverage ratio (debt/assets) of 92 percent.

Apex invests primarily in mortgage-backed securities that are backed by either adjustable-rate (0.38 percent) or fixed-rate mortgages (99.61 percent, on December 31, 2002). Other fixed-income securities composed 0.1 percent of the portfolio. These securities may be agency pass-throughs or CMOs or private-label MBSs. The private-label MBSs may be senior or subordinate class. Subordinate classes of MBSs—along with leveraged MBSs, such as interest-only and principal-only strips, inverse floaters, and lines of credit to mortgage warehouse facilities—are part of what Apex refers to as "other mortgage securities." This portion of its assets is capped by management at 10 percent of total mortgage-related assets. When measured at par value, agency pass-through securities made up 98.98 percent of Apex's holdings of fixed-income securities on December 31, 2002, and AAA-rated CMO securities comprised 0.53 percent. The carry values and percentages of three investment categories of Anthracite Capital Inc. as of December 31, 2002, were: commercial real estate securities ($894 million), 36.1 percent; commercial real estate loans ($74 million), 3 percent; and residential mortgage-backed securities ($1.5 billion), 60.9 percent. Anthracite invests in the entire credit spectrum of commercial MBSs, concentrating those investments in the sub-investment-grade classes (rated BB+ or less). When it invests in commercial MBSs below investment grade that are in the first-loss position relative to the other classes of securities issued by the trust, Anthracite acquires a majority of the first-loss position—the controlling interest in the trust—which assures it of the right to control the work-out process, which includes appointing a special servicer. The responsibilities of the special servicer include advancing funds to the trust to fill in temporary liquidity problems and managing the loan loss mitigation process when necessary.

The $330.2 billion of federally related mortgage pools securitized in 2003 and the $259.8 billion of asset-backed securities issued in the United States in 2003 (Flow of Funds Accounts of the U.S. Board of Governors of The Federal Reserve) were purchased because they offered value to investors relative to other fixed-income securities. Managers of fixed-income portfolios compete for the discovery of value, and it is this competition that drives the prices for pass-through securities, collateralized mortgage obligations, and the myriad tranches of asset-backed securities to market clearing levels. Arbitrageurs in the market who are in constant search of securities that are inconsistently priced pull and push values through their trading activity back to what is considered fair value by investors.

Managers of fixed-income portfolios price prospective investments off of the Treasury yield curve. Segments of the mortgage- and asset-backed securities market that satisfy the general credit and liquidity criteria of a fixed-income manager will be searched for value relative to the comparable Treasury securities and prospective investments securities in other market segments that satisfy the manager's general investment criteria.

Since the market for asset- and mortgage-backed securities covers the entire credit duration and convexity spectrums, the market appeals to a broad range of investors from money market funds to pension funds to high-yield portfolios and hedge funds. Federally related mortgage-backed securities and asset-backed securities represented approximately 54 percent of total financial sector credit outstanding in 2003 according to the U.S. Flow of Funds Accounts of the United States. (Table L.3 in the 2004 Flow of Funds Accounts)

Managers of fixed-income funds construct and run their portfolios to track or exceed the performance of an index composed of a sector or subsector of the fixed-income market. For example, the Lehman Aggregate Index is designed to measure the performance of the U.S. investment-grade fixed-rate bond market, and The Lehman Mortgage Index is designed to measure the performance of mortgage-backed pass-through market. Neither of the indices can purchase directly but can be used as benchmarks for fund managers. One manager may allocate funds to planned amortization classes of private-label REMICs rather than the pass-through market. Another manager may sell pass-throughs and purchase principal-only strips. The pass-through market is the core of the MBS market, and managers trying to outperform this market will do so by reallocating funds from the pass-through market to other segments of the MBS market.

Securitization offers value to companies that need to refinance pools of financial assets because it offers an alternative to the route of the firm's balance sheet to the capital markets. The only way that securitization can offer value to the securitizer is if the MBS and ABS issued in the securitization process offer value to investors. Securitization is flexible enough that the design of MBS and ABS can be tailored to meet the needs of investors with different objectives and expectations regarding default rates, interest rates, and prepayment rates. Value is offered to investors by creating securities that fill their needs. Securitization is used to distill and reallocate the value embedded in pools of mortgages, auto loans, dealer floor plan loans, credit card receivables, and an array of other finance receivables. Financial engineers working with traders and salespeople create classes of securities to satisfy demand.

> The Company divides its below-investment-grade CMBS [commercial MBS] investment activity into two portfolios, Controlling Class CMBS and other below-investment-grade CMBS. The distinction between the two is in the controlling class rights. Controlling class rights allow the Company to control the work out and/or disposition of defaults that occur in the underlying loans. These securities absorb the first losses realized in the underlying loan pools. Other below-investment-grade CMBS have no right to control the work out and/or disposition of underlying loan defaults; however, they are not the first to absorb losses in the underlying pools. (Anthracite Capital, Inc., 10-K, December 31, 2002)

Interest-Rate Risk

MANY COMPANIES, from insurance companies to mutual funds, manage interest-rate risk by setting duration targets, or specific objectives regarding the price sensitivity of a fixed-income security to changes in interest rates. One approach to creating a portfolio with a specific duration target is to invest in planned amortization classes (PACs), the features of which are described in Chapter 4. A PAC is structured such that within a specified constant prepayment rate (CPR) range, the cash flows (interest and principal) are known ahead of time and are not affected by fluctuations in prepayment rates, allowing the duration target to be met.

An investor in MBSs whose goal is to have a portfolio with zero duration can take a short position in Treasuries. When rates increase, the value of the MBSs decreases because of the discount effect, whereas the value of the short position in Treasuries increases, off-setting the decrease in MBS value.

Reinvestment of Cash Flow

Chapter 3 discusses the differences between corporate bonds and pass-through securities. Typically, a corporate bond (or government bond) pays a semiannual coupon (interest only) and the total principal amount at maturity. A pass-through security pays interest and some principal every month. As discussed in Chapter 3, the investor in the pass-through security therefore must deal with reinvestment issues each month, for both the interest and principal received.

A sequential-pay structure can redistribute the prepayment risk and the reinvestment risk among the different classes. In an A-B-C-D structure, for example, where all principal from the underlying asset is first allocated to class A and subsequently to classes B, C, and D, the prepayment risk is first absorbed by class A. As market rates decrease, mortgagors increase their prepayment, and investors in class A receive their principal sooner than expected, exposing them to the risk of having to reinvest it at a lower market rate. The investors in class A will demand a higher spread above Treasuries to compensate for the prepayment/reinvestment risk they have taken.

As noted above, investors who want to avoid prepayment risk could purchase PACs. However, some reinvestment risk still exists in PACs, and those investors trying to avoid this risk entirely should invest in Z-bonds. Z-bonds, unlike corporate bonds or pass-through securities, pay no interest or principal as long as other classes are outstanding. The interest due on the Z-bonds accrues and is paid, together with its principal, after all other classes are paid. A Z-bond is purchased at discount, like a zero-coupon bond.

Of course, investors seeking higher yields will choose classes with greater prepayment and reinvestment risk.

Investors expecting lower market rates, and therefore higher prepayment rates, may invest in principal-only (PO) securities. The amount of principal to be received is independent of prepayment rate, but the period over which it is paid to the investor is a function of the prepayment speed. The faster the prepayment speed, the sooner the principal is paid to the investor and the sooner he can reinvest it. On the other hand, when the prepayment rate is low, investors receive and are able to reinvest the principal more slowly, and they are faced with an "opportunity cost" for missed investment possibilities while their money is tied up in the PO.

Interest-Only Strips as a Hedging Tool

For those investors whose goal is to invest in a portfolio partially hedged against interest-rate risk, interest-only (IO) securities can be a useful tool. Chapter 3 reviews how the value of bonds decreases with the increase in market rates, and how the value of IO securities first increases and, after reaching a maximum, starts to decrease when market yields increase. Following is a portfolio that satisfies the investor seeking an interest-rate hedge, one created by combining bonds and IOs.

Combining Bonds and IOs
The bonds for the hedged portfolio have the following characteristics. (For more details in how to value a bond, see Chapter 3.)

Bond XXX
Face value = $100,000
Coupon rate = 10%
Coupon = $10,000
Number of years to maturity (n) = 30
k = discount rate
V = value (see Exhibit **9.9**)

The IO strips for the hedged portfolio are derived from 9.5 percent FNMA pass-through securities backed by a pool of one hundred fixed-rate mortgages with a 10 percent weighted average coupon (WAC), and each with a $100,000 original balance, amortizing over a period of thirty years.

EXHIBIT 9.9

Price/Yield Relationship for Bond XXX

k	V
5%	$176,862.26
6%	$155,059.32
7%	$137,227.12
8%	$122,515.57
9%	$110,273.65
10%	$100,000.00
11%	$91,306.21
12%	$83,889.63
13%	$77,513.04
14%	$71,989.34
15%	$67,170.10

Source: Stone/Zissu

Let's say that Institution ZZ has $4,741,700 to invest. Institution ZZ is presented with two possible investments:

1   $4,741,700 in bonds with 9 percent yield (this amounts to forty-three XXX bonds); or

2   $4,741,700 in the described IO securities, with 9 percent yield.

Institution ZZ looks at the values of those bonds and IO securities under different prepayment/yield scenarios, shown in EXHIBIT **9.10** and graphed in EXHIBIT **9.11**.

Institution ZZ realizes how vulnerable it is to changes in market rates. By investing the $4,741,700 in bonds, it would benefit only from decreases in market rates, while by investing that same amount in IO securities, it would benefit from increases in market rates up to 14 percent, after which it would observe a decrease in the investment value.

For the 5 percent to 15 percent market-rate range, the portfolio in 100 percent bonds has a minimum value of $2,888,314.88 and a maximum value of $7,605,076.97, while the portfolio in 100 percent IOs has a minimum value of $2,673,037.00 and a maximum value of $6,500,172.00.

EXHIBIT 9.10

Alternative Prepayment/Yield Scenarios

CPR	k	V (IO)	V (BOND)
30%	5%	$2,673,037.00	$7,605,076.97
25%	6%	$3,005,091.00	$6,667,550.96
20%	7%	$3,428,711.00	$5,900,766.31
15%	8%	$3,985,186.00	$5,268,169.37
10%	9%	$4,741,685.00	$4,741,767.12
7%	10%	$5,224,437.00	$4,300,000.00
5%	11%	$5,496,260.00	$3,926,166.92
1%	12%	$6,500,172.00	$3,607,254.18
0%	13%	$6,487,446.00	$3,333,060.71
0%	14%	$6,107,613.00	$3,095,541.77
0%	15%	$5,766,230.00	$2,888,314.38

EXHIBIT 9.11

Comparative Portfolio Values of Bonds and IO Securities

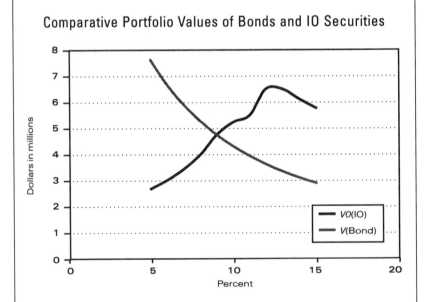

The institution's objective is to preserve its capital. For that purpose, it can create a portfolio of 50 percent bonds and 50 percent IOs ($2,370,850 of each). EXHIBIT **9.12** shows the values of that portfolio

---
EXHIBIT 9.12

Portfolio Values under a Range of Market Rates

k	PORTFOLIO (50/50)
5%	$5,139,056.99
6%	$4,836,320.98
7%	$4,664,738.66
8%	$4,626,677.68
9%	$4,741,726.06
10%	$4,762,218.50
11%	$4,711,213.46
12%	$5,053,713.09
13%	$4,910,253.35
14%	$4,601,577.39
15%	$4,327,272.19

Source: Stone/Zissu

under market rates between 5 percent and 15 percent. Within that range, the portfolio has a minimum value of $4,327,272.19 and a maximum value of $5,139,056.99.

From the standard deviations of each portfolio value as a function of market rates (EXHIBIT **9.13**), institution ZZ understands already that in order not to be exposed to interest-rate risk, the best of the three portfolios is the one with 50 percent invested in IOs plus 50 percent invested in bonds (lowest standard deviation). This is shown in EXHIBIT **9.14**, which graphs the value of the hedged portfolio (50 percent bonds and 50 percent IOs) together with the alternative two portfolios (100 percent bonds and 100 percent IOs).

EXHIBIT 9.13

Standard Deviations of Portfolio Values

PORTFOLIO	100% IO	100% BONDS	50% IO + 50% BONDS
Standard deviation	1,389,438	1,540,871	223,663

Source: Stone/Zissu

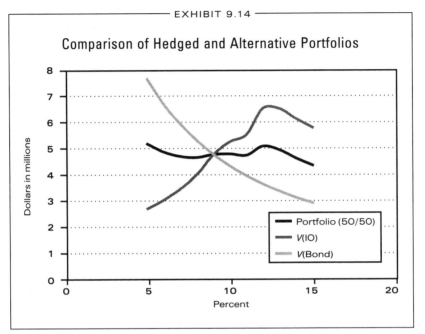

Institution ZZ has created a portfolio that is partially hedged against interest rates over a range of market rates. Because of the IO's characteristics, the hedge breaks apart after reaching a market rate of 14 percent, because the discount effect becomes stronger than the prepayment effect and the IO starts to behave like a regular bond.

Banks that derive income from servicing a portfolio of mortgages are, in effect, long IO strips. Servicing fees are calculated as a percentage of the principal serviced. When serviced principal is prepaid, the total servicing fee is diminished. The value of a servicing portfolio could be hedged with Treasury strips. Adding Treasury strips to a portfolio of servicing contracts would hedge the servicer from losses caused by unexpected declines in interest rates that, in turn, provoke increases in prepayment rates.

Hedging FNMA 9.5 Percent Pass-Through Securities with IO Securities

Institution ZZ has an additional $10,249,561 to invest and again seeks a portfolio hedged against interest-rate risk. Listed below are three possible portfolios, including corresponding values for each with changes in market rates above and below the initial 9 percent. The

---
EXHIBIT 9.15

Portfolio Values

k	PORTFOLIO 1	PORTFOLIO 2	PORTFOLIO3
15%	6,661,656	12,464,202	9,562,929
14%	7,106,920	13,202,131	10,154,525
13%	7,609,888	14,023,172	10,816,530
12%	8,289,428	14,050,681	11,170,054
11%	9,132,169	11,880,639	10,506,404
10%	9,725,030	11,293,070	10,509,050
9%	10,249,562	10,249,560	10,249,561
8%	10,629,240	8,614,322	9,621,781
7%	10,902,292	7,411,454	9,156,873
6%	11,107,139	6,495,763	8,801,451
5%	11,266,176	5,777,999	8,522,088
4%	11,393,110	5,201,383	8,297,247
3%	11,496,726	4,728,517	8,112,621
2%	11,582,888	4,333,960	7,958,424
1%	11,655,654	3,999,877	7,827,765

Source: Stone/Zissu

9.5 percent FNMA pass-through securities are backed by a $10 million pool of mortgages. The values of each portfolio are listed in **EXHIBIT 9.15** and graphed in **EXHIBIT 9.16**. Portfolio 3, which is invested in half of the 9.5 percent FNMA pass-through securities plus 50 percent of 2.161586 times the 9.5 percent IO securities backed by the $10 million-pool of mortgages, is partially hedged against interest rates.

➤ *Portfolio 1:* 100 percent in 9.5 percent FNMA pass-through securities = $10,249,561

➤ *Portfolio 2:* 2.161586 times 9.5 percent IO securities = $10,249,561

➤ *Portfolio 3:* 50 percent in 9.5 percent FNMA pass-through securities plus 50 percent of 2.161586 times 9.5 percent IO securities = $10,249,561.

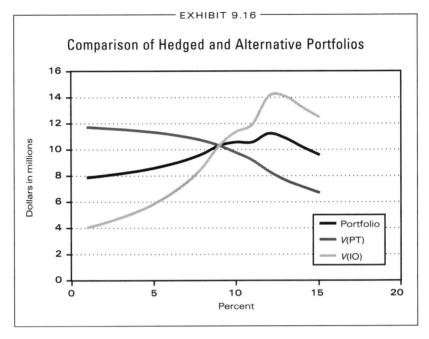

EXHIBIT 9.16

Comparison of Hedged and Alternative Portfolios

EXHIBIT 9.17

Portfolio Values

k	PORTFOLIO 1	PORTFOLIO 2	PORTFOLIO 3	PORTFOLIO 4
15%	6,661,656	12,464,202	9,562,929	8,112,2932
14%	7,106,920	13,202,131	10,154,525	8,630,723
13%	7609888	14023172.4	10816530	9,213,209
12%	8,289,428	14,050,681	11,170,054	9,729,741
11%	9,132,169	11,880,639	10,506,404	9,819,286
10%	9,725,030	11,293,070	10,509,050	10,117,040
9%	10,249,562	10,249,560	10,249,561	10,249,561
8%	10,629,240	8,614,322	9,621,781	10,125,511
7%	10,902,292	7,411,454	9,156,873	10,029,582
6%	11,107,139	6,495,763	8,801,451	9,954,295
5%	11,266,176	5,777,999	8,522,088	9,894,132
4%	11,393,110	5,201,383	8,297,247	9,845,178
3%	11,496,726	4,728,517	8.112.622	9,804,674
2%	11.582.888	4.333.960	7.958.424	9.770.656
1%	11,655,654	3,999,877	7,827,765	9,741,710

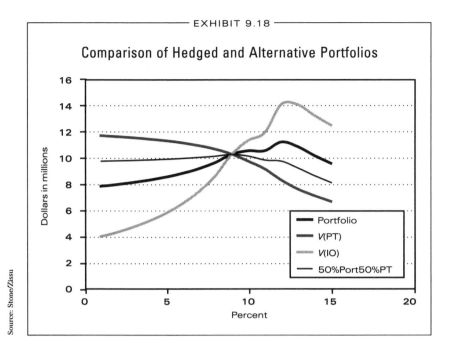

EXHIBIT 9.18

Comparison of Hedged and Alternative Portfolios

Dollars in millions

Percent

Legend:
- Portfolio
- V(PT)
- V(IO)
- 50%Port50%PT

Source: Stone/Zissu

Institution ZZ is not yet satisfied with portfolio 3, and decides to create a portfolio with a better hedge. It can refine portfolio 3 by creating portfolio 4 as follows:

Portfolio 4 = 50 percent of portfolio 1 + 50 percent of portfolio 3. The four portfolios considered by institution ZZ are valued and graphed in EXHIBITS **9.17** and **9.18**. Observe that portfolio 4 is the best in achieving an almost perfect hedge against interest-rate risk, at least in the 0 percent to 11 percent range.

Principal-Only Strips as a Hedging Tool

A BANK funding FNMA pass-through certificates, collateralized by premium mortgages, with certificates of deposit (CDs) is exposed to prepayment risk. If rates fell faster than expected, mortgagors would exercise their prepayment options sooner and in greater volumes, while at the same time people would be reluctant to cash out their CDs in the lower-interest-rate environment. The bank could hedge its exposure to prepayment risk and interest risk by buying principal-only (PO) strips. EXHIBIT **9.19** computes the yield of a pass-through

---
EXHIBIT 9.19

Yield on FNMA 10% POs with FNMA
10% Pass-Through Certificates

CPR	0%	5%	10%	15%	20%	25%
PT	9.88	9.83	9.79	9.74	9.69	9.64
PO	1.86	3.40	5.41	7.66	10.00	12.37
PT + 2% PO	9.91	9.89	9.89	9.89	9.89	9.89

Source: Stone/Zissu

certificate that is trading at premium (101) and a PO that is trading at 67.4 (yielding 10 percent for 20 percent prepayment rate) across different prepayment levels. As prepayment rates increase, the yield on the pass-through certificate decreases while the yield on the PO increases.

Hedging each FNMA $5 pass-through certificate with $0.10 of FNMA 10 percent POs (row 3) shows how the yield on the bank's assets could be maintained at 9.89 percent across a wide band of interest-rate and prepayment-rate combinations. Speculators who take positions in POs provide important liquidity to the market so that banks can efficiently put in place this type of hedge and unwind it when expectations regarding interest rates and mortgagor behavior are revised.

Inverse Floaters as a Hedging Tool

IOs DECREASE in value as interest rates decrease, because higher prepayment leads to less outstanding principal. To hedge against interest-rate risk, a portfolio manager who invested in IOs could add some inverse floaters to the portfolio. When interest rates decrease, inverse floaters increase in value for two reasons:

1   the amount of the future cash flows increases (the leverage determines the increased cash flows), and

2   the future cash flows are discounted at the lower market interest rate.

A regular IO decreases in value as interest rates decrease, causing an increase in prepayment level and a decrease in outstanding principal. An inverse IO would still leave reduced principal in a higher prepayment environment, but the inverse IO coupon would increase. For example, it could go from:

9.5% × $100,000 = $9,500, to
12% × $90,000 = $10,800, or, for very high prepayment rates, to
12% × $80,000 = $9,600.

When interest rates increase, it causes the prepayment rate to decrease and therefore the value of IOs to increase. However, as rates keep going up, eventually prepayment levels stabilize, and inverse IOs become affected only by decreasing coupons (in other words, going in the opposite direction of the market rates), moving as fast as the leveraged coupon allows. For example, it can go from:

9.5% × $100,000 = $9,500, to
8% × $95,000 = $7,600.

This is a potential negative effect. A second such effect is that the reduced future cash flows to be received by the inverse IO holders are now discounted at the higher market rate, reducing the value of the certificate.

EXHIBIT 9.20 presents a summary description of an inverse IO security. The issuer is FNMA, and the inverse IO was stripped from a 6.25 percent pass-through security issued in March 2003.

Floater formula: −1 × one-month Libor + 765 bp
Cap = 7.65%
Floor = 0%

EXHIBIT 9.21 shows the coupon-rate behavior of the inverse IO securities under different Libor (index) scenarios.

When Libor is 0 percent, the inverse IO coupon is capped at 7.65 percent. When Libor is 7.65 percent or above, the inverse IO coupon is floored at 0 percent. **EXHIBIT 9.22** shows the relationship between Libor and the inverse IO coupon rate.

EXHIBIT 9.20

Summary Description of an Inverse IO Security

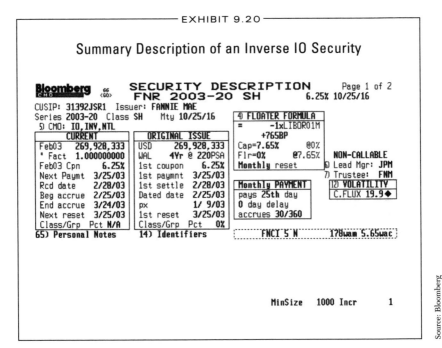

EXHIBIT 9.21

Inverse IO Coupon Rates under Different Libor Scenarios

Libor (Index)	0%	1%	6%	7.65%	8%
Inverse IO Coupon	7.65%	6.65%	1.65%	0%	0%

EXHIBITS 9.23 through **9.26** show the expected cash flows of the inverse IO security. Observe that as market rates increase from 1.3375 percent to 8 percent, prepayment rates decrease, going from 325 PSA to 0 PSA, which is a positive element for an IO investor. Note also that even though the PSA decreases, the cash flows expected to be received decrease as well, because the inverse IO security receives lower coupon rates, which are inversely tied to the performance of the one-month Libor. The area under the curve decreases as PSA decreases.

EXHIBIT 9.22

Inverse IO Coupon Rate vs. Libor

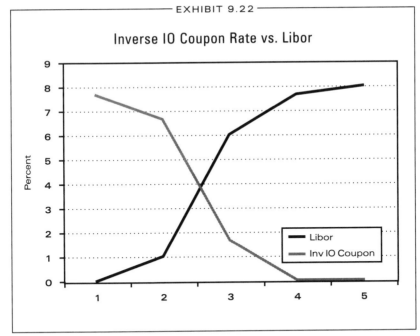

EXHIBIT 9.23

Expected Cash Flows of Inverse IO Security
at Market Rate of 1.3375%

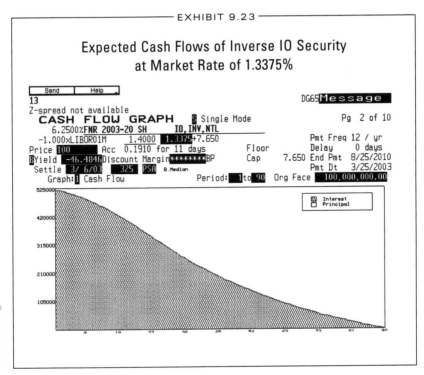

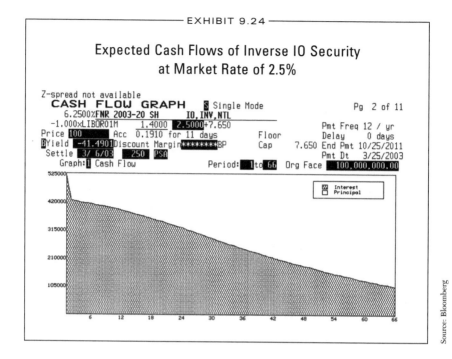

Source: Bloomberg

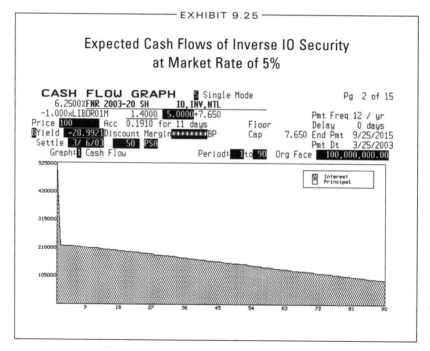

Source: Bloomberg

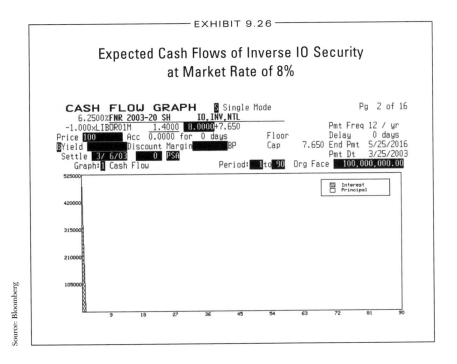

Hedging CMOs with Options on Treasury Bonds

THE CMO classes absorbing the higher prepayment risk compensate investors with a higher yield. Those investors interested in buying such classes of CMOs, because of the higher yield, can hedge the prepayment and reinvestment risks by buying options on Treasury bonds.

If market rates decrease, prepayment rates increase, and the investor receives more principal upfront that can be reinvested at the lower market rate. On the other hand, at lower market rates the price of Treasury bonds increases, but the investor who has bought call options on Treasury bonds has locked in a price and can exercise the call option to offset the losses on the CMO investment.

If market rates increase, the CMO class is less affected by prepayment and increases in value. At the same time, the call option, being out of the money, would not be exercised, and the premium paid to purchase the call option would be offset by the increase in value of the CMO class.

Chapter Notes

1. This is the number of securities issued within transactions, not the number of securitization transactions.

2. Lehman Brothers Intermediate Aggregate Index covers the intermediate U.S. investment-grade fixed-rate bond market, including government and corporate securities, agency mortgage pass-through securities, asset-backed securities, and commercial mortgage-based securities.

Chapter Ten

Credit Risk

INSTITUTIONS CONSTRAINED by the ratings of their investments must understand the different types of credit enhancement provided in securitization as well as the factors in the achievement of the different ratings. When financial assets are securitized, a significant portion of the equity of the issuer that formerly supported the various risks associated with the assets must be raised from a third party or reconstructed from the assets themselves and financed via the capital markets. The function of equity is to finance unexpected losses. The losses may be temporary, when due to delinquencies, or permanent, if caused by defaults. In a securitization transaction, both the unexpected and expected losses will be financed directly or indirectly by investors willing and able to assess and manage these risks.

Direct Financing of Risk versus Buying a Financial Guaranty

DIRECT FINANCING of risk may be arranged by issuing two or more tranches of securities supported by the pool of assets. Each tranche differs with respect to the level of delinquency and default it will finance and its priority vis-à-vis the other classes of securities. This is known as the senior/subordinate structure. Investors value the credit risk of senior tranches issued by the special-purpose vehicle (SPV) based on the adequacy of the equity protecting their interest.

An alternative to raising equity for a securitization transaction by means of issuing subordinate securities is to buy a financial guaranty that assures investors that interest and principal will be paid on schedule. The scope of the guaranty can range from a conditional partial guaranty to a full unconditional guaranty of the timely payment of interest and principal for a class of securities. A subordinate class of securities issued by a securitization vehicle is similar to a partial guaranty in the sense that it finances losses on the asset pool up to a specified limit.

An important distinction between the way a subordinate class of securities and a financial guaranty perform is liquidity. The ability of a financial guarantor to make timely payments of interest and principal does not depend on the cash flows of the specific pool of assets. In contrast, a problem arises if the interest and principal payments made by obligors are disrupted because a component of the securitization structure fails to perform as required, or defaults, and delinquencies on the underlying assets are excessive. The level of credit enhancement, although sufficient from a credit perspective, may be insufficient to assure investors of timely receipt of interest and principal. Since subordinate securities are structured from the securitized assets, the cash flows that can be diverted from the subordinate class to pay the senior tranche are then limited by the cash flowing into the securitization vehicle.

Unlike banks or insurance companies, the U.S. monoline insurers cannot put their AAA rating at risk. U.S. monoline financial guarantors are either AAA or are out of business. Monoline financial guarantors have been designed with a system of internal and external checks and balances to ensure that their capital is more than adequate to service their commitments through simultaneous events creating stresses on income and value, up to those that exceed a multiple of expected worst-case historical records in both magnitude and duration. Each monoline insurer is ringed by four sets of constraints that ensure that their capital is adequate to preserve their AAA-rating claims-paying ability. The four constraints are: (1) statutory capital regulations, (2) rating agency capital requirements and underwriting criteria, (3) the capital markets, and (4) internal controls.

A Financial Guaranty Is Not an Insurance Contract

A COMMON ERROR that is often made when market participants discuss the guaranties issued by the companies that comprise the U.S. monoline bond insurance industry is to confuse a guaranty with an insurance contract, specifically pool insurance. Pool insurance contracts were a common credit-enhancement technique used in the U.K. mortgage-backed security (MBS) market before most of the U.K. firms providing pool insurance were downgraded. Underwriting insurance is based on the law of large numbers. Risk is reduced to a predictable level by spreading it across a large number of separate policy holders.

Financial guaranties, on the other hand, are underwritten based on the premise of zero expected losses. Underwriting credit risk on the basis of zero expected losses implies that risks must be at least investment grade before they are guaranteed. The premium charged by the monoline is not for funding expected losses, as with insurance, but for enhancing an investment-grade security to a AAA level. In effect, the principal "rents" the credit rating of the financial guaranty insurer for the term of the transaction, thus gaining access to the capital markets on the guarantor's credit strength.

The premium charged by the guarantor is compensation for this AAA access. Unlike the monoline guaranty companies, pool insurance is supplied by composite (multiline) insurers. This implies that pool insurance policies, along with other lines of insurance, are supported by the same capital base. Losses in one business can be offset with profits in another.

In addition to the differences between underwriting principles for pool insurance and financial guaranties, there is an important functional difference. Pool insurance policies are designed to ensure that the interest and principal due to investors are ultimately paid, while a financial guaranty is designed to assure investors of the *timely* receipt of interest and principal. Supplementing a pool insurance policy with a liquidity facility provided by an adequately rated third party would minimize, although not eliminate, the differences between guarantied securities and insured securities.

Subordinate securities will assure investors in the senior classes of timely payment of interest and principal only to the extent that the funds have been received by the securitization vehicle and thus are available to be diverted to the senior classes. As in the case of pool insurance, it will be necessary to supplement the senior/subordinate structure with a liquidity facility. The liquidity facility separates the periodic performance of the securitized assets from the ability of the SPV to service its obligations. The subordinate class of securities is relied on for credit support rather than as a source of liquidity. The liquidity provider expects to be compensated by the subordinate class of securities.

Selecting Efficient Forms and Levels of Credit Enhancement

ENHANCING THE credit quality of money- and capital-market instruments entails interposing an additional layer of equity between the debtor and the creditor. This additional layer of equity may be supplied by a third party in the form of a guaranty or insurance policy or may be derived from the value of the assets that the instrument has been issued to finance. The latter form of credit enhancement falls into the broad category referred to as internal credit enhancement.

The primary forms of internal credit enhancement are creating a subordinate class of securities to fund the credit risk and collateralizing the securities with assets that exceed the value of securities issued (overcollateralization). Enhancing the credit quality of a security is equivalent to reducing the leverage of the equity. In the case of a securitization transaction that has been structured as a true sale of assets, credit enhancement is the process of structuring and raising an equitylike interest to fund the purchase of the assets. A true sale of assets implies that the equity of the originating financial institution is no longer a source of funds and cannot absorb unexpected losses.

Investors in the securities issued by the SPV have direct recourse to the assets, guaranties, and reserves owned by the fund but not to the originator of the assets. Should the originator of the assets become insolvent, the performance of the securities issued by the SPV would not be affected. The principal and interest payments made by the obligors (in this case, the mortgagors) are collected by the servicer (typically but not necessarily the originator of the assets) and subsequently distributed to the investors via a paying agent under the auspices of a trustee.

Rating agencies base their assessment of the credit quality of the securities issued by the SPV on the likelihood that obligors will be able to service their loans, that collateral value will be maintained, and that parties to the transaction—the servicer, paying agent, trustee, management company, depositary, swap counterparties, suppliers of liquidity, financial guaranties, and the like—will be able to perform their designated functions in a manner that ensures the flow of interest and principal from obligors to investors according to a well-defined and predetermined schedule.

When planning a securitization transaction, the group responsible for structuring the transaction has the responsibility to the issuer of designing and arranging the most efficient form and level of credit enhancement. Efficiency in this respect can be defined as the quantity and level that maximizes the value received by the issuer in return for refinancing the pool of assets or stream of future receivables by means of securitization. The choice of the form and level of credit enhancement is constrained by the market and the rating agencies, as has been noted. As the value between one rating category and another (for example, AAA and AA) decreases the marginal cost of financing, the additional credit enhancement may exceed the marginal value of the higher rating. Although the *structurer* cannot affect the value the market places on different rating categories, it may be able to obtain a higher rating for a lower cost by choosing or constructing one form of credit enhancement in lieu of another.

Relative Value in Credit-Enhancement Structures

As has been discussed, it is common for the institution that has originated and securitized a pool of assets to retain a residual interest in the pool of assets. A residual interest may take the form of a reserve or spread account, zero-coupon note, overcollateralization, or excess servicing. The residual is designed to absorb the first tranche of losses due to default and delinquency. If losses are less than expected (that is, if assets perform better than expected), the return on the residual will be positive. The residual is the mechanism through which the issuer can extract profits from the transaction.

The relative value of two asset-backed securities (ABSs) that were identical in all respects except for the source and form of equity used to finance credit risk would be based on perceived or actual functional differences between the two credit-enhancement structures. Assuming for the moment that there were no legal, tax, transaction cost, or asymmetric information considerations differentiating the two sources of equity (financial guaranty and subordinate security), investors would choose the two ABSs equally.

If the securities guaranteed by an insurer sell at a discount to the securities supported by subordinate securities, it implies that the market perceives a difference in the ability of the two forms of credit enhancement to finance the same level of defaults and delinquencies. Let's say investors can agree that the financial guaranty supplied, and the equity raised, by the SPV via the issuance of various classes of subordinate securities are both structured to finance the same level of defaults and delinquencies experienced by the assets, and are equivalent in all other relevant dimensions. It would then be a simple matter for the most efficient form of credit enhancement to be used for each transaction by comparing the costs of the two forms of credit enhancement.

It is precisely the differences in form and function between external, or indirect, credit enhancement and internal, or direct, credit enhancement that make the decision between the two approaches more opaque and less straightforward. Equality between the value of bond insurance and the senior/subordinated structure is a condition that would exist only if the market for credit enhancement were perfectly competitive—that is, if the market for credit enhancement consisted of products that were perfect substitutes. Listed below are some of the reasons that cause the relative value of the two forms of credit enhancement, financial guaranty insurance and the senior/subordinate structure, to diverge:

Relatively risky assets or complex structures cause the rating agencies to require a higher level of credit enhancement to attain a desired rating. If the marginal cost of the larger subordinated note exceeds the marginal premium charged by monoline guarantors, the issuer would prefer financial guaranty insurance. Why should the bond insurers be willing or enabled to finance the additional risk at a lower cost than the market? It could be that the financial guarantor excels at understanding, evaluating, and redistributing the risks associated with complex ABSs.

By splitting the pool into a senior class and a subordinate class of securities, prepayment risk and early amortization risk is shifted to the senior class. If the prepayment risk premium is excessive, guarantied securities may sell at a premium to the senior classes created by means of subordination. The additional prepayment risk associated with the senior class would be reflected in a narrowing of the spread on the senior note above the comparable Treasury security relative to the spread required on the subordinated note.

The securities guaranteed by one of the U.S. monoline financial guarantors have a AAA rating that is transparent and durable. Investors in senior notes supported by subordinate securities must monitor the subordinate tranche to value the level of credit protection that still exists. An increase in the subordinate tranche will narrow the yield difference between the A-note (senior note) and B-note (subordinated note), increasing the relative value of the financial guarantee.

Finally, an important consideration is the risk-based capital requirement for investors in different tranches of ABSs. The cost borne by investors due to such capital requirements is reflected in the investors' required yield. An increase in the cost of funding subordinate securities for financial institutions will increase the required yield on these securities.

Index

About Bloomberg

Bloomberg L.P., founded in 1981, is a global information services, news, and media company. Headquartered in New York, the company has sales and news operations worldwide.

Bloomberg, serving customers on six continents, holds a unique position within the financial services industry by providing an unparalleled range of features in a single package known as the BLOOMBERG PROFESSIONAL® service. By addressing the demand for investment performance and efficiency through an exceptional combination of information, analytic, electronic trading, and Straight Through Processing tools, Bloomberg has built a world-wide customer base of corporations, issuers, financial intermediaries, and institutional investors.

BLOOMBERG NEWS®, founded in 1990, provides stories and columns on business, general news, politics, and sports to leading newspapers and magazines throughout the world. BLOOMBERG TELEVISION®, a 24-hour business and financial news network, is produced and distributed globally in seven languages. BLOOMBERG RADIO℠ is an international radio network anchored by flagship station BLOOMBERG® 1130 (WBBR-AM) in New York.

In addition to the BLOOMBERG PRESS® line of books, Bloomberg publishes *BLOOMBERG MARKETS®* magazine. To learn more about Bloomberg, call a sales representative at:

London: +44-20-7330-7500
New York: +1-212-318-2000
Tokyo: +81-3-3201-8900

FOR IN-DEPTH MARKET INFORMATION and news, visit the Bloomberg website at **www.bloomberg.com**, which draws from the news and power of the BLOOMBERG PROFESSIONAL® service and Bloomberg's host of media products to provide high-quality news and information in multiple languages on stocks, bonds, currencies, and commodities.